Hospitality Sales

Hospitality Sales: A Marketing Approach

Margaret Shaw
Susan V. Morris

John Wiley & Sons, Inc.
New York, Chichester, Weinheim, Brisbane, Singapore, Toronto

Thanks Bob. Thanks Chip.

This book is printed on acid-free paper. ∞

Copyright © 2000 by John Wiley & Sons, Inc. All rights reserved.

Published simultaneously in Canada.

This publication is designed to provide accurate and authoritative information in regard to the subject matter covered. It is sold with the understanding that the publisher is not engaged in rendering professional services. If professional advice or other expert assistance is required, the services of a competent professional person should be sought.

Library of Congress Cataloging-in-Publication Data:

Shaw, Margaret, 1949–
    Hospitality sales: a marketing approach / by Margaret Shaw and Susan
  V. Morris.
      p. cm.
    ISBN 0-471-29679-1 (cloth : alk. paper)
    1. Hospitality industry—Marketing. I. Morris, Susan V.
  II. Title.
  TX911.3.M3S53   1999
  647.94'068'8—DC21   98-53410

Printed in the United States of America.

10 9 8 7 6 5 4 3 2 1

Contents

Preface

Much has been written about hospitality marketing. The trade press, journals, books, and textbooks have covered the subject widely. We, as authors, felt what was missing was a text focusing on sales and marketing. Sales is very much a part of marketing. But somehow sales has not received the attention we feel it deserves. Personal selling—the sales process, sales management, sales and technology—is the cornerstone of what this book is all about. Reaching out to the customer and saying, yes, we have what you are looking for. Sales is also an integral part of operations. In many ways, sales is the link between operations and marketing.

We introduce the concept of sales and marketing in Part I of the text. We call this section "Setting the Stage." In Part II, "The Players," hospitality customers and businesses are addressed. Part III, is what we consider the heart of the text, "Personal Selling and Sales Management." In this section, the nuts and bolts of hospitality sales are presented, including two chapters on sales and technology. Part IV, "Intermediaries and Partnerships," is the final section. Intermediaries are important customers in hospitality and are the subject of Chapter 11. Chapter 12 takes a closer look at the growing presence of supplier partnerships and relationship marketing.

Each chapter highlights key terms when first introduced throughout the text. Each term is boldfaced and included in the Glossary at the end of the text. Chapter summaries and discussion questions are presented at the end of each chapter. International examples are used throughout the text. Gained from our hospitality sales and marketing teaching experience, we draw heavily on examples to help explain concepts and practices.

The sales and technology chapters were challenging—challenging in that technology is evolving so quickly that we knew much would be missing by the time this book went to press. Nonetheless, technology is so much a part of today's hospitality sales, we would be remiss not to have it as a major subject of the text. The sales technology section is divided into two parts. Part A, Chapter 9, looks at management and operations, including sales office automation, yield management technology, point-of-sale systems, guest service technology, and property management systems. Part B, Chapter 10, addresses reaching out to the hospitality customer, including central reservation systems, global distribution systems, database marketing, sales support tools, and the Internet and World Wide Web.

USAGE OF THE BOOK

This book can be used at several levels. For community colleges, it can be used for an introductory course in hospitality sales and marketing. Sales is an applied subject and works well at this level. For third- and fourth-year courses at the university level, this text could be the basis for an elective course in hospitality sales. We encourage the use of field projects to supplement the text at this level. The text could also serve as a basis for introductory sales training in the hospitality industry.

ACKNOWLEDGMENTS

We appreciate the many contributions to this book. Industry, in particular, was very supportive, as evidenced by the many examples scattered throughout the text. We also cite often from journals and the trade press, which are referenced in notes at the end of each chapter.

Specifically, we would like to acknowledge Nicole Bruce and Emily Smith. They are both hospitality students who helped with selecting glossary terms and developing end-of-chapter discussion questions. Who better than students could give excellent input to these important areas of textbook development. Thank you Nicki and Emily for a job well done.

We also appreciate the support and time afforded us by the University of Guelph and Marriott. Colleagues from both these institutions gave us feedback and encouragement throughout the development process of putting the book together. Thank you.

Margaret Shaw
and
Susan V. Morris

PART ONE

Setting the Stage

Introduction to Sales and Marketing

LEARNING OBJECTIVES

1. *To grasp the basic tenet of hospitality sales and marketing*
2. *To understand the relationship between sales, marketing, and operations*
3. *To appreciate characteristics unique to the service industry, including hospitality*
4. *To understand what is meant by hospitality marketing management*
5. *To become familiar with the component parts of a marketing plan*

"IBM Plans to Revamp Sales Structure" reads the headline of the *Wall Street Journal*,[1] reporting that IBM sales account executives will now be organized by industry and not the more traditional geographic territory approach. Similarly, "Hyatt to Realign Reps," in *Business Travel News*,[2] reports that Hyatt Hotels sales representatives will be more industry specific as well as specific account focused for its 600 sales account executives nationwide. "Rebirth of a Salesman" from the *Canadian Business Journal*[3] reports on the burgeoning growth of sales force automation (SFA) including laptops, e-mail, modems, and the like, increasingly being used by sales reps throughout North America.

In the 1990s, sales forces across many industries including hospitality are mobilizing, reorganizing, and realigning their teams and their efforts to better achieve the ultimate goal of capturing the customer. Sales representatives, also referred to as sales account executives, sales managers, and sales associates, are energetic, aggressive, and taking the sales challenge seriously. Indeed, the publications noted previously, and others including *Fortune, Business Week*, the *New York Times,* and *Nation's Restaurant News* report regularly on the restructuring of sales and marketing efforts to address the needs of today's changing consumer.

SALES AND MARKETING

Sales and marketing are related concepts and each is an art and a science. Sales flows from marketing. **Marketing,** as stated by Lewis et al., "is communicating to and giving target market customers what they want, when they want it, where they want it, and at a price they are willing and able to pay."[4] The primary focus of **sales** is on the communication aspect of marketing. It involves direct personal selling to potential customers that you and your organization have the right product, in the right place, at the right time, and at the right price—be it a hotel, a restaurant, a casino, or contract foodservices.

Marketing is getting and keeping a customer, a macro approach to managing a successful business. In a broad sense, marketing is the development and delivery of a successful product, that is, the development and delivery of a satisfied customer. Sales entails finding that customer and matching his or her specific needs with the right product offering, a micro or "one-on-one" approach to customer satisfaction. For example, a meeting planner from Texas Instruments (TI) is planning an annual sales meeting to be held in Dallas, Texas. From a macro perspective, this planner has selected the city and is searching for full-service lodging accommodations for 200 TI sales representatives for a five-day conference. From a micro perspective, he or she visits several hotel alternatives and meets with the hotel sales representatives to find the best "fit." Various aspects of the meeting being planned are discussed including dates, rates, guest room accommodations, function room requirements, food and beverage services, and so forth. It is the job of the hotel **sales manager** to learn the specific needs and wants of the planner and "create" the right product, place, time, and price for a successful conference.

A successful conference is what the planner is really buying, not bricks and mortar. Thus, successful selling is understanding the real needs of the buyer, communicating how your product and service can best respond to those needs, and then delivering it. In another context, McDonald's Golden Arches markets fun, simplicity, good service, and a good price. McDonald's sells friendly service, good value for price paid, convenient locations, and those delicious golden chicken nuggets on which many of us grew up. Ronald McDonald is an ancillary product, a public relations endeavor, that augments and supports the idea or concept of kids and why they are special.

Public relations, advertising, and special promotions often support the selling effort. Figure 1.1 shows a Ritz-Carlton advertisement directed at its business traveler clientele. It depicts both the selling and the marketing of this upscale hotel chain. The ad is selling hotel rooms to busy business executives and marketing a hotel that "remembers your needs." The actual purchase of the hotel room, however, may have been handled by a travel agent, a corporate travel manager, or a secretary. Thus, the advertisement supports the sale, in this case a hotel room, but it does not actually make the sale happen.

SALES AND OPERATIONS

Sales is the critical link between marketing and operations. Although marketing is espoused by hospitality professionals, all too often it gets purged in the daily hustle and bustle of operations. It is the role of sales to help bridge this gap.

Selling starts by prospecting, making contacts, establishing relationships with clients, and uncovering their specific needs and wants. But it doesn't end there. Sales is the host or hostess greeting restaurant patrons. Sales is the front-desk clerk welcoming a guest at the local Holiday Inn or at the Waldorf Astoria in New York City. Sales is the housekeeping staff delivering the extra set of towels requested by a guest. Sales is the sommelier in a gourmet restaurant recommending wines to complement an entree choice.

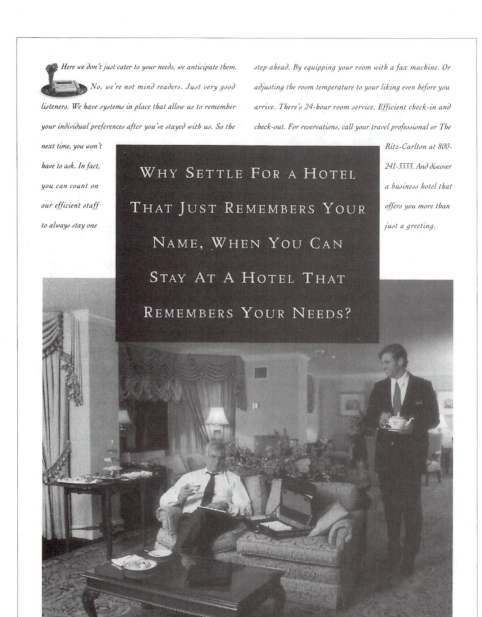

FIGURE 1.1 *The Ritz-Carlton Hotel advertisement. (Courtesy of the Ritz-Carlton Hotel Company. © 1992 The Ritz-Carlton Hotel Company. All rights reserved. Reprinted with the permission of The Ritz-Carlton Hotel Company, L.L.C. The Ritz-Carlton® is a federally registered trademark of The Ritz-Carlton Hotel Company, L.L.C.)*

Taco Bell, emerging as a major player in the fast-food industry, has redesigned its operations to put more emphasis on the service aspect of the frontline employee. Referred to as its "value strategy," much of the back-of-the-house operations such as shredding lettuce and chopping tomatoes has been outsourced. This action not only reduced cost but, more important, gave employees more time on the frontline serving customers. As noted by Schlesinger and Heskett:

> [It] shifted the focus of both frontline workers and their managers from manufacturing meals to serving customers. The ratio of front-of-the-house personnel to back-room factory workers has been turned upside down, and employee job descriptions increasingly focus on the limited but crucial service dimensions that drive the bottom line.

Taco Bell's value strategy also gave more credence to its employee selection process, training efforts, and pay scale and bonuses. Management at Taco Bell also lowered prices to meet the value-conscious demands of the 1990s consumer.

FIGURE 1.2 *Highlights of the Taco Bell story. (Source:* L. A. Schlesinger and J. L. Heskett, "The Service-Driven Service Economy," *Harvard Business Review,* September–October 1991, p. 78. This article is recommended reading for more detail on the Taco Bell Story.)

Sales is the front-office cashier saying "Thank you for staying with us. We hope you enjoyed your stay." It is amazing how a simple thank you can express appreciation for a customer's patronage and bring that person back.

Personal selling is performed either consciously or unconsciously by all client-contact personnel of a hospitality organization. This includes the credit manager. One of the authors nearly lost a $100,000 per year account when a poorly trained credit manager called the client to collect a payment that had not yet been billed. A well-trained and motivated employee is key to successful selling. Though the many facets of human resources are beyond the scope of this book, its importance to guest satisfaction cannot be overstated. Taco Bell, the fast-food chain, has made major inroads in its selling efforts by focusing on its human resources management. Highlights of these efforts are shown in Figure 1.2.

Hospitality is very much a part of the service industry. Characteristics unique to the service industry product include perishability, simultaneity, heterogeneity, and intangibility. **Perishability** refers to the short shelf life of the hospitality product. If it is not sold today, the potential revenue from the sale of that product is gone. A hotel room has a 24-hour shelf life. A restaurant seat has a two-hour shelf life. Manufactured goods have a much longer period of durability. If a television set is not sold today, it can be sold tomorrow or next week. The potential revenue from the sale of that product is not lost. But a Tuesday night hotel room cannot be resold on Wednesday. Tuesday has come and gone. If the hotel guest room goes unsold Tuesday, the potential revenue lost from that vacant room cannot be recouped.

Simultaneity means that production and consumption occur at the same time. How can you produce a guest experience without the guest? Our customers, in a sense, are part of the assembly line. They need to be present for final production of the product offering. A vacant guest room produces nothing. Yes, the carpeting is installed, the bed is made, and the bathroom plumbing works. But it all just exists until a guest arrives to use it. Simultaneous production and consumption is a unique challenge for successful operations in hospitality management.

Relatedly, **heterogeneity** is another service characteristic in hospitality. Heterogeneity refers to the variability of service delivery. Guest service agents have their moods. Customers have their moods. All have personalities of varying shapes and sizes. Hospitality is a very people-oriented business. Service personnel change from shift to shift, typically on an eight-hour schedule. Although operational manuals exist in most hospitality establishments, rarely are policies and procedures followed in an exact manner. Guests' "personalities," too, can change throughout their stay, and it may have nothing to do with how they were treated by service personnel. Dealing with heterogeneity in service operations is dealing with reality. Mistakes will happen. But, more important, mistakes can be addressed. Often a simple apology can win back a customer regardless of who was at fault when the mistake occurred.

Intangibility is a fourth major characteristic of the service product. Some consider it the most important component to recognize. Intangibility refers to the highly intangible nature of the service product offering. Intangibility is a feeling; it is having a sense about something that one cannot fully articulate. The intangible nature of the service product cannot be prejudged. Consumers cannot really see, touch, smell, hear, or taste a service product prior to consumption. They can only anticipate. One can test drive a car before an automobile purchase is made to see what it "feels" like to drive. But a hospitality customer cannot "test drive" a hotel weekend package or a restaurant meal prior to consumption. The intangibility aspect of hospitality emphasizes that service delivery is critical to customer satisfaction. Most customers have an idea of what to expect. But, in the end, they are really not sure of what they are buying until the hospitality experience actually takes place.

The essence of marketing is finding and keeping a customer. Operation's most important role is the keeping of that customer—having that cus-

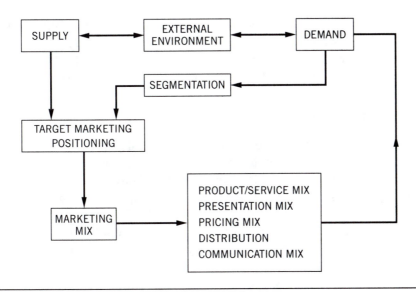

FIGURE 1.3 *Conceptual model of marketing management.*

tomer walk away with a positive and memorable experience and want to return again.

SALES AND MARKETING MANAGEMENT

The cornerstone of good sales and marketing is a basic understanding of the concept of **marketing management.** Shown in Figure 1.3 is a conceptual model of marketing management, which is discussed in more detail next.

Supply-and-Demand Analysis

Marketing management starts with an analysis of supply and demand in the marketplace. The demand side represents current and potential customers. Who are they? What are their needs? What are their wants? Are their needs and wants changing? Are demographics changing? Are the attitudes, interests, and opinions (or psychographics) of today's consumer changing? Careful analysis of current marketplace issues from a demand-side perspective is paramount to what successful marketing is all about.

Analysis of supply looks at both your firm and your major competitors. Who are you? Who are they? What are your strengths and weaknesses? What are their strengths and weaknesses? Who is your clientele and how are they similar and/or different from those of your competitors? It is important that an objective assessment be made. If your competition clearly has a distinct advantage, say an extensive business center for its business clientele, then strategies would have to be developed to combat the situation.

External Environment Analysis

The external environment assessment is an integral part of the supply-and-demand analysis. Key issues to examine include economic, political, technological, sociocultural, regulatory, and ecological environs. This assessment is sometimes referred to as **environmental scanning.** In a way, it is a checklist or means to ensure that external factors impacting the marketplace are included in the supply-and-demand analysis. It is normally conducted at the local, regional, and/or national levels. For many hospitality organizations in the 1990s, external environment assessments are conducted at the international level as well. When McDonald's first entered the former Soviet Union, it assigned employees to teach the Russian potato farmers how to grow a better potato in order to meet its strict quality standards to produce the world-renowned McDonald's french fry.

An economic example of environmental scanning might be a pending recession in the Southwest corridor of the United States, slowing down consumer spending patterns including the number of meals eaten away from home on a weekly, monthly, or annual basis. An ecological example might be mandatory recycling regulations for commercial business operations, forcing hotel and restaurant owners to rethink their current waste management procedures, as well as customer concerns on the issue. Indeed, the Delta Meadowvale Hotel near Toronto proacted (prior to mandatory legislation) by placing a separate "blue box" in each of its guest rooms asking guests to separate recyclable waste. Many, if not most, of the loyal customers at this property supported the effort and applauded management for being environmentally concerned.

Environmental scanning is a means to reach out and search for opportunities and threats in the marketplace. It needs to be done on a continuous basis as we simply do not live or operate in a static environment. Crystal balls only exist in fantasy; that is, predicting the future is not an exact science. Nonetheless, a regular and thorough monitoring of the marketplace can only enhance sales and marketing efforts for hospitality firms.

Segmentation, Target Marketing, and Positioning

Segmentation is the act of dividing a market into meaningful groups or segments of buyers having similar needs and wants. Business travelers have different needs and wants than pleasure travelers. Families with young children have different needs and wants than singles or empty nesters. Planners of large conventions have different needs and wants than independent travelers. Segmentation helps the sales and marketing manager more clearly identify who the various buyers in the marketplace are and what they really want. Based on the results of the supply-and-demand analysis and an appropriate segmentation of all potential buyers, target marketing and positioning decisions are made next.

Target marketing is choosing which segments of demand you are going to go after, or "target." To put it simply, family restaurants target families. Four Seasons and Hyatt hotels target upscale business travelers. Casinos offer entertainment and target singles, families, and convention goers who are looking for gaming to relax and have fun.

Positioning is a more elusive concept. It refers to how consumers actually perceive your product, be it real or their own personal point of view. What "image" does your product have in the marketplace—expensive? cheap? gourmet? friendly and fun? stuffy? relaxing? refined? a dump? In essence, "market positioning means creating an image in the consumer's mind."[5] What's important here is that it is not what management perceives the product to be but, rather, what the consumer believes to be true. Marketing mix decisions play an important role in creating the image you want to portray and are discussed next.

The Marketing Mix

The hospitality **marketing mix** includes product/service, price, presentation, distribution, and communication decisions. Each flows from the target market(s) and positioning decisions outlined previously and includes both the tangible and intangible aspects of the product offering.

The **product/service mix** refers to the actual products and/or services developed and offered to your guests. In hotels, the product/service mix not only includes beds, pillows, cleanliness, friendly service, and so forth; it may also include ancillary services such as transportation to and from the airport, fax services, concierge services, or no services at all. For some segments of demand, offering limited service or no service at all is a service in itself. This is a marketing choice done quite successfully by budget hotel operators such as Motel 6, Super 8, and Formule 1 of Group Accor in France.

The **presentation mix** refers to how these products and services are presented. Examples include the dress and attire of employees; the location and decor of the restaurant or hotel; the atmospherics such as lighting, sound, colors, and textures; and the actual customers who frequent the hospitality establishment. A bar full of college students sounds good to other college students, but this is probably not the case for a business professional looking for a quiet place to relax and have a glass of wine. Again, it all leads back to target marketing and positioning decisions. Who is our target market? How do we position ourselves? What do our customers want? And what don't they want?

The **pricing mix** decision refers to what price, what level of pricing, and, most important, what price the customer is really willing to pay. A $150 hotel room or an $18.50 steak may seem appealing and communicate a top-quality hotel stay or fine-dining experience, but an incorrectly targeted customer may simply not want to foot the bill. Pricing decisions are difficult and are an integral part of the positioning statement as well as the presentation mix. In the preceding case, the $18.50 steak may look great on the menu but the customer may opt for the $7.95 burrito and a bottle of beer. Management of this restaurant may be trying to attract too broad an audience by positioning itself as "we appeal to everyone" and by presenting a menu that is too widely diffused in pricing and menu choice.

Applebee's menu is shown in Figure 1.4. It is a good menu, nicely balanced, reasonably priced, and appealing to its target audience—the mid-priced restaurant goer looking for a pleasant meal at a fair price with an agreeable number of menu choices from which to choose.

All too often, pricing decisions are made on a cost-plus basis. This simply doesn't work from a sales and marketing perspective. The hotelier or restaurateur must first determine who the target markets are, what they are willing to pay, and then design the specific product offering to suit their needs and pocketbooks. Understanding the budget of the customer must come first. Then, and only then, can pricing decisions be made.

The **distribution mix** deals with the issue of accessibility and availability of the hospitality product to its target markets. For example, Holiday Inn has a strong international distribution system and is accessible to loyal patrons worldwide. Central reservation systems and intermediaries such as travel agents and tour brokers make Holiday Inns readily available to these customers. For local independent restaurant operators such as Judy's in Amherst, Massachusetts, or Anthony's Pier 4 in Boston, distribution issues are not a major concern to management. Yet, for chain operations such as Hilton and Sheraton hotels or Pizza Hut and Movenpick restaurants, they are. From a sales perspective, especially for hotels, distribution can be a critical link to reach targeted customers and make a sale. Computer technology has had a tremendous impact on hospitality distribution and is discussed later on in Chapters 9 and 10.

The **communication mix** addresses the question of how can we best communicate to our target markets that we have the right product, in the

FIGURE 1.4 *Excerpt from Applebee's menu. (Courtesy of Applebee's. Reprinted with permission.)*

TABLE 1.1   *Sample Marketing Plan Table of Contents*

Executive summary
Market overview
Competitor analysis
Positioning statement and target market identification
Goals and objectives
Action plans
Budget projections

---

right place, at the right time, and at the right price. Tools include advertising, direct mail, public relations, brochures, merchandising, special promotions, and personal selling. A detailed discussion of these communication tools is the subject of Chapter 2.

THE MARKETING PLAN

A **marketing plan** is a formal document detailing the marketing management decisions of a hospitality establishment. It is prepared on an annual basis for the upcoming year and is the responsibility of the **director of marketing**. Marketing plans are typically 30 to 40 pages in length. It is a working document reviewed on a monthly or quarterly basis. When necessary, changes are made to reflect unforeseen realities of the marketplace. Shown in Table 1.1 is a sample marketing plan table of contents. Formats will vary among hospitality establishments; however, the content is consistent. Sections of the plan include the executive summary, market overview, competitor analysis, positioning statement and target market identification, goals and objectives, action plans, and budget projections. Following is more detailed discussion of each of these sections of the marketing plan.

Executive Summary

An **executive summary** is a brief yet concise summary of the entire plan. It is a recap or brief statement of the main points covered in the plan. Although the executive summary is the lead section of a marketing plan, it is prepared last. The purpose is to enable the reader to quickly grasp the sales and marketing thrust for a hospitality establishment. Executive summaries are normally one page, rarely exceeding two pages. They are confidential to the owners and management of the operation, as is the entire marketing plan.

Market Overview

This section presents the analysis of supply and demand and environmental scanning of the marketplace. A detailed product analysis is included as well. In other words, this section of the marketing plan looks at the strengths and weaknesses of the current product offering plus opportunities and threats in the marketplace environment. This section is sometimes referred to as a **SWOT analysis** which is an acronym for *S*trengths, *W*eaknesses, *O*pportunities, and *T*hreats.

A tabular format is a helpful way to present the SWOT analysis. Following is a simplified hypothetical example demonstrating this approach:

Strengths
- Excellent downtown location
- Newly refurbished guest rooms
- Modern business center
- Good food and beverage facilities

Weaknesses
- Function rooms need upgrading
- Parking garage too small
- Audio-visual equipment outdated

Opportunities
- New convention center recently opened nearby
- Untapped potential for exhibit and trade show market

Threats
- New competitor opening nearby in next six months
- Pending recession; stagnant economy

This is an easy-to-read format, capturing key areas for management to focus its attention. In this example, the exhibit and trade show market may emerge as a new target market. If so, particular attention would most likely be given to refurbishing the hotel's function rooms and upgrading the current audiovisual equipment.

Competitor Analysis

A separate section analyzing the competition is common in marketing plan development. Although it is part of the market overview, the competitor analysis is usually quite detailed and, thus, warrants a separate section. It is important that the competition be analyzed by the market segments they serve. This is done by categorizing the competition into primary and secondary competitors. Primary competitors are those firms that are in the same product class having similar target markets. Secondary competitors are firms that are in the same general location but are in a different product class and/or have different target markets. Focus of the analysis is then placed on the primary competition.

For example, a downtown Hilton hotel focusing on the convention market may compete directly with a Sheraton hotel two blocks away targeting the same market. A Four Seasons hotel in the next block targets upscale individual travelers and would be considered a secondary competitor. The Hilton and the Sheraton would consider each other to be a primary competitor.

The content of a competitor analysis includes information such as the size of the establishment, target markets served, services offered, level of service, price comparisons, and physical facility comparisons. Information on competitors can be obtained in several ways. These include visits to the establishment, news clippings, the local chamber of commerce and convention and visitors bureau, conversations with managers and employees of your establishment and the competitors', brochures, and even customers. If you have lost business to a competitor, it is very important to find out *why*. At most hotels, lost business reports that track what business is lost to whom and why are mandatory. They are analyzed and used to revise the current marketing plan and/or to develop next year's plan.

Positioning Statement and Target Markets Identification

Positioning and target market identification are based on the results of the market overview and competitor analysis. The positioning statement should be concise and succinct and reflect the needs of the target markets selected. For example, a positioning statement might read: "ABC is a first-class, full-service hotel accommodating the lodging needs of the upscale business traveler conducting business in the local community."

The target market in this example is clearly the upscale business traveler. Added to this may be more specific details including individual or group needs (such as in-room fax machines or quality soundproof meeting rooms), the geographic location of major sources of business (such as the Northeast corridor including Boston, New York City, and Washington, DC), and positions held by the clientele (such as senior management, vice president, and CEO). Specific industries that the business travelers represent (such as the banking, finance, and legal professions) may also be included. Well-defined target market identification is paramount in successful marketing plan development.

Goals and Objectives

Established objectives and ways in which achievement will be tracked need to be clearly articulated in the plan. Sales managers often have revenue goals for specific target markets to be achieved over a given period. Goals based on revenue generated from new business versus repeat business are often included as well. Goals can also be set for various times of the year. For example, October may be a busy time of year when higher room rate goals are established. January may be a slow time of year when room-night generation is the objective with less emphasis on higher rated business. In other words, different goals are often set for different times of the year, even for different days of the week. (A more detailed discussion on goal setting is included in Chapter 8.)

Action Plans

This section of a marketing plan outlines specific action steps felt necessary to reach stated goals and objectives. It essentially spells out who is going to do what and how. Sales managers are often assigned specific target markets from which to solicit business. Each sales manager then develops a detailed plan for his or her assigned market.

The communication mix introduced earlier (and the subject of Chapter 2) is the framework from which the action plan evolves. Personal selling, advertising schedules and media placement, travel and trade show attendance, and direct-mail campaigns are common component parts of the action plan. Table 1.2 gives a sample action plan for a hotel sales manager targeting the upscale individual business traveler. Note that completion dates are included for various parts of the plan.

Budget Projections

Revenue forecasts and expense estimates comprise the budget projections. Revenue forecasts are presented by target market and on a month-to-month basis. Often the previous year's actual revenues and expenses are included in this section. Quarterly and end-of-year comparisons are made. These include comparing this year's actual revenues and expenses to this year's bud-

---

TABLE 1.2 *Sample Action Plan*

Sales Manager:	Susan McCutcheon
Target Market:	Upscale individual business traveler
Objective:	Generate $175,000 revenue for peak periods of demand and $110,000 revenue for off-peak periods of demand for the current year.
Geographic Locations:	Boston, New York City, Washington, DC
Level of Management:	Senior-level, vice presidents, and CEOs

Action Plan

Personal Selling:	Sales calls on current and prospective client companies based in Boston, New York City, and Washington, DC (ongoing throughout year).
Advertising:	Research and identify publications in each locale frequently read by target market such as the *Boston Globe*, the *New York Times*, the *Washington Post, Fortune, Business Week* (by March 31st).
	Contract with advertising agency for advertisement development and placement (by May 15th).
Direct Mail:	Develop direct-mail campaign (by June 15th). Use current direct-mail listing developed in-house the previous quarter. May have updates.
	Review final version and send to press (by July 1st).
	Mail out (by August 1st).

---

get and to last year's actual figures. The director of marketing is held accountable for meeting the projected budget.

Expense estimates in the marketing plan are not expenses incurred by the entire operation. They are specific marketing expenses including sales manager and administrative staff payroll expenses, related travel expenses, public relations expenses, advertising and direct-mail expenses, and brochures and other collateral expenses. The marketing expense budget, on average, is 5 to 7 percent of total revenue projections. When opening a new hospitality establishment, it is usually higher.

SUMMARY

This chapter has laid the foundation for hospitality sales and marketing. First and foremost, sales flows from marketing. If management doesn't have a marketing mindset, then sales efforts will be all for naught.

Marketing is giving the targeted customers what they want, when they want it, where they want it, and at a price they are willing and able to pay. Sales is direct communication with potential customers, letting them know we have what they want. In many respects, sales is the link between marketing and operations. Operations is essentially the delivery component of marketing and the final determination of a happy (or unhappy) customer.

Marketing management entails an analysis of supply and demand, an external environment analysis, followed by segmentation, target marketing, and positioning decisions, and marketing mix decisions. The marketing mix areas include product/service, presentation, price, distribution, and communication.

The marketing plan is a formal document detailing the marketing management decisions of a hospitality establishment. The contents of a marketing plan include an executive summary, market overview, competitor analysis, positioning statement and target market identification, goals and objectives, action plans, and budget projections. It is a working document frequently reviewed by management. Marketing plans are confidential to the owners and management team of the firm.

Marketing begins, transcends, and ends with the consumer—sales makes sure it happens.

DISCUSSION QUESTIONS

1. Why is marketing considered a "macro" approach while sales is considered a "micro" approach in hospitality sales and marketing?
2. From an economic perspective, supply and demand are important concepts. Discuss how these concepts relate to hospitality sales and marketing.
3. Discuss how sales and marketing are connected using both hotel and restaurant examples.
4. How, in the 1990s, has environmental scanning had an impact on the hospitality industry?
5. Compare and contrast segmentation and target marketing. How are they similar? How are they different?
6. Discuss the concept of positioning. Is it important to create an image in the customer's mind of the product you are offering? If so, how do you create this image?
7. How does marketing management relate to the development of the marketing plan?

NOTES

1. B. Ziegler, "IBM Plans to Revamp Sales Structure to Focus on Industries, not Geography," *Wall Street Journal*, May 6, 1994, p. B1.
2. D. Long, "Hyatt to Realign Reps," *Business Travel News*, July 25, 1994, p. 8.
3. J. Lorine, "Rebirth of a Salesman," *Canadian Business Journal*, Spring 1994, pp. 22, 24, and 26.
4. R. C., Lewis, R. E. Chambers, and H. E. Chacko, *Marketing Leadership in Hospitality: Foundations and Practices*, 2nd ed., Van Nostrand–Reinhold, New York, 1995, p. 3.
5. Ibid., p. 343.

Chapter 2

The Marketing Communication Mix

LEARNING OBJECTIVES

1. *To better understand what is meant by the communication mix of marketing*
2. *To become familiar with the communication tools in hospitality marketing, which include*
   - *Personal selling*
   - *Advertising*
   - *Direct mail*
   - *Public relations*
   - *Brochures and other collateral*
   - *Merchandising*
   - *Special promotions*

In Chapter 1, we stressed the importance of understanding and appreciating the link between sales and marketing. In this chapter, we look at the communication mix of marketing. This deals with the myriad ways of communicating with current and potential customers of a hospitality establishment. Communication tools of marketing include personal selling, advertising, direct mail, public relations, brochures and other collateral, merchandising, and special promotions. Each of these components is an integral part of the sales efforts for all major players in the hospitality industry including hotels, restaurants, resorts, conference centers, contract foodservices, casinos, and so forth. Table 2.1 highlights key aspects of these component parts of the communication mix. A more in-depth discussion of each follows.

PERSONAL SELLING

Personal selling is direct, person-to-person, oftentimes face-to-face, interaction with a prospective customer. The term prospective customer is important here because it signifies that a sale has not yet been made. Sales man-

TABLE 2.1 *Highlights of the Marketing Communication Mix*

Personal Selling

Direct/personal and/or face-to-face communication between potential buyer and seller

Advertising

Indirect/nonpersonal communication between potential buyer and seller

Direct Mail

Direct/nonpersonal communication between potential buyer and seller

Public Relations

Direct/personal or indirect/nonpersonal communication directed at community at large to enhance public image, goodwill, and/or support the positioning statement of the hospitality establishment

Brochures and Other Collateral

Indirect/nonpersonal printed and/or audiovideo material describing the hospitality product offering

Merchandising

Direct/personal or indirect/nonpersonal communication directed at in-house captive audience designed to stimulate purchase behavior

Special Promotions

Special promotion of a short-term product offering designed to stimulate sales on a short-term basis

---

TABLE 2.2　*Five-Step Process to Personal Selling*

---

1. *Open the Relationship:*
   Current customers, prospecting, leads, and referrals.
2. *Qualify the Account:*
   Determine needs and wants, both tangible and intangible, both past and present.
3. *Present the Message:*
   Provide "solutions" to "problems" through features and benefits of the hospitality product offering.
4. *Close the Sale:*
   Ask for the business and "book" the account.
5. *Service the Account:*
   Deliver as promised.

---

agers talk with potential clients, reservationists talk with potential customers, waiters and waitresses talk with restaurant patrons who have not yet ordered their meal. The abbreviated Texas Instruments (TI) example described in Chapter 1 dealt with a hotel sales manager interacting directly with a TI meeting planner—a potential client—in order to make a sale.

Personal selling is a one-on-one, direct process of matching the needs and wants of buyers and sellers. A buyer may want to hold his or her organization's annual training conference the third week in September, but a preferred facility may only have the second and fourth weeks available. Should this seller offer other desirable attributes such as a good price value, a good location, and good conference facilities and services, the buyer may forego the preferred dates and accept an offer for the second week in September.

There is a five-step process to personal selling and key elements of this process are shown in Table 2.2. Each of these basic tenets is discussed next.

Open the Relationship

Opening the relationship is the first step. There are numerous sources for finding new business and the best place to start is with current customers. These current accounts are loyal customers who have used your product in the recent past. Trace dates, tickler files, or bring file forward (BFF) systems are commonly used by sales managers as reminders to periodically check with these regular accounts about upcoming events, meetings, or newly planned conferences.

Other sources include prospecting, leads, and referrals. Prospecting is calling on potential customers who have not met previously at your facility but have the potential for doing so. For example, if a new division of Procter and Gamble recently relocated to your area, a sales manager should make a sales call to learn about its off-premise meeting and catering activity, who plans these events, and when and where these events typically take place. **Off premise** refers to scheduled events that take place at a location other than that of the organization. Prospecting is oftentimes initially done by telephone (also known as telemarketing) and then followed up with a personal sales call to identified potential clients.

Leads and referrals are opportunities for potential business from an outside source. Sources here include local convention and visitors bureaus, national sales offices for hospitality chain operations such as Marriott and Hilton hotels, satisfied customers, and colleagues from the business community. Indeed, family, friends, and neighbors can generate leads for sales account executives to pursue.

Qualify the Account

Qualifying a potential account is twofold. First, the current needs and wants, including both physical and psychological, must be identified. The physical needs refer to the largely tangible aspects of an event such as number of persons, duration of the event, food and beverage requirements, audiovisual needs, and so forth.

The psychological needs are more intangible yet are just as important. Examples include: What are the underlying objectives? Is the purpose of the event "serious" or "fun," or a combination of both? Are spouses invited and/or encouraged to attend? Probing to learn as much as possible about the upcoming event is critical to this stage of the sales process. Sales managers who don't probe, but simply take orders, often lose the business to a competitor who has similar facilities but has a staff that is better trained and more aggressive in the art of probing.

Second, qualifying a potential account includes learning about similar events that the planner may have held in the past. Was the planner satisfied? Why or why not? What changes are being made? How can the catering or lodging establishment help the planner better meet the overall objectives of the event? When planning a banquet, for example, the type of linen being used may be particularly important to one client, whereas an extensive wine list may be more critical to another. Some planners may simply want the food and beverage or catering director to make all of the detailed decisions for them. Probing helps a sales manager learn as much about the real needs of a planner (including a planner's time). The key issue is what will it take to insure a truly successful event from the buyer's perspective?

Present the Message

Once the needs and wants—both tangible and intangible—have been identified, the sales manager is now in a position to present the message. This is the third step of the sales process. It is usually done in person, on site, and then followed up with a written proposal or contract. This contract includes all pertinent items discussed in the negotiations. Once both parties have signed the contract, it then becomes binding. In restaurant sales, a simple phone call reserving a table for four near the window is all that it takes to make a "contract." More complex events such as banquets, weddings, conferences and conventions require formal contracts.

A key point in presenting the message is that the sales manager provides "solutions" for the buyer's "problems." The tenet of marketing is that you—the supplier—can provide the customer with what she or he needs or wants. In hotel sales, for example, it is the facilities and services of a lodging establishment that are provided to house, feed, and entertain the attendees of a meeting or convention. The meeting planner sets the objective(s), not the management of the hotel. The job of the hotelier is to provide the planner with the facilities and services needed to help ensure a successful event.

Close the Sale

"Book it" is hospitality sales vernacular for closing the sale. It means that a signed contract has been received and reservations are "on the books." The event may be scheduled for two months away or 10 years out—which is the case for the annual convention of the 12,000-member American Bankers Association. It may take a sales manager anywhere from one day to two weeks to two years or more to open a relationship, qualify an account, present a message, and close a sale. One of the authors spent three years developing a five-year contract with the Harvard Business School of Harvard University for the Hyatt Regency Cambridge in Greater Boston—no small task.

Service the Account

Servicing the account, the fifth step, refers to service delivery and is largely accomplished by the operations side of management.

For complex events, this entails collecting all of the many details that need to be pulled together prior to an event's taking place. These include such items as food function menus, rooming lists, credit arrangements, billing instructions, ground transportation requests, schedule changes, specific audiovisual requirements, VIP lists, and so on. It is a cumbersome job and takes a detail-oriented person to do the job effectively. Some say being part magician helps, too.

Servicing the account may or may not be the responsibility of the hotel sales manager. In larger hotels, the booking is often turned over to the convention services department. The sales manager, however, continues to keep in touch with the customer even if he or she now shares joint responsibility with a convention services manager assigned to the account.

Sales Management Versus Personal Selling

Sales management is an important part of hospitality sales leadership and is a somewhat different concept from that of personal selling. **Sales management** deals with training, motivating, and directing the sales force of a hospitality organization. We bring this up now hopefully not to confuse the reader but, rather, to distinguish the basic difference between these two concepts early in the text. Personal selling is the direct interaction between buyer and seller that we just introduced and is developed more fully in Chapters 6 and 7. Sales management is assisting the sales account executive to better do his or her job of making the sale happen and is the subject of Chapter 8.

ADVERTISING

Advertising is indirect, nonpersonal communication to prospective customers through various media including radio, television, newspapers, billboards, and the like. Advertising provides an opportunity to reach large audiences and, at the same time, to inform them that your establishment has the right product, at the right time, at the right place, and at the right price. There are important decisions to consider when developing a good advertising campaign and they include the following:

- Who is the target audience?
- What is the general message?
- How can the message be best presented?
- When and how often (reach vs. frequency) should the ad be run?
- Where should the ad be placed?

Shown in Figures 2.1 and 2.2 are hospitality advertisements for Lufthansa German Airlines and the Hotel Marquis Reforma of Mexico, respectively. A discussion of the preceding considerations using these examples follows.

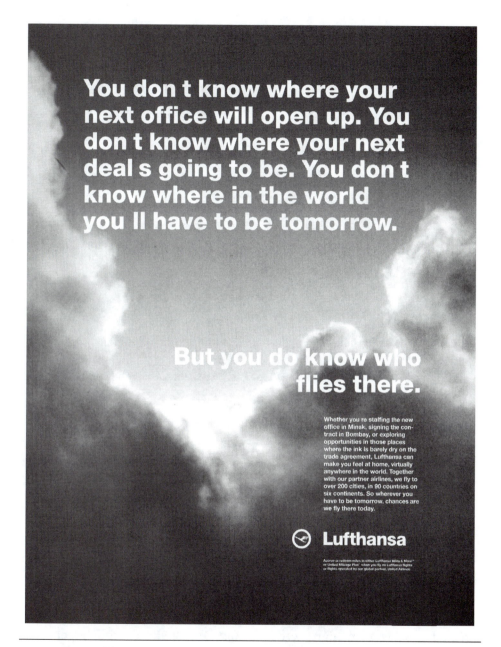

FIGURE 2.1 *Lufthansa German Airlines advertisement. (Courtesy of Lufthansa German Airlines. Reprinted with permission.)*

FIGURE 2.2 *Hotel Marquis Reforma advertisement. (Courtesy of Hotel Marquis Reforma. Reprinted with permission.)*

Target Audience

Any advertising campaign needs to start with defining the target audience. The Hotel Marquis Reforma ad is directed at the upscale business or pleasure traveler planning a trip to Mexico. The Lufthansa ad is aimed at the international business traveler who conducts business all over the world.

General Message

The general message should convey in plain, simple language what it is that you want the targeted audience to hear or see. The general message in the Lufthansa advertisement is especially clear. It is communicating to the targeted audience that Lufthansa flies worldwide "to over 200 cities, in 90 countries on six continents." The Hotel Marquis Reforma is presenting a message of a small, refined, prestigious hotel. Note that this advertisement indicates that the Hotel Marquis Reforma is a member of "The Leading Hotels of the World" and "Small Luxury Hotels." These are upscale consortia that are well known to the target market. Consortia are loosely knit groups of similar, yet independently owned and operated hotels that share joint marketing efforts such as advertising and central reservation systems.

Presenting the Message

Similar to personal selling, presenting the message is an important part of developing an advertising campaign. In advertising, which is more limited and constrained than personal selling, careful consideration has to be given as to *how* you state or say your message. The Lufthansa advertisement is well presented. The global-reach message is clear, concise, articulately stated, in large print, easy to read, and softened with a background of light clouds and blue skies, implying comfort and safety. The targeted audience can easily grasp what it is that Lufthansa has to offer.

Reach Versus Frequency

In advertising, reach refers to how wide an audience you want to "reach," and frequency refers to how often. The target market may be families with small children and a reach decision may be to all families of this type in the Northeast, just the East Coast, or the Long Island area only. The frequency considerations might include once or twice daily, once a week, or once a month. The time of day, day of the week, or month of the year will all be selected according to the audience you want to reach. Budget considerations weigh heavily in these types of decisions as well.

The Lufthansa and Hotel Marquis Reforma ads were run monthly and biweekly in *Fortune* and *Business Week* magazines, respectively. Both campaigns were conducted in the mid-1990s, reaching nationwide to their target markets. Many U.S. national publications, including those mentioned previously, offer advertisers regional distribution with reduced-rate options when only a specific geographic segment is being targeted.

Placement

Placement refers to where in the publication, where in the radio broadcast, or on which highway billboard you want to place your message. Certain restrictions apply, of course, in the case of billboards. The state of Vermont, for example, doesn't allow highway billboards at all.

The Lufthansa and Hotel Marquis Reforma advertisements were placed midsection in the publications selected. The prized placement (and most expensive) for magazines is the inside and back covers where exposure to an advertisement is highest. Similarly, and not surprisingly, the most expensive placement in television advertising is "prime time."

Bartering Practices in Advertising

Advertising, similar to personal selling, is not cheap. The use of bartering or trading for advertising in the hospitality industry is commonplace. **Bartering** essentially entails the exchange of goods or services between two business organizations with no cash transaction. An example would be, say, trading $25,000 in hotel rooms and/or food and beverage services over a one-year period in exchange for $50,000 worth of advertising. This is called a trade-out.

In a study conducted at Michigan State and Central Michigan Universities,[1] researchers estimated that up to 80 percent of the lodging establishments surveyed practiced bartering, mostly in advertising. This practice is ethical, makes sense, and is a way for hospitality operators to "trade" space that may otherwise go empty, especially in periods of low demand. As discussed in Chapter 1, hospitality is part of the service industry and therefore is a highly perishable product.

Personal Selling Versus Advertising

Advertising and personal selling are the primary selling tools in hospitality and usually comprise a major portion of the marketing budget. Yet, needless to say, there are advantages and disadvantages to each.

Advertising works best when the product is basic and simple such as a Big Mac, Coke, and fries. Personal selling works best when the product is more complex and attention to numerous details is essential to the closing of a sale. Conferences and conventions are complex purchases that require much custom designing, and personal selling is the most effective communication tool for these types of purchases.

The primary advantage of advertising is reach. Large numbers of potential customers can be reached through advertising with a single message. From this perspective, the cost per person in advertising is relatively low. Personal selling, on the other hand, has the advantage of flexibility and immediate feedback. Overcoming potential objections of a prospective buyer can be addressed on the spot, and adjustments, if necessary and justifiable, can be made immediately.

A hospitality firm rarely uses just one or the other of these two communication tools of marketing. Personal selling can support an advertising thrust, as is often the case for the restaurant industry and individual guest room sales for the lodging industry. On the other hand, advertising can support the personal selling effort, as is done for conference and convention sales and foodservice management contracts. It is a matter of (1) degree of product complexity and (2) target audience that determine where the marketing communication budgeted dollar is best spent. The marketer needs to decide which communication tools will work best and determine the appropriate balance for each.

DIRECT MAIL

Direct mail is a form of advertising. It is nonpersonal, non-face-to-face, yet direct communication with a clearly identified target audience. It is widely used and often developed and implemented by the sales staff. As noted by Irma Mann, a well-known marketer in hospitality, "[i]t's an efficient, cost-effective way to deliver your message and it has immediate, measurable returns, which is why it has become such a popular choice."[2]

Direct mail is written communication promoting a product—a letter, a special promotion, an electronic message—sent to regular and/or potential clients. In hospitality, it is a relatively simple task to develop a mailing list, especially a listing of your current clientele. In the restaurant business, for example, the names and addresses of regular customers can be garnered while patrons are dining at the restaurant over a specific period of time, say, two weeks or one month. With this listing, a direct-mail campaign can be developed and sent out to promote future special events such as a Friday Night Jazz Festival or a Mother's Day Special. A simple "thank you for your patronage" letter isn't a bad idea, either.

In the hotel business, developing a direct mail listing is even easier. The names and addresses of all customers are already available from the front-office guest registration. Efficient hotel operations categorize or code all guest registrations by target market such as "C" for a corporate client, "A" for an association delegate, or "WP" for a weekend packager. Business cards from clients and potential clients are also a means from which to develop a direct-mail listing for a corporate target market.

Figure 2.3 shows a sample direct-mail form letter to be sent to prospective customers. This particular letter is used by a sales manager as a result of prospecting. A potential client has been identified but this prospect has no immediate plans to host an event. A thoughtful, "personalized" follow-up letter is sent saying, "We look forward to future opportunities to serve you." Note that a convention brochure will be enclosed with the letter.

FIGURE 2.3 *Sample direct-mail form letter. (Courtesy of Marriott International. Reprinted with permission.)*

```
DATE

PROSPECTIVE CLIENT NAME
COMPANY NAME
COMPLETE ADDRESS

Dear _____,

Thank you for giving me a chance to introduce myself to you
recently. We would look forward to any opportunity to serve as the
host hotel for **COMPANY NAME** and providing your managers with
the quality service and accommodations they expect and deserve.
Our goal is to provide our guests with the level of service which
assures us of being your ''preferred'' hotel in central New
Jersey.

Enclosed please find a copy of our convention brochure which
highlights the physical facilities available here at the Marriott
Hotel. However, we like to believe that the ''real'' Marriott is
not something that can be sent through the mail. You cannot
describe it accurately with pictures and physical dimensions
because it is a group of people and their attitude towards
hospitality. We believe that our dedication to our guests is what
sets us apart from other hotels.

Marriott prides itself on hosting successful meetings, and we
look forward to future opportunities to serve you. If I may be of
any assistance to you with your plans, please feel free to call.

Best Regards,


Sales Manager
MARRIOTT HOTEL
```

Direct mail is often used to get people to respond to a specific product offering or special promotion. This kind of direct mail requires pretesting prior to a large mailing to make sure the design is appropriate and effective. Tom McCarthy, another well-known hospitality sales marketer, offers the following:

> One of the great things about direct mail is that you can test several advertising approaches before determining which will be used.... Many hoteliers who try direct mail claim that it doesn't work very well. Often they don't give any thought to testing more than one approach. It's a good idea to send two different letters with postage-paid cards to see which draws a larger return. Don't guess at what the best approach is; wait until the results are tabulated.[3]

Direct mail, when well thought out, properly implemented, and followed up, can be an excellent communication tool in hospitality. Whether the purpose is to introduce a new product, to promote a special weekend package, to generate leads, or to promote goodwill in the local community, direct mail is cost-effective and can work well. With the advent of database marketing (discussed in more detail in Chapter 10), we are seeing an increased use of direct mail in the hospitality industry to support the sales effort.

PUBLIC RELATIONS

Public relations (or PR for short) can be a direct/personal or an indirect/nonpersonal form of communication to the community at large. This could be a local community, a national community, or a worldwide community. The purpose of PR is to enhance the public image and goodwill of the hospitality establishment. Good public relations also supports the sales activity of the organization.

An example of personal communication from a PR perspective would be a general manager's direct involvement in a fundraiser for a local United Way campaign. This helps position a hotel or restaurant as a good citizen, involved, and caring about the community in which it operates. This, of course, enhances its public image and supports a positive relationship with the local community. Relatedly, good public relations can generate referral business as well.

Publicity is the indirect/nonpersonal side of public relations. It most often is a "story" (good or bad) reported in the media about the organization, a person in the organization, or an activity at the hospitality establishment. Following the previous example, a local newspaper or radio station may report positively on the general manager's involvement with the United Way campaign. Should the hotel or restaurant also host a fund raising banquet for United Way, this may be considered "news" and be covered by the local media as well.

Another way to build PR is to organize events that "create" news. These include special events, media events, and community-relations events. Organizing and hosting a 5-K "run-for-health" event to support the American Heart Association, for example, can produce both direct and indirect public relations opportunities. This type of special event can enhance community relations by involving other local organizations such as the Chamber of Commerce, hospitals, businesses, schools, local police, and the like. With this kind of support from the local community, media from the local and regional levels will probably take note.

It is important to remember that public relations is managed; it doesn't just happen. Public relations may result from planned or from unplanned events such as a fire or an unexpected celebrity showing up at your establishment. Unplanned events such as these need to be managed nonetheless. When public relations is poorly managed or not managed at all, it makes the job of the sales account executive all the more difficult to open, present, and close a sale. Good PR, on the other hand, makes the job that much easier. Not that selling is easy! It is not. But well-managed public relations is essential to a solid-based communication mix for hospitality sales and marketing.

BROCHURES AND OTHER COLLATERAL

Brochures and other print collateral, videos, and CD-ROM describe a hospitality product offering and support the selling effort. Other promotional materials used to increase awareness include flyers, cocktail napkins, t-shirts, computer mouse pads, key chains, commuter coffee mugs, posters, and, indeed, airplane banners commonly seen at college football games on Saturday afternoons. These promotional tools, similar to advertising and public relations, will not close a sale. Yet, they can be important support materials to help make a sale.

Figure 2.4 shows a sample two-sided flyer for a wine festival event promoted by Canadian Pacific Banff Springs Hotel. It is a special weekend promotion including wine tastings, food seminars, a dinner dance, a fashion show, and overnight accommodations. This flyer conveniently fits into a standard #10 business envelope. Thus, it can be enclosed easily with letters of various sorts to prospective customers.

An important consideration for all collateral is the design. It should be easily readable, capture the reader's attention, be coordinated with other pro-

FIGURE 2.4 *Canadian Pacific Banff Springs Hotel wine and food festival flyer. (Courtesy of Canadian Pacific Hotels. Reprinted with permission.)*

motional materials, include photos (or a good sketch), and reflect as much as possible the "personality" of the hospitality product offering.

MERCHANDISING

The purpose of **merchandising** is to stimulate the purchase behavior of an in-house captive audience. Merchandising can be personal and/or nonpersonal communication directed at this target audience. Merchandising is widely used in hospitality, especially for restaurant and foodservice sales.

Personalized merchandising is largely done by the waitstaff in restaurants or by the front office guest service agents in hotels. This, in concept, is really personal selling and often referred to as "upselling." A waiter bringing a dessert cart to a table and highlighting the contents of each item is personal/direct merchandising. Those fresh strawberries and cream look so good, the customer can hardly resist! A waiter or waitress bringing sample wines to a table and offering vintage wine by the glass is another example of personal merchandising.

Nonpersonal merchandising is commonplace in hospitality as well. The dessert cart mentioned is often prominently placed near the host or hostess stand for customers to see as they are escorted to their table. Pasta displays in restaurants, show kitchens, photos of in-house restaurants and/or menu displays in hotel elevators are also examples of nonpersonal merchandising. The familiar table tent card in restaurants, lounges, and hotel guest rooms is a form of indirect merchandising. Pizza Hut, as shown in Figure 2.5, developed a tent card showing how easy it is to have your favorite pizza delivered "right to your room."

Creativity is a key ingredient for hospitality merchandising. The Royal Garden Hotel of Hong Kong developed a special cocktail created by the bartenders that became a national drink. Successfully promoted with special tent cards in the lounge:

> [The] Hong Kong cocktail, made from vodka, Drambuie, Angostura bitters and Southern Comfort and garnished with red azalea, bamboo leaves and a lemon section, won a cocktail competition in Hong Kong last May and is being used as Hong Kong's new national drink.[4]

Merchandising is an excellent communication tool and, similar to brochures and other collateral, can be an integral part of the sales effort. Caution is urged, however, about the overuse of tent cards. This can be frustrating to the customer and unproductive. One of the authors on a business trip angrily removed over a dozen hotel tent cards from the desk and table in the guest room to make space for her handbag and briefcase. Too many tent

FIGURE 2.5 *Pizza Hut room service delivery tent card. (Pizza Hut® and the Pizza Hut logo are registered trademarks of Pizza Hut International, L.L.C. Reprinted with permission.)*

cards, in this case, cluttered the room, produced no incremental sales, and, perhaps more important, resulted in a displeased customer.

SPECIAL PROMOTIONS

Special promotions are short-term product offerings designed to stimulate sales on a short-term basis. They can help fill low-demand periods, and can help build continued patronage from a loyal customer base on a long-term basis. Special promotions are communicated to an identified target market via personal selling, advertising, direct mail, and/or merchandising. In a sense, a special promotion is really a product and not a communique per se. They are typically included as part of the communication mix because of their short-term nature.

Special promotions abound in the restaurant business. McDonald's offers "Happy Meals," Arby's offers "Value Combos," table service restaurants offer "early bird" specials, and many fine-dining establishments offer "prix compris," a fixed price for a complete meal. This is often a special of the day that includes appetizer and/or salad, main course, dessert, and coffee or tea. These promotions are commonly offered on a regular basis, especially discounted specials for the price-conscious consumer of the 1990s.

Hotels frequently offer special promotions for the same reasons as restaurants. Weekend package specials are especially commonplace for downtown city hotels. Regular business customers are, for the most part, absent on weekends. Many of these hotels switch their weekend target marketing efforts to the more price-sensitive weekend pleasure traveler. This type of discounted special promotion can help fill otherwise empty guest rooms.

Frequent-traveler programs at hotels have become a typical product offering for hotel chain operations. We purposely do not include them here as a special promotion. Frequent-traveler programs have become simply a part of the basic product offering, as is the case for the airline frequent-flyer programs, too. As a reminder, the very definition of a special promotion is short term.

Excerpts from a special promotion offered by Hyatt Hotels & Resorts to meeting planners is shown in Figure 2.6. The purpose was to stimulate business after a period of extensive hotel renovations. The full promotion piece was a prominent enclosure in widely read publications by meeting planners across North America and was complemented by direct mail campaigns offering AT&T calling cards with 10 free units of calling time.

SUMMARY

The communication mix—personal selling, advertising, direct mail, public relations, brochures and other collateral, merchandising, and special pro-

COMPLETE AND RETURN, TODAY.

NAME

TITLE

COMPANY NAME

ADDRESS

CITY _____ STATE _____ ZIP

TELEPHONE (___) FAX (___)

PLEASE TELL US ABOUT YOUR NEXT OPEN MEETING DATES:

DESTINATION	MONTH/YEAR	TOTAL # OF ROOMS	# OF ROOMS/ PEAK NIGHT	LENGTH OF STAY	PLEASE CONTACT ME BY MONTH/YEAR
1.					
2.					
3.					

Complete and return by mail (postage-paid), or fax to 402-593-4030.
To receive your Free slide calculator, reply card must be filled out completely. Thank you!

RMN46

TWO FREE OFFERS—

ONE FROM HYATT,

THE OTHER FROM AT&T—

THAT CAN HELP YOU MAKE

MORE EFFICIENT USE OF HYATT'S

NEWLY RENOVATED SPACES.

GET THIS FREE CALLING CARD
BY CALLING
1-800-383-6163, EXT. 14485.

GET "THE ARRANGER" FUNCTION SPACE
SLIDE CALCULATOR — FREE WHEN YOU
COMPLETE AND RETURN THIS FORM.

HYATT TOUCH
CALLING CARD
10 units ☏ AT&T

Hyatt is proud to offer AT&T Long
Distance Service. That means you can
use your AT&T **TrueChoice** Calling
Card, wherever and whenever you
travel to keep in touch. Call to learn
about the features that make this card
simple to use. And when you order
your **TrueChoice** Calling Card, you'll
receive a Hyatt Touch
Calling Card with 10 Free
units of calling time. Call
1-800-383-6163, ext. 14485.

AT&T
Your True Choice™

NO POSTAGE
NECESSARY
IF MAILED
IN THE
UNITED STATES

BUSINESS REPLY MAIL
FIRST-CLASS MAIL   PERMIT NO. 75   OMAHA, NE

POSTAGE WILL BE PAID BY ADDRESSEE

HYATT HOTELS & RESORTS®
ATTN RENOVATED HOTEL ADVERTISING
9805 Q ST
OMAHA NE 68127-9997

FIGURE 2.6 *Hyatt Hotels & Resorts special promotion. (Courtesy of Hyatt Hotels & Resorts. Reprinted with permission.)*

motions—is an important tool in the overall selling effort in hospitality. It is an integral aspect of getting and keeping customers.

Personal selling is one on one and especially effective for complex purchases. Advertising is nonpersonal and has the advantage of reaching large audiences at the same time with a single message. Direct mail, a form of advertising, is gaining in popularity largely because of the ability to track its effectiveness and the relative ease with which a mailing list can be compiled in hospitality. Public relations plays an important supportive role in the communication mix by enhancing the public image and goodwill of the hospitality establishment. Brochures and other collateral are used to describe the product offering, to increase awareness, and to support the sales effort. Merchandising is personal or nonpersonal communication to an in-house captive audience and is widely used in our industry. Special promotions are short-term product offerings designed to stimulate sales on a short-term basis and to enhance loyal customer patronage on a regular long-term basis.

This chapter introduced the communication mix components and emphasized the importance and interrelatedness of each. While the focus of this book is on personal selling, sales management, and related activities, all of the component parts of the communication mix need to be well-coordinated with specific sales activities. At the same time, sales activities need to be clearly integrated with the marketing communication mix.

DISCUSSION QUESTIONS

1. Briefly describe the communication tools of the hospitality marketing communication mix.
2. When is personal selling more appropriate for reaching a targeted audience?
3. How does personal selling differ from sales management?
4. Discuss important decisions that need to be considered when developing an advertising campaign.
5. What are the advantages and disadvantages of both personal selling and advertising? Is either one of these communication tools more effective than the other?
6. As a restaurant owner planning a grand opening celebration, how would you go about reaching your target audience?
7. Develop a special promotion for a hotel or restaurant of your choice. What are some key issues that need to be considered? (*Hint*: How does this question differ from question #4?)

NOTES

1. J. W. Damitio and R. S. Schmidgall, "Bartering Practices in the Lodging Industry," *Hospitality Research Journal*, Vol. 17, No. 3, 1994, pp. 101–110.
2. I. S. Mann, "Direct Marketing," *Hotel & Resort Industry*, March 1995, p. 12.
3. T. T. McCarthy, "Testing Ideas Can Help Improve Sales," *Hotel & Resort Industry*, May 1994, p. 17.
4. M. Scoviak-Lerner, "A Recipe for Better Beverage Sales," *Hotels*, November 1993, p. 76.

PART TWO

The Players

Chapter 3

Hospitality Customers: The Buyers

LEARNING OBJECTIVES

1. *To gain an appreciation for the many and varied types of hospitality customers*
2. *To become familiar with major customer segments in hospitality, which include:*
   - *Individual business customers*
   - *Business groups, conferences, and conventions*
   - *Exhibit and trade shows*
   - *Institutional market*
   - *Leisure customers*

Customers for hospitality are numerous. In the broadest sense, they include business and leisure customers, meeting and convention planners and attendees; exhibit and trade show planners and attendees, and institutions such as schools and hospitals. This chapter addresses these hospitality customers. Later on, in Chapter 11, intermediaries such as travel agents, independent meeting planners, and tour wholesale operators, who assist in the hospitality purchase, are discussed.

Individual customers are essentially those customers who travel independently and make their own travel arrangements. They may or may not, however, be the actual decision maker for part or all of the planned itinerary. Individual customers are sometimes referred to as **free independent travelers (FITs)**. They are also referred to as **transient customers**.

Many travelers attend organized events such as a meeting being held by a corporation or a convention being held by an association. These events are put together by planners who make most, if not all, decisions for the event. These planners are at various times referred to as meeting planners, association executives, and the like. In other words, these customers make decisions for end users who are also customers.

A key point here is distinguishing between the planner, the decision maker, and the end user. Knowing who makes the decision and how, when, and why it is being made is imperative to successful selling. All too often too much time is spent by a sales manager talking to the wrong person at the wrong time.

Table 3.1 captures the essence of the various types of customers who generate demand for the hospitality industry. The purpose of the purchase is first divided into business or leisure markets. Business markets are then subdivided into individual travel, meetings and conventions, exhibits and trade shows, and institutional markets. The leisure market is divided into individual and group travel. Following is a more detailed discussion of each of these segments of demand.

INDIVIDUAL BUSINESS CUSTOMERS

The individual business customer comes from all walks of life—male, female, corporate executive, entrepreneur, single, married, children, no children, doctor, lawyer, 20-something, 60-something, politician, college educated, perhaps an MBA, perhaps a Ph.D. Though differing on demographics, geographic origins, business trade, and so forth, the one thing they have in common is that they are indeed traveling primarily for business purposes. Hotel business centers, guest rooms with well-designed work space, voice mail, dataports, fax machines, even an in-room supply of staples and paper

TABLE 3.1   *Customers Segmented by Purpose of Purchase*

Purpose of Purchase

Business
Individual travel
Meetings and conventions
Exhibits and trade shows
Institutional market

Leisure
Individual travel
Group travel

clips, are amenities expected by today's business traveling customer. As noted by Darryl Hartley-Leonard, former president of Hyatt Hotels:

> Years ago, hotels tried to make their guests feel right at home. We still do, but times have changed, and today our guests tell us that what they need during a hotel stay are services that allow them to be as productive on the road as they are in the office—24 hours a day, if necessary.[1]

And, when conducting business, business travelers want air travel to be hassle-free. Shown in Figure 3.1 are sample British Airways advertisements directed at the business professional who wants to arrive home from that hectic trip abroad rested and relaxed.

Advertising is a widely used communication tool to capture the attention of the individual business traveler. The market is too large and too dispersed to make personal selling to all potential individual customers cost effective. Figure 3.2 depicts a Sheraton advertisement clearly aimed at today's business traveler. Advertising is effective for less complex product purchases such as the individual business (or leisure) trip. Regardless of who makes the decision, arrangements for these kinds of trips are less complex than, say, for the five-day Texas Instruments annual sales conference introduced in Chapter 1. Personal selling is essential for conference sales, but not necessarily required for transient business sales.

Corporate individual business travel, on the other hand, can become complex because of the sheer volume of travelers from just one company. In large corporations, there is often a **travel manager** (or **travel coordinator** as they are sometimes called) who negotiates for the best price and other value considerations with suppliers such as hotels, airlines, and car rental agencies. In these negotiations, buyers negotiate rates, fares, and/or fees in exchange for volume. For example, IBM may negotiate discounted rates with Hilton Hotels in exchange for a promise of a minimum of 5000 room-nights over a

ARRIVE HOME READY TO MAKE THAT IMPORTANT PRESENTA-TION.

FIGURE 3.1 *British Airways advertisements. (Courtesy of British Airways. Reprinted with permission.)*

FIGURE 3.1   *(continued)*

FIGURE 3.2 *Sheraton advertisement. (Courtesy of Starwood Hotels & Resorts. Reprinted with permission.)*

given period of time (such as one year) at designated properties across the United States. In these situations, the decision maker was not the individual traveler, but, rather, the company for whom this traveler works. Often corporate travel managers negotiate rates with several suppliers, giving their business travelers options from which to choose. Our IBM traveler may have a choice of Delta or Continental airlines for air transportation; Hilton, Hyatt, or Sheraton hotels for lodging accommodations; and Alamo or Hertz rental car companies for ground transportation.

BUSINESS MEETINGS AND CONVENTIONS

The **meetings and conventions market** includes 85 million delegates attending over one million meetings each year. By the early 1990s, total annual expenditures for corporate and association off-premise meeting activity topped $40 billion.[2] Essentially, this market is defined as groups of 10 or more people meeting together for a common purpose. Corporate, association, and government segments make up the bulk of this market and following is a discussion of each.

Corporate Meetings Market

The types of meetings planned by the **corporate market** include training meetings, sales meetings, new product introductions, management meetings, stockholders meetings, and so forth. There are many reasons for these meetings and goals to be achieved including to motivate, educate, network, team build, bond, and reward. Meetings may be held quarterly, semiannually, annually, or, simply on an ad hoc basis as the need arises. Stockholders meetings are typically held annually as mandated by the FTC (Federal Trade Commission) in the United States and by the Canadian Business Corporations Act in Canada.

In large corporations, these meetings are often planned by a designated meeting planner from that organization. In smaller companies, the individual responsible for planning a meeting may be the person who is hosting the meeting or someone assigned to handle the specific event. Sometimes **independent meeting planning firms** are called in to orchestrate logistics for the event—travel arrangements, lodging, food and beverage, function rooms, ground transportation—where as the meeting agenda specifics are usually set by the company.

At Nestlé Canada, for instance, the travel coordinator is responsible for the majority of meeting planning activity. The specific objective and budget for each meeting are determined by the division head conducting the meeting. This individual contacts the travel coordinator to arrange the details. A designated **meeting planner** at Kraft–General Foods typically receives a detailed meeting agenda from a department head and then the meeting planner is responsible for booking and coordinating accommodations, meeting space, food and beverage, transportation, and so forth.

In one year alone, IBM held over 1000 meetings at Marriott hotels. These meetings were planned, however, by 650 different people and the meetings ranged in size from 10 to 5000 attendees. Although there is a growing trend to consolidate the planning and purchase of corporate meeting activity, it currently remains a decentralized function. As a result, few corporations really know how many meetings they hold on an annual basis and they often rely on suppliers such as hotel companies for this information.

Attendance at corporate meetings, not surprisingly, is usually compulsory. From a supplier perspective, this is advantageous in that forecasting hotel room occupancy, airline load factors, and banquet attendance can be done with a high degree of accuracy.

Corporate meeting planners have their own associations including Meeting Professionals International (MPI) and Professional Convention Managers Association (PCMA). They meet on a regular basis to exchange thoughts, ideas, and technological advances for the meeting planning industry. Association executives (meeting planners for the association market) often join these organizations as well.

Association Market

The **association market** comprises state, regional, national, and international associations. These organizations are formed to serve the common interests and objectives of its individual members. Most associations fall into one of the following categories: trade associations; professional societies; and associations representing nonprofit organizations such as educational, religious, and fraternal groups.

Trade associations largely represent the corporate sector of the economy including the manufacturing, retailing, and service industries. Examples here include the American Bankers Association, the Hospitality Sales and Marketing Association International, and the Grocery Product Manufacturers Association. Professional societies are organized to benefit such professions as law, accounting, and medicine. Examples here include the Canadian Institute of Chartered Accountants, the American Cancer Society, and the Society of Petroleum Engineers.

Associations representing nonprofit organizations have relatively limited budgets. Nonetheless, they are valued customers in that they have large memberships and they often meet during traditionally off-peak periods in the hospitality industry such as summer months and weekends. Hotels, resorts, and conference centers, in particular, actively solicit this market by offering discounted rates during the slower periods.

Most large national associations have full-time meeting planners, typically referred to as **association executives**. These planners, along with a site selection committee and board of directors, take on the meeting planning task of the annual convention, board meetings, regional meetings, special committee meetings, educational seminars, and the like.

The most arduous, of course, is the annual convention. Depending on the size of the association, this process can take anywhere from two days to six months to ten years to complete. For example, attendance at the American Bankers Association (ABA) annual convention is 10,000+ attendees. The ABA's planning horizon usually involves a 10-year advanced booking with a convention center and a headquarters hotel selected at a chosen destination such as Los Angeles, Chicago, Atlanta, or Boston. In the United States, the annual convention typically rotates to various parts of the country each year.

Some associations have their own meeting facilities. The Canadian Institute of Chartered Accountants (CICA) uses its on-site meeting facilities at CICA headquarters whenever possible. These facilities include 12 meeting rooms, catering facilities, and state-of-the-art audiovisual equipment. Off-premise facilities are used when a group is larger than on-site facilities permit (more than 40 attendees) or if the purpose of the meeting could be better served by being held away from its Toronto-based headquarters.

The association market, similar to the corporate meetings market, has its own association—the American Society of Association Executives (ASAE). The ASAE is a large, influential organization based in Washington, DC, home of the majority of associations in the United States. Much is published by ASAE regarding specifics in its field including the *Encyclopedia of Associations*. This publication lists all associations registered in the United States, their home base, officers of the organization, membership size, and so forth. It is a worthwhile investment for hospitality suppliers targeting this market.

Government Market

The **government market** is large. It is made up of persons working for local, state, federal, and related government agencies who attend off-premise government-sponsored meetings each year. Most government meetings are educational seminars or training programs. The planning and timing of these meetings depends on need, and they are not necessarily scheduled on a regular basis.

All government employees who travel on official business have daily spending allowances known as per diems, which cover food, lodging, transportation, and related expenses. Per diems for government employees vary depending on the employee's position and travel destination.

A good source for government-type accounts is the *Encyclopedia of Associations* under the listing "Legal, Government, Public Administration and Military Organizations." These include the Department of Commerce, the Internal Revenue Service, Peace Corps, U.S. Environmental Protection Agency, U.S. Secret Service, and so forth. There is also the *United States Government Manual,* which includes a listing of major federal agencies and departments and describes the functions of each. Similar to corporate and association meeting planners, government planners have their own association, the Society of Government Meeting Planners.

EXHIBITS AND TRADE SHOWS

Exhibits and trade shows are big business. Two well-known events for the hospitality industry are the National Restaurant Association (NRA) Show and the International Hotel/Motel and Restaurant Show (IHMRS) held each year in May and November, respectively. Literally thousands of hoteliers, restaurateurs, club managers, institutional foodservice directors, and the like, attend these shows to view and purchase products and equipment for their businesses. Suppliers such as computer companies, kitchen manufacturers, glassware vendors, and linen suppliers display their goods with an army of salespersons to "sell" their wares.

Larger trade shows, such as the NRA Show and IHMRS mentioned, previously book at major convention centers such as McCormick Place in Chicago, the Javits Center in New York, and the Hynes Convention Center in Boston. Shows of this magnitude need a large amount of square footage for exhibitors to display their wares and to meet face-to-face with prospective customers.

Exhibitors are, indeed, salespeople. Trade shows are an excellent venue to communicate directly with potential customers about product and service offerings. As noted in a recent publication on international trade shows:

> To sales and marketing professionals, these three to four days of frenzied activity represent paradise. It is the ideal stage for doing what they do best—qualify leads, find distributors, sell goods, introduce new products, monitor current trends and check out the competition.... And it's done in person—one on one—without anything or anyone getting in the way.[3]

International trade shows or trade fairs are flourishing and stretch around the globe, ranging from the Geotechnica/Information Technology trade fair in Cologne, Germany, to the Tokyo Motor Show/Automotive trade fair in Tokyo, Japan, to the Expocorma/Forest Products trade fair in Santiago, Chile, to the Expocomer/Consumer products trade fair in Panama City, Panama.

INSTITUTIONAL MARKET

Players in the **institutional market** are largely comprised of institutional organizations such as colleges and universities, hospitals and health care centers, primary and secondary school systems, and corporate facilities. They are major providers as well as purchasers of foodservice operations. Many manage their own foodservice operations. Yet there is a growing trend to outsource the business of feeding employees, students, or hospital patrons to companies that are in the business of providing this service. These include suppliers such as ARAMARK and Marriott contract foodservice companies of the United States, and Beaver Foods and Cara foodservice operations of Canada.

For example, ARAMARK has a contractual agreement with Saint Joseph's Health Center in Kansas City, Kansas, to manage its on-premise food court for patients and their families at this health care facility. ARAMARK's client is the health care center. The end users are the patients, families, and friends who patronize the food court services. It is the satisfaction of both these customers that determine the true success of this partnership.

LEISURE CUSTOMERS

By the mid-1990s, "[U.S.] pleasure travel, including visiting friends/relatives, outdoor recreation and entertainment, accounted for 781 million person-trips."[4] **Person-trips**, a common industry statistic, is one person traveling 100 miles or more away from home one way. The **leisure market** can be segmented into singles, couples, families, and the mature market. Following is a more detailed picture of these customers. (As noted at the beginning of this chapter, a detailed discussion of tour wholesale operators—intermediaries whose primary market is the leisure travel market—is presented in Chapter 11.)

Singles, Couples, and Families

"Vacationing Families Head Downtown to Welcoming Arms of Business Hotels" read a recent headline in the *Wall Street Journal*.[5] To cater to the needs of families, Hyatt Hotels inaugurated "Camp Hyatt" in the early 1990s, offering a range of organized activities for family entertainment. And, as reported in the *International Herald Tribune*, Pippa Pop-ins is a "[h]otel for the under—12 set." Located in London, England, it is "apparently the only children's hotel in the world."[6]

Singles, couples, and families purchase hospitality products for myriad reasons including rest, relaxation, fun, adventure, escape from boredom, visiting friends and relatives, and the get-away-from-it-all syndrome. Leisure, in this context, refers to an evening out, a weekend at Opryland, a trip to grandmother's, or New Year's Eve in Paris. To a child, a trip to Disney World is, indeed, a trip to fantasyland. To hard-working 20-something young professionals, a night out is sometimes fantasyland, too.

GNO—or Girls Night Out—is a group of MBA graduates from New York University who have been getting together every two months for the past 13 years for an evening out. They exchange thoughts, views, and ideas, are a source of support for each other, and share career-building goals and frustrations. They are also part of the leisure let's-go-out-for-dinner market. Over the years, several of these women have become mothers and now you see "infant seats under the table," too.[7]

Restaurants, hotels, campgrounds, and so forth cater to the needs and desires of the leisure market. Revisiting the "Vacationing Families Head Downtown," Camp Hyatt, and Pippa Pop-ins introduced earlier, there are several trends of significance here. First, dual-career couples with kids are traveling more and more as a family. It may be a two-week vacation in Europe or a four-day weekend getaway in downtown Chicago. Strollers are starting to clog the elevators. And, as reported by James Hirsch:

> The Hyatt Regency Reston in Reston, Va. uses its 21 executive suites for weekend slumber parties. The kids, no more than 10, throw down their sleeping bags in the living room, and the grown-ups stay out of harm's way in an adjoining bedroom.[8]

Second, sometimes family members need a break from each other, and the concept of babysitting has been around for along time. But a hotel for children only? Why not. Pippa Pop-ins was the innovation of Pippa Deakin, a former teacher and nanny. She opened her hotel for tots as a licensed nursery, which has a three-night maximum stay. "Just what kind of parents send their child to a hotel overnight? . . . it's more likely to be parents with a big night out."[9] The children play together, eat supper together, choose their own beds, are squeaky clean from bubble baths, have organized pillow fights, and often don't want to leave in the morning when it's time to go home.

A third issue is that families are eating out together, a lot. Chain restaurants such as Red Lobster, Ponderosa, and Friendly's actively seek this market. These casual-dining establishments are gaining in popularity with families as well as with singles and couples. As noted by Bill Saporito of *Fortune* magazine:

Movable Feasts: More People Dine and Drive

FIGURE 3.3 *Dine-and-drive market illustration. (Source: Wall Street Journal*, January 4, 1994, p. B1. Courtesy of Richard Bennett. Reprinted with permission.)

The fastest growing segment of the restaurant industry: casual dining, where sales are increasing at double-digit rates. This nomenclature includes such settings as Chili's, Applebee's, and Outback Steakhouse, where vittles come with a relaxed atmosphere. The concept here: not-so-fast food for aging boomers who may still crave a burger but now want to sit down and eat it from a plate, perhaps with a glass of wine. And the kids? Sure, bring 'em. [10]

Also mobilizing is the dine-and-drive crowd. Shown in Figure 3.3 are examples of these diners—the busy on-the-road sales executive, a 50-

something vacation couple, and, of course, soccer mom and the gang on the way home from the game. By the early 1990s, one in ten meals purchased in a restaurant was consumed in the car. "When snacks from convenience stores are included . . . the incidence of eating and driving may be as high as one in six meals."[11]

Our habits are changing. Meals eaten away from home and takeout meals brought into the home continue to rise. The hospitality industry is responding to these emerging needs, wants, and desires of the energetic, fast-paced demands of today's consumer.

Specialized and/or individualized vacation travel is on the rise, too. Ecotourists are looking for true back-to-nature, nonurbanized travel such as backpacking, canoeing, and cattle ranching—anything away from the city, suburbs, and civilization in general. Adventure seekers are rock climbing, bungie jumping, sky diving, and exploring icebergs in Antarctica.

Directed-play vacations are also a growth market. Upscale travelers, in particular, are drawn to themed events for a holiday excursion. As noted by Keri Culver, a spa director for Sonnenalp Resort Spa in Vail, Colorado, "[f]rom intensive language clinics to athletic camps to writer's workshops, upper-end guests are seeking 'directed play' vacations."[12] Shown in Table 3.2 are topic ideas for camps, clinics, and workshops suggested by Culver in her article in the *HSMAI Marketing Review.*

Some vacationers simply seek peace and quiet. One couple we know recently spent a week's holiday at a rented villa on the tiny island of Montserrat. What is there to do on Montserrat? Nothing. Nothing except enjoy the beautiful sunny days and quietly soak up the sun, read a novel, take a dip in the private pool, play a game of tennis, dine on the patio by moonlight. Where is Montserrat? Never mind, it's a secret.

Mature Market

Not in the history of leisure travel has the mature market been such a tremendous force in the hospitality business. Their reasons for travel are as varied as the singles, couples, and family markets. And because of their sheer size, a separate discussion is warranted.

The **mature market** is generally considered to be pleasure travelers aged 50 and over. Aptly stated by Irma Mann, who heads her own strategic marketing firm specializing in hospitality:

> The 25-year-old skinny-dipper at Woodstock is now the 50-year-old insurance executive, and a member of the American Association of Retired Persons (AARP). The generation that witnessed "The Greening of America" is now taking part in its graying. And for all the ballyhoo and media attention directed toward Generation X, the children of baby boomers, "mature" Americans will be the growth market for the travel industry.

TABLE 3.2 *Sample Ideas for Directed Play Vacations*
Writer's Workshop
with a renowned author
Golf Instruction—Women Only or Co-Ed
excellent demographic and interest is already very high
Photography Workshop
perhaps color photography in spring, black and white in autumn
Language Program
with cultural activities—dancing, special foods, speakers
Surfing/Windsurfing Camp
with a competition at the end of the week
Stress Management and Wellness Clinic
with guided imagery classes, yoga, hiking
Cycling Week
with an Olympian on a road bike or a rebel with a mountain bike
Women's Fitness Quest
with athletic and bonding activities
Political or Topic-Based Forum
in a symposium format with speakers, panel discussions, and round tables
Awakening the Artist Week
featuring numerous artistic endeavors, plus speakers and rituals
Swimming Camp
for triathletes and masters swimmers
Wild Man Retreat
on the level of Iron John and similar activities, to reveal the wild spirit of males
Women's Adventure Week
including rock climbing, kayaking, horseback or mountain bike riding
Senior's Longevity Week
with one of the new low-impact, lifestyle fitness modalities, for example Pilates, Feldenkrais, The Egoscue Method, Larry Lane, or Debbie and Carlos Rosas.

Source: Keri Culver, "Directed Play Vacations," *HSMAI Marketing Review,* Winter 1996, pp. 21–24. Reprinted with permission.

"People over 50" applies to 26 percent of the United States population, and comprises almost one-third of American households. This is a population that controls three-quarters of all domestic material wealth, and is responsible for two-thirds of discretionary spending. Last year there were more mature Americans than teenagers, and by the turn of the century, 60 million Americans will be age 55 or older.[13]

Although age is used as the primary market segmentation variable to define this market, other attributes, such as income level, education level, lifestyle, and so forth, offer important ways to further segment this market. As noted by Forbes and Forbes:

It is no longer possible to look at age as the sole clue to the lifestyle that an individual or age group is currently involved in. In today's society of later marriages, multiple marriages, early retirement, reentry into the workforce after retirement, and lifelong learning, it is no longer logical to attribute specific interests and activities to a mature adult by age.[14]

These authors suggest segmenting by life changes and recommend five distinct market segments for the mature market: "the 50–55 active employed, the 55–60 pre-retired, the 60–65 approaching retirement or semi-retired, the 65–75 retired or semi-employed, and the 75+ retired."[15] They then label the age 50–60 group as more similar to the "boomer" generation (age 35–50) since they are still, for the most part, actively employed. Mann similarly suggests that "for purposes of marketing, most hotels and airlines have defined the 'mature' traveler as between the ages of 60 and 75."[16]

The 60+ mature market travelers have more time to travel, more flexibility in when they choose to travel, and more discretionary income to spend on travel. That is not to say that this market spends freely! Quite the opposite. They are most protective of their hard-earned dollars and choose very carefully how that "nest egg" is going to be spent. Indeed, many senior citizens choose not to travel at all.

For those that do, there are myriad ways in which they select and plan their travel itineraries. Some make all the decisions themselves, and then find a travel agent to book their preplanned itinerary for them. Some join travel clubs and pick and choose which travel excursions they want to participate in. University alumni groups, hobby clubs, art galleries, Smithsonian museums, and even banks are getting into the travel game targeting the mature market.

[U.S.] Banks started setting up discount-travel clubs in the early 1980s as a way to lure older depositors. Now the clubs are gaining popularity, and banks are planning more elaborate trips to outdo one another. Banc One's Classic One club recently sent 200 older depositors to Australia, at $5,000 a person. First State Bank in Barbersville W.Va., sponsored a two-week trip to Europe.[17]

Sometimes they know their travel companions well; sometimes not. In the latter instance, part of the reason for travel is to meet new people and make new friends, especially with those who enjoy similar travel experiences.

No matter how you fine tune or subsegment the mature market, their presence is formidable. Again, the sheer magnitude of this market make it worthy of much fuss by all hospitality players.

Group Leisure Market

Many associations are created around people's personal interests and hobbies, and regularly hold annual conventions. Examples include the National Bridge Club Association, the Star Trek "Trekkie" Association, the U.S. Figure Skating Club of America, and the National Amateur Rose Growers Association. Name any hobby and chances are there is a state, regional, and/or national association for these enthusiasts.

Much like the association market for nonprofit business organizations, leisure association membership is typically price sensitive. Delegates attending these conventions are not on expense accounts and personally pay their association annual dues, travel expenditures to attend meetings and conventions, and so forth, out of their own pocket. But they do travel, attend their annual conventions, and enjoy every minute of it.

The Hyatt Regency Cambridge of Greater Boston once booked the Northeast Amateur Rose Growers Association for a Labor Day weekend at significantly reduced rates. Not only did the hotel achieve 100 percent occupancy over the long-weekend period (which typically ran 20 to 30 percent), the hotel staff enjoyed a beautiful array of bright fragrant roses brought in by association members artistically displayed throughout the entire hotel.

Travel clubs (mentioned earlier in the mature market segment) also generate business within the group leisure market. Family reunions, weddings, and bar mitzvahs are part of this market, too. A key point to remember is that the reason for travel is pleasure and not business. Yet a growing number of travelers combine these two purposes into one trip. A businessperson might travel to the West Coast to conduct business Thursday and Friday, and then be joined by his or her spouse for a weekend getaway in the same locale.

SUMMARY

Customers in the hospitality industry are many and diverse. Broadly speaking, people travel for business or leisure purposes. The needs, wants, and desires of the leisure travel market are quite different from the business travel market. The successful sales manager recognizes these differences and he or she approaches these varied markets accordingly.

Several business market segments were introduced in this chapter including individuals, meetings and conventions, exhibits and trade shows, and institutional markets. Major players in the business arena include corporate, association, and government markets. For the meetings and conventions market, meeting planners and association executives who plan meetings are the customers that hospitality sales managers call on to solicit this business. In large corporations, travel coordinators or travel managers often negotiate with hospitality sales managers for volume discounts for the travel needs of their employees.

Another business segment is the government market. Government employees travel for both group and individual purposes for local, state, federal, and related government agencies. They travel on a per diem, which is a preset spending allowance for daily food, lodging, and transportation expenses.

Exhibitions and trade shows are, for the most part, held for business purposes. Often held on an annual basis, these shows offer suppliers in a given industry the opportunity to display and market their products to prospective buyers. Personal selling is the primary communication tool used by exhibitors at these shows to sell their goods and services.

Many institutions are providers as well as purchasers of foodservice operations. Some manage their own operations, while others outsource this task to companies that are in the business of providing this service. In this chapter, we gave the example of ARAMARK managing the on-premise food court services for Saint Joseph's Health Center of Kansas City, Kansas.

The leisure segment is made up of singles, families, couples, and the mature market. They travel for fun, relaxation, excitement, to get away from it all, and a host of other reasons. Increasingly, we see dual-career couples taking time away from work and home to travel with their young children. Casual-dining establishments are also gaining in popularity with families as well as singles and couples. The dine-and-drive crowd is alive and well, too.

The mature market is another growth market for both individual and group leisure travel. The 60+ mature market, in particular, has more time to travel and more flexibility in when they choose to travel. Although their discretionary income is, for the most part, higher than the boomers and Generation X, they nonetheless watch their travel spending quite closely.

Group leisure markets include the mature market as well as leisure associations, travel clubs, family reunions, weddings, bar mitzvahs, and so forth. These groups sometimes make their own arrangements and sometimes work with a travel agent. Regardless, they are major players in the growing leisure segment of the hospitality industry.

DISCUSSION QUESTION

1. We do not market hotel rooms to business travelers, we help improve their productivity when traveling for business purposes. Discuss.
2. How do the needs of business and leisure travelers vary?
3. Compare and contrast the corporate and association meetings and conventions markets. How are they similar? How are they different?
4. What are exhibits and trade shows? What is their purpose?
5. Who are the major players in the institutional market and what are their basic needs?
6. Discuss current trends and issues in the leisure market.

NOTES

1. The Frequent Traveler [advertising supplement], *Business Week*, April 18, 1994, p. 3.
2. Loren G. Edelstein and Carla Benini, "Meetings Market Report 1994," *Meetings & Conventions*, August 1994, pp. 60–61 and 64–74.
3. "International Trade Fairs [advertising supplement], *Canadian Business Journal*, January 1995.
4. "American Travelers Set Record Numbers," *Hotel & Motel Management*, November 6, 1995, p. 64.
5. James S. Hirsch, "Vacationing Families Head Downtown to Welcoming Arms of Business Hotels," *Wall Street Journal*, June 13, 1994, p. B1.
6. Emily L. Baker, "For Overnight Pop-Ins: A Hotel for the Under-12 Set," *International Herald Tribune*, November 25, 1994, p. 10.
7. Sue Shellenbarger, "Five Friends Get the Lift They Need from Girls Night Out," *Wall Street Journal*, May 29, 1996, p. B1.
8. Hirsch, "Vacationing Families Head Downtown," p. B1.
9. Baker, "For Overnight Pop-Ins," p. 10.
10. Bill Saporito, "What's for Dinner? The Battle for Stomach Share," *Fortune*, May 15, 1995, pp. 50–51, 56, 60, and 64.

11. Kathleen Deveny, "Movable Feasts: More People Dine and Drive," *Wall Street Journal*, January 4, 1994, p. B1.

12. Keri Culver, "Directed Play Vacations," *HSMAI Marketing Review*, Winter 1996, pp. 21–24.

13. Irma S. Mann, "Tapping into the Mature Market," *Hotel & Resort Industry*, May 1994, p. 30.

14. Robert J. Forbes and Maree S. Forbes, "The Mature Market: Prime Travelers Who 'Do It Their Way,' " *HSMAI Marketing Review*, Fall 1994, p. 18.

15. Ibid., p. 19.

16. Mann, "Tapping into the Mature Market," p. 30.

17. Daniel Pearl, "More Seniors Taking Travel Plans to the Bank," *Wall Street Journal*, September 6, 1994, p. B1.

Chapter 4

Hospitality Businesses: The Suppliers

LEARNING OBJECTIVES

1. *To become familiar with the major players in the lodging and foodservice side of hospitality businesses*
2. *To better understand the hotel, resort, and conference center businesses in lodging hospitality*
3. *To better understand the restaurant, catering, and contract foodservice businesses in hospitality*

"Gaming Still Drives Worldwide Expansion," "Hotels Contracting Out Food and Beverage Operations," "Ramada Revives with Three Tiers," "Successful Timeshare Conversion of World-Class Resorts," "New U.K. Theme Park Follows Trend to Tap Europe's Fun-Seekers"—each of these headlines in publications around the world reflects today's dynamic happenings in hospitality. Suppliers are as numerous and varied as customers. This and the following chapter take a closer look at suppliers in the hospitality arena. This chapter covers hotels, resorts, and conference centers and restaurants, catering, and contract foodservices. Chapter 5 includes convention centers, casinos and gaming, timeshare and vacation ownership, cruise lines, country inns and bed-and-breakfasts, theme parks, and tourism destinations. Each has sales teams, marketing plans, selling strategies, and promotional campaigns to reach out to its target markets and to get and keep a customer.

HOTELS, RESORTS, AND CONFERENCE CENTERS

Hotels, resorts, and conference centers are probably the most visible, the most written about, and the most likely to be a household word. They are all in the business of supplying lodging accommodations, food and beverage services, and other amenities to the traveling public. As defined by the *Random House Dictionary*, a hotel is a "commercial establishment offering lodging to travelers . . . often having restaurants, meeting rooms, stores, etc., that are available to the general public."[1] Lodging establishments emerge as separate and distinct entities because of varying target markets and specific product offerings.

Hotels

Hotels are typically categorized in several ways including property type, location, and size. This is commonly referred to as **product segmentation**. Shown in Table 4.1 is a widely accepted product segmentation approach separating hotels by property type: budget/economy (limited and full service), mid-market (limited and full service), upscale/first-class, and luxury. Property type is largely a differentiation by price level (the room rate range of guest rooms at the property) and by service level. Limited service implies that there is little or no function space and limited food and beverage facilities.

Product segmentation categories for location usually include down-

---

TABLE 4.1 *Product Segmentation by Property Type*

Property Type	Examples
Budget/economy (limited service)	Motel 6, EconoLodge, Travelodge, Super 8, Knights Inn, Formule 1 (Europe)
Budget/economy (full service)	Days Inn, Rodeway Inn, Howard Johnson, Journey's End by Choice (Canada)
Mid-market (limited service)	Comfort Inn, Fairfield Inn, Shoney's, Hampton Inn, Holiday Inn Express
Mid-market (full service)	Best Western, Courtyard, Holiday Inn, Ramada, Posthouse (Great Britain)
Upscale/first-class	Doubletree, Hilton, Hyatt, Marriott, Radisson, Sheraton, Omni, Delta, Sofitel (France)
Luxury	Four Seasons, Ritz-Carlton, Savoy Group of London, Oberoi (India)

Source: Adapted from National Hotel Realty Advisors, Hotel & Motel Brokers of America, Hospitality Evaluation Services. Reported in Patrick Ford, ''Real Estate in Transition,'' *Lodging,* May 1996, pp. 53–60.

---

town, suburban, highway, airport, and resort. Size categories are typically defined as under 75 rooms, 75 to 150 rooms, 150 to 300 rooms, 300 to 500 rooms, and over 500 rooms.

Product segmentation categorization helps make statistical information more meaningful to hospitality management. Industry statistics on occupancy and **average daily rates (ADRs),** for example, are regularly produced for comparison purposes by organizations such as Smith Travel Research and the American Hotel & Motel Association (AH&MA). An urban upscale property such as a Sheraton or Westin hotel is clearly going to have a higher ADR than a suburban limited-service budget property such as a Motel 6 or Super 8 hotel. Tables 4.2 and 4.3 give examples of commonly reported figures in the trade press. Sometimes general statistics with no product segmentation are reported. This is often done to give an overall picture of the industry, especially over a period of time. Table 4.4 gives an example adapted from a *Wall Street Journal Europe* article reporting on new optimism in the hotel sector in the United States. As the author noted, ''[t]he hotel industry in the U.S. has benefited greatly from the general economic recovery of the 1990s, and the corresponding increase in demand for hotel accommodations.''[2]

Budget/economy hotels are largely the domain of the interstate highway. Demand is generated, for the most part, by the interstate traveler who is looking for a place to stay for the night that is inexpensive, safe, simple, and clean. Many of these travelers, whether for business or for pleasure, are in transit, that is, trying to get somewhere or just passing through en route to a final destination. There was substantial growth for this sector throughout

TABLE 4.2   *Hotel Operating Performance Statistics by Location*

Location	Occupancy Percentage		Average Room Rate	
	1997	1998	1997	1998
Urban	69.8%	69.7%	$114.80	$106.56
Suburban	65.9%	66.3%	$72.23	$68.31
Airport	70.5%	71.0%	$77.98	$72.11
Highway	60.8%	61.7%	$55.16	$52.46
Resort	69.7%	69.1%	$114.85	$108.69

Source: © 1998 Smith Travel Research. Reprinted with permission.

the 1980s and it appears to be leveling off in the 1990s (at approximately 20 percent of total U.S. lodging industry revenues). As noted by Randell Smith, president and founder of Smith Travel Research:

> [T]he reasons [for this] are difficult to pinpoint. The travelers who prefer economy/budget hotels have perhaps been diverted by the discounts offered by mid-price properties. Or they may not be taking as many trips as before the recession in spite of a high level of consumer confidence.[3]

Nonetheless, relatively new entrants are feeling confident about the budget/economy sector in the U.S. market including Knights Lodging Systems (KLS) based in Cleveland, Ohio. KLS is a growing chain, currently at 180 properties, and was one of the first chains to introduce its own credit card. KLS teamed up with Huntington National Bank and MasterCard to

TABLE 4.3   *New Property Construction by Property Type and Location*

By Property Type	1989	1995
Budget/economy	40.1%	22.9%
Mid-market	30.8	51.1
Upscale/first-class	20.4	24.9
Luxury	8.7	1.0
	100.0%	100.0%
By Location	**1989**	**1995**
Urban	6.3%	1.2%
Suburban	39.3	48.2
Highway	45.7	48.2
Airport	5.6	1.6
Resort	3.1	.7
	100.0%	100.0%

Note: 1989 total: 827 units; 1995 total: 562 units.
Source: © 1997 Smith Travel Research. Reprinted with permission.

TABLE 4.4   *Total U.S. Hotel Occupancy and Average Room Rates*

Year	Occupancy	Average Daily Rate
1990	63.5%	$57.96
1991	61.8%	$58.08
1992	62.6%	$58.91
1993	63.5%	$60.53
1994	64.7%	$62.86
1995	65.1%	$65.81
1996	65.0%	$70.81
1997	64.7%	$75.16
1998[a]	63.9%	$78.84

[a]Projected.
Source: © 1998 Smith Travel Research.

offer a credit card "emblazoned with the logo of [the] hotel franchising company . . . one of several new marketing programs rolled out by KLS to bolster brand awareness" for this new entrant in the budget/economy sector.[4]

Holiday Inn, Ramada, Best Western, and the like, are well-known mid-market hotel chains throughout the United States, Canada, and worldwide. They are readily visible on major highways, in the suburbs, and in downtown locations of small-to-medium-sized cities such as Northampton, Massachusetts, and Shawnee Mission, Kansas. They are emerging in metropolitan areas such as Atlanta, Chicago, and San Francisco, and at major airports, too. Properties in these metropolitan locations are slightly larger, 100+ rooms, but account for less than 20 percent of all mid-market lodging establishments in the United States.[5] Overall, supply and demand growth for the mid-market sector was modest yet steady by the mid-1990s.

What's new in the mid-market? Wingate and AmericInn are good examples. Wingate is a new brand and a division of Hospitality Franchise Systems (HFS) that was launched in 1995. The Wingate concept is an all-new-construction product being developed as a "limited-service, mid-market chain that will feature sophisticated in-room technology . . . that cater[s] to the needs of the business traveler."[6] HFS is anticipating 300 properties by the year 2000.

AmericInn, started in the early 1990s, has grown from 21 properties in 1992 to a forecasted 100 hotels by the mid-to-late 1990s. Its current strongholds are Minnesota, Wisconsin, and Iowa, and it is looking to expand to new geographic areas. AmericInn is competing across the "luxury-economy and mid-market segments . . ." with rates ranging from $50 to $80 and a room mix that "includes suites with whirlpool, refrigerator and microwave."[7] The masonry-and-concrete construction promises a quiet room; swimming pools, saunas, and/or game rooms promise opportunities for relaxation.

The upscale/first-class product segment sector is alive and well. Although down in the 1980s, average rates and occupancies emerged stable and steady by the early 1990s and are expected to continue on this upbeat trend. According to Smith Travel Research, the ADR for this segment was in the $80+ range by mid-1990.[8] Shown in Figures 4.1 and 4.2 are examples of Marriott and Sofitel advertisements for this sector. Marriott's ad is targeting the first-class business meeting planner; Sofitel's is aimed at the upscale, transient guest. First-class hotels are primarily located in large downtown urban centers and in secondary cities where corporate business activity is high such as Hartford, Connecticut, and Somerset, New Jersey. Major suburbs with burgeoning business centers and/or corporate industrial parks, such as Naperville, Illinois, are also home to upscale lodging establishments. The primary target market for these hotels is, indeed, business travel.

Convention hotels are large first-class operations catering to the needs of the association and convention markets, and are often selected as headquarters hotels for major exhibits and trade shows, too. The Chicago Hilton, for example, is located in the heart of downtown Chicago. It has over 2000 rooms, with multiple function rooms and ballrooms, and specifically targets the large convention market. The Opryland Hotel, an independent operator located on the outskirts of Nashville, Tennessee, is a major convention hotel player. Recent developments at this property are compelling:

> Perhaps the most captivating project in the hospitality industry is the just-completed Delta expansion at the Opryland Hotel. The project, which opens this month [June 1996], features 988 new guestrooms (for a total of 2,879), more than 300,000 square feet of new meeting and exhibit facilities (for a total of more than 600,000 square feet), and the Delta itself. The Delta is a 4.5 acre, glass-roofed interiorscape complete with shops, restaurants, meeting rooms, and a river.[9]

Opryland, Hilton, and a host of others that target the convention market are complex operations. They also rely heavily on personal selling as the major communication tool to attract and keep customers.

Luxury hotels, needless to say, are the high end of the hotel sector. Whether traveling for business or for pleasure, luxury hotels are prepared to pamper the elite, the jet-setters, the CEOs, or whomever, who are willing and able to pay the price. Average daily rates at these establishments hover in the $250+ range, depending on what part of the world one is traveling to. Examples of these "grande dames" in the United States include the independently operated Plaza and Carlisle in Manhattan. Probably the best

FIGURE 4.1 *Marriott Hotels, Resorts and Suites advertisement. (Courtesy of Marriott International. Reprinted with permission.)*

FIGURE 4.2   *Hotel Sofitel advertisement. (Courtesy of Hotel Sofitel. Reprinted with permission.)*

known luxury chain-operated hotels in North America are the Ritz-Carlton and Four Seasons brand names. Inter-Continental Hotels operates several luxury hotels in Europe and Asia including the recently opened Hotel Inter-Continental Singapore.

Corporate retreats for senior-level management are frequently held at luxury properties and are target markets for sales managers at these hotels. Altoon + Porter Architects of Los Angeles, for example, hold company retreats twice a year at luxury hotels, lasting three to four days. As reported in *Corporate Meetings & Incentives*, Ronald Altoon, president of the firm, comments that, "we meet as partners [six of us] two times a year for tactical and strategic planning . . . [a]nd we feel that the ambience at the hotel is critical to us."[10] Succinctly stated by the author of the article, "[f]or some corporate executives, holding a meeting at a top-rated hotel is not an option, but an absolute necessity for achieving their business objective."[11]

All-suite hotels and the extended-stay market represent a growth area in hospitality. Unique to the all-suite hotel is the guest room configuration, which is actually two rooms—sleeping accommodations plus a living space area. Sometimes the living room includes a pullout sleep sofa. Most all-suite accommodations include a kitchen workspace area, a refrigerator, and a microwave oven. These hotels may or may not offer food and beverage services on the premises. In other words, there is a range of all-suite hotels just as there is for traditional hotels. For example, research has shown that "this group accounts for one in five of the hotels in the luxury and upscale price-level segments."[12]

All-suites target families as well as businesspersons traveling to an area for an extended period of time. This type of business traveler has come to be known as the **extended-stay market.** This market is described as business-people who stay at a lodging establishment five nights or longer.

Several hotel chains are going after this business market including Marriott with its Residence Inn brand, MainStay Suites by Choice Hotels, and Hawthorne Suites by US Franchise Systems. They, and others, are specifically targeting corporate employees in training, relocating, or on special project assignments. And, as noted by Rufus Schriber, brand vice president at Residence Inns by Marriott, "[t]here are a lot of companies outsourcing. . . . It is an important notion for business going forward and a healthy sign for extended-stay [hotels]."[13] Outsourcing, as a reminder, is when one company hires another company to do work that was previously done in-house. Like consulting, it is often a special assignment of a short-term nature. And, of course, these people need a place to put down their toothbrush and hang their hat.

Homewood Suites is also active in the all-suite/extended-stay marketplace. Figure 4.3 shows one of its frequent advertisements in *Hotel & Motel Management* luring investors to strongly consider the Homewood Suite brand as the better choice by which to enter this growing market.

Product-Line Development

Thus far, we have looked at hotels from a product segmentation perspective, that is, the budget/economy, mid-market, upscale/first-class, and luxury seg-

FIGURE 4.3 *Homewood Suites advertisement. (Courtesy of Promus Hotels, Inc. Reprinted with permission.)*

ments. We then addressed the all-suite/extended-stay grouping. At this point, it is important to introduce and address product-line development in the industry.

Hotel chains such as Sheraton, Hyatt, and Marriott, originally entered the hotel industry in the upscale/first-class segment. Holiday Inn (HI) first entered in the mid-market sector. Throughout the 1980s and continuing into the 1990s, these hotel companies, among others, are expanding across product segments. Hotel companies have a mandate for growth, as does any business enterprise, and a good portion of this growth in hospitality has been through product-line development.

Product-line development is when a company that is in a core business, such as lodging, develops product concepts that reach out to separate and distinct markets. Continuing with the HI example, this hotel chain developed and introduced the Holiday Inn–Crowne Plaza upscale hotel in the mid-1980s. Subsequently, it expanded its product line further to include HI Sunspree Resorts and Holiday Inn Express—a budget/economy product.

DoubleTree Hotels, initially in the first-class hotel market, recently expanded into the upscale all-suite sector. Descriptions of each of these product lines are shown in Figures 4.4, and 4.5 respectively.

Marriott has developed product lines in several lodging sectors. These range from the budget/economy brand, Fairfield Inns, to the luxury product line called J. W. Marriott Hotels. Table 4.5 gives a more detailed picture of Marriott's product-line development.

Sheraton continues with its first-class hotels and is aggressively promoting its "The Luxury Collection," which includes the St. Regis in New York and the Royal Orchid in Bangkok (see Figure 4.6). Sheraton has its mid-market Four Points brand in its product-line portfolio, which is described in Figure 4.7. In this case, however, the Four Points product-line development is really a renaming of its Sheraton Inns brand which had a confusing image in the marketplace. As articulated by Glenn Withiam, senior editor of the *Cornell Quarterly*:

> ITT Sheraton rolled out a new midscale franchise only flag in April 1995. The new chain, Four Points Hotels, will comprise full-service properties aimed at both business and leisure travelers. In part, Four Points was created to reduce the potential market confusion created by the Sheraton Inn name. Sheraton's description of the new chain makes it appear to be a direct competitor with Courtyard by Marriott and other "garden" type hotels.[14]

Not all Sheraton Inns are automatically converted to the Four Points brand. Certain standards have to be met, which are slightly higher and more stringent than the previously set standards for Sheraton Inns. Sheraton's strategy is to eventually phase out its Sheraton Inn properties altogether.

One smart business call.

That's all it takes to put you in touch with over 60 Doubletree Hotels from coast to coast, where you'll enjoy the luxuries you like at rates that will let you rest easier.

And at every Doubletree, you'll find the kind of personal service and special attention that will bring you back again and again. And it begins the very first night with our welcoming chocolate chip cookies.

So. You don't have to give up the great restaurants, swimming pools, and health clubs that make business trips bearable. Because now, you've got the right connection. Doubletree Hotels. It's a smart call.

DOUBLETREE
H   O   T   E   L   S

We're waiting to welcome you at over 60 Doubletree Hotels from coast to coast.

FIGURE 4.4 *DoubleTree Hotels advertisement. (Courtesy of Promus Hotels, Inc. Reprinted with permission.)*

Resorts

Resorts are first-class hotels located in rural areas typically offering some level of outdoor recreational facilities such as swimming, golf, tennis, or horseback riding. Because of their isolated location, a full array of food and beverage services are normally offered. Historically, resorts catered to the upscale leisure traveler on vacation—the resort was a destination in itself. Today, they continue to target this market yet also target the meetings and conventions markets.

Well-known independent resorts include the Greenbriar in White Sulphur Springs, West Virginia, the Homestead in Hot Springs, Virginia, and the Broadmoor in Colorado Springs, Colorado. The "Springs" locations themselves depict the idyllic settings of these classic resort facilities.

Several chain-operated hotel companies own and/or manage resort op-

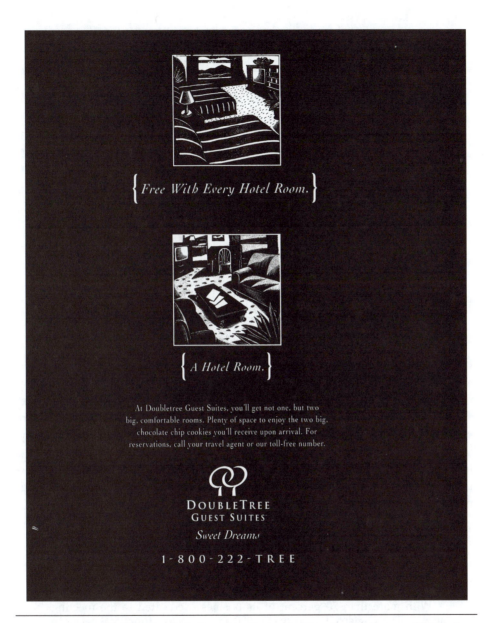

FIGURE 4.5 *DoubleTree Guest Suites advertisement. (Courtesy of Promus Hotels, Inc. Reprinted with permission.)*

TABLE 4.5   *Marriott Lodging Product-Line Development*

Lodging Sector	Product Line
Budget/economy	
Hotel	Fairfield Inns by Marriott
All-suite	Fairfield Suites by Marriott
Extended stay	TownePlace Suites by Marriott
Mid-market	
Hotel	Courtyard by Marriott
Extended stay	Residence Inns by Marriott
All-suite	SpringHill Suites by Marriott
First-class/upscale	
Hotel	Marriott Hotels
	Renaissance Hotels
All-suite	Marriott Executive Apartments
Luxury	J.W. Marriott Hotels
Super luxury	The Ritz-Carlton Hotels
Resort	Marriott Resorts
	Renaissance Resorts
	The Ritz-Carlton Resorts
Resort timeshare	Marriott Vacation Club International

Source: Marriott International.

erations. Hilton Hotels is now Hilton Hotels and Resorts, a trademark signifying that it is in the resort side of the business, too. Marriott references Hotels • Resorts • Suites in many of its advertising campaigns (see Figure 4.1). Registry Hotels and Resorts follows a similar strategy. This company, like others, targets both the leisure and business markets. Following is a description of its Everglades property from a *Worldwide Resort Guide* advertising supplement depicting how it can meet the needs of both these segments:

> The Registry Resort in Naples [Florida] is a world-class property known for its casual elegance, luxurious accommodations, exceptional restaurants, and state-of-the-art conference facilities. Designers and architects created the resort to coexist with a fragile environment of clear water, unspoiled mangrove-lined beaches, and lush, green flora.
>
> With more than 70 percent of its business dedicated to the meetings market, The Registry Resort has 38,000 square feet of function space conveniently situated on one level. The resort's Crystal Ballroom accommodates up to 1,500 persons and features sophisticated audiovisual equipment and full-size staging.[15]

In 1995, Hyatt announced a new marketing program and a new positioning thrust for its 16 resort properties. As reported by Tom O'Toole, vice president of marketing for Hyatt, all resorts would now be marketed under

Oh, how the demands and pressures of the day can take their toll.

To ease the burden, we offer The Luxury Collection, an assembly of the world's most elite hotels and resorts. Landmarks of distinction, they have welcomed kings and queens, presidents and prime ministers, literary giants and theatrical immortals.

While guests are treated like royalty, it isn't a requirement for staying here. In fact, many of our exclusive leisure packages are (dare we say it) quite affordable, such as the

FOR THOSE WHO LIVE A LIFE OF POLO MATCHES AND CHARITY BALLS, A CHANCE TO ESCAPE THE DAILY GRIND.

Romance Package, a two-night visit replete with Champagne, flowers and a sumptuous breakfast in the privacy of your room.

So, for reservations in the U.S. or Canada, call *800-325-3589*. Or have your butler contact us at www.luxurycollection.com.

We'll make you feel right at home, whichever of your homes that may be.

THE LUXURY COLLECTION
ITT SHERATON

Clockwise from top left: Hotel Danieli, Venice · Hotel Imperial, Vienna · Hotel Principe di Savoia, Milan · Sheraton Kuwait, Kuwait City
© 1998 ITT Sheraton Corporation

FIGURE 4.6 *The Luxury Collection advertisement. (Courtesy of Starwood Hotels & Resorts. Reprinted with permission.)*

FIGURE 4.7 *Four Points Hotels advertisement. (Courtesy of Starwood Hotels & Resorts. Reprinted with permission.)*

one umbrella, separate from the Hyatt Regency and Park Hyatt brands. A separate resort division was formed to help streamline these efforts for Hyatt's growing presence in the resort marketplace.

Conference Centers

The conference center concept first emerged in the 1970s. Conference centers are lodging facilities specifically designed for especially small-to-medium-sized meetings as opposed to individual guests. Some truly "dedicated" conference centers do not even accept individual travelers. The International Association of Conference Centers (IACC) defines a dedicated conference center as

> a specialized hospitality operation dedicated to facilitating and supporting conferences . . . geared toward accommodating these conferences from the design of the facility, to the professional support services, the specialized training of the staff, and the packaging of the product.[16]

IACC was formed to enhance the emergence of conference centers as a mature and serious player in the hospitality industry.

Informally, there are four basic types of conference centers. These include the executive conference center, the corporate conference center, the resort conference center, and the not-for-profit/educational conference center. The executive conference center offers upscale facilities and accommodations for senior-level-management-type meetings. The Harrison Conference Center Inn (197 guest rooms and 30 meeting rooms) of Glen Cove, New York, and the Hamilton Park Executive Conference Center (219 guest rooms and 31 meeting rooms) of Florham Park, New Jersey, are examples of this type of facility.

Corporate conference centers are owned and managed by a corporation. Examples here include the Xerox Training and Conference Center (800 guest rooms and 115 meeting rooms) located in Leesburg, Virginia, and the General Electric Leadership Development Center (146 guest rooms and 44 meeting rooms) in Croton-on-Hudson, New York.

The resort conference center classification is a center that has one or more major resort amenities like golf or skiing and a combination of amenities like swimming, tennis, or a health club. Doral Arrowood (276 guests rooms and 36 meeting rooms) of Rye Brook, New York, and the Scottsdale Conference Resort (360 guest rooms and 45 meeting rooms) of Scottsdale, Arizona, are prime examples of the resort approach to conference center development.

Not-for-profit/educational conference centers are predominantly located at institutes and on university campuses. Marriott is manager of such facilities at Georgetown University and the University of Maryland. The University of Michigan School of Business Executive Residence is an example of a self-operated educational conference center.

The IACC, which has grown to over 300 members, has established "Universal" criteria that distinguish bona fide conference centers from other types of hospitality operations. These criteria include such items as climate control, ergonomic chairs, and appropriate lighting in all meeting rooms. Figure 4.8 gives a more detailed picture of these strict guidelines for IACC conference center designation.

As also suggested by IACC, there are four key points for a good conference center site or location. These include[17]:

FIGURE 4.8 *International Association of Conference Centers (IACC) required criteria for IACC designation (Courtesy of International Association of Conference Centers. Reprinted with permission.)*

Universal Criteria applicable to all conference centers regardless of category are:

1. A minimum of 60 percent of net facility space devoted to meeting space that is dedicated, single-purpose conference space

2. A minimum 60 percent of total sales generated by conferences

3. Conference room design incorporating the following:

   - A majority of conference setups using ergonomic chairs with a minimum comfort rating of six hours
   - A majority of conference setups using tables designed for meetings, providing a hard writing surface
   - Appropriate light 50–70 foot-candles at tabletop, adjustable
   - Climate-controlled conference rooms
   - Wall surfaces suitable for tacking or other mounting of flipchart-type sheets
   - Appropriate acoustics for conference communication
   - Adequate electrical, audiovisual, and telephone outlets

4. Conference rooms available to clients on a 24-hour basis for storage of materials, and other preparations

5. An average group size of 75 people or less

6. A package plan that includes conference rooms, three meals, continuous refreshment service, conference services, and basic audiovisual equipment.

- Proximity to a major concentration of corporate headquarters and/
  or regional offices
- Proximity to an airport servicing major carriers (within an hour's
  drive)
- Easy access to major highways (within 15 minutes of a major artery)
- A setting that allows for a distraction-free environment

Growth and interest in conference center facilities continues. As reported in *Meetings & Conventions*, "[i]n response to increased demand for
high-level meeting facilities, conference center companies are expanding the
number of properties they manage or own."[18] These companies include Marriott, Benchmark Hospitality, and Dolce International. Marriott currently
manages 28 centers and plans to own and/or operate an additional 20 in the
not-too-distant future. Benchmark is planning to double its presence in the
resort conference center market to 20+ facilities over the next five years.
Dolce International "has in the past 14 months doubled its portfolio; the
company now owns and manages two conference centers, manages another
seven and expects to take on three more management contracts [soon]."[19]
Professional conference center management is clearly in a growth mode, giving customers in the meetings industry even more options from which to
choose.

As discussed thus far, hotels, resorts, and conference centers are many
and varied. They each have their own particular niche they are trying to
pursue—be it for the business and/or leisure and the individual and/or
group markets. Yet these suppliers represent only one aspect of the hospitality industry.

RESTAURANTS, CATERING, AND CONTRACT
FOODSERVICES

We have all eaten in restaurants, most of us since we were children. What
kind of restaurant? A fast-food outlet? An upscale restaurant? A pizza place?
A cafeteria? At the club? A family/casual-dining restaurant? A food court at
the campus center or in the mall? There are myriad ways to define and
categorize restaurants much less the foodservice industry. Similar to the hotel
business, there is no clearcut easy way to do this.

As William Fisher, former executive vice president of the National Restaurant Association (NRA), succinctly states, "[t]he restaurant and foodservice industry provides food and beverage prepared outside of the home for

public consumption.''[20] Short and sweet, to the point. The NRA suggests the following seven foodservice categories[21]:

- Restaurants, cafeterias, fast food, bars, taverns
- Foodservice in hotels, motels, and motor hotels
- Foodservice sales in retail stores
- Vending and nonstore retailers
- Contractors and caterers
- Recreation and sports
- Institution operating own foodservice

Another approach, for restaurants in particular, is the traditional triad—quick service, midscale, and upscale. A recent *Cornell Quarterly* publication suggested expanding this typology to include (1) quick service, (2) midscale, (3) moderate upscale, (4) upscale, and (5) business dining.[22]

A key point here is that there are a multitude of foodservice businesses and almost as many ways to categorize these players. Our approach will be to take an introductory look at hospitality from a restaurant, catering, and contract foodservice perspective.

Restaurants

Americans are spending close to $.50 of each dollar they spend on food in restaurant purchases. Many restaurants are independent operations. Chain restaurants, especially in fast food and casual/family dining, keep growing. Hotels are in the restaurant business, too. Each of these sectors—independent, chain, and hotel restaurant—is discussed in more detail next.

Independent restaurants are just that, independent. They are privately owned and have no chain or brand-name affiliation. They may be a small family restaurant, a tavern-style pub, or a large 700-seat steak house such as the Hilltop Steak House in Saugus, Massachusetts, just north of Boston.

Emir's is a small, family-owned and operated independent restaurant in Guelph, Ontario, specializing in Lebanese cuisine. Initially offering eat-in or takeout services in its 30-seat restaurant, its offerings have expanded to include off-premise catering and delivery services. Now in its seventh year of operation, Emir's has developed a loyal following of customers who keep coming back again and again. The Emir family motto? ''For an adventure, take your taste buds to the land of falafels and a piece of heaven.''

Demand for meals to go or ''home-meal replacement'' is on the rise in North America. Eatzi's, an independent operation developed by Brinker International and recently opened in Dallas, Texas, is going after this market in a big way, literally.

> The 8000-square-foot Eatzi's unit opened January 15 [1996] with 45 chefs preparing food on-premises and such features as a scratch bakery, produce, a coffee bar, beer and wine, and a floral department. There are more than 100 meal choices . . . including sushi, lasagna, turkey with dressing, and Swedish meatballs and noodles.
> So far the store is drawing 2,000 customers daily . . . The unit has only 20 seats.[23]

And, as commented by Lane Cardwell, chief administrative officer of Brinker International, "[o]ur customers know what to do—leave and eat."[24]

Successful independent restaurants often become chains. The first A&W Root Beer stand was opened in 1919. Little did the co-owners know that A & W would become the first franchised quick-service restaurant (QSR) and one of the first chain operations in the hospitality industry. Today, A&W has franchises worldwide, including over 700 restaurants in the Pacific Rim region of Southeast Asia.

Chain restaurants are now ubiquitous in the United States and have a growing presence in Europe. For fast food or QSRs, McDonald's continues to lead the pack. Its global reach includes 14,000 stores in 73 countries on every continent except Antarctica. Foreign operating revenues are now 50 percent of total revenues for the chain. McDonald's is also expanding its type of location in the United States including retailers such as Wal-Mart, Home Depot, and Amoco and Chevron gas stations.

A relatively new concept in the QSR arena is "wraps." "From California to Atlanta, chefs and chain kitchen managers increasingly are rolling multi-course meals into edible wrappers or wraps—that is, flavor-infused tortillas and unleavened flatbreads."[25] The price range for these wraps is $5 to $7. San Francisco–based World Wrapps offers wraps such as grilled salmon, peppercorn relish, snap peas, and roasted garlic mashed potatoes or grilled vegetables, spanish rice, and goat cheese in a tomato tortilla. Atlanta-based Great Wraps, a 50-unit quick-service chain, will wrap up your choice of salad, too.

Table service restaurant chains include well-known brands such as Friendly's, Denny's, Ponderosa, Pizza Hut, Red Lobster, and Olive Garden, to name a few. Eat 'N Park is a regional 56-unit family restaurant chain spread across Pennsylvania, Ohio, and West Virginia. Outback Steakhouse, specializing in steaks with an Australian theme, is strong in Florida and expanding into the Midwest and Northeast. Ruth's Chris Steak House recently opened its 48th unit, the first in Canada, in Toronto.

Many U.S. chains have expanded into Europe, including T.G.I. Friday's and Planet Hollywood, both having opened in Paris. There are over 15,000 restaurants in Paris and the idea of chain development is starting to take hold in this renowned international "city of lights." Chez Rebert, for example, is a five-unit restaurant chain with all five outlets in Paris. Specializing in couscous (a Middle East semolina pasta), the restaurant concept is somewhat upscale, offering a friendly and lively atmosphere. Ten of us enjoyed a delightful New Year's Eve dinner at the Chez Rebert Batignobles location. The place was packed.

Hotel restaurants are well known to the traveling public. Some are good, some are very good, and some have a lot of room for improvement. They are always a challenge to hotel management. Hotel restaurants not only target the in-house guest but also look to the local market. They increasingly and aggressively compete with local restaurant establishments for both of these market segments.

In the midscale category, such as Holiday Inn, the typical hotel restaurant offers a fairly broad-based, medium-priced menu and is open all day long. In the upscale category, new concepts emerge every three to four years at hotels to replenish somewhat tired and typically themed restaurants. Today, an international theme approach is not uncommon. For example, the Asian influence is strong in the United States and American Southwest cuisine is emerging in the Middle East. At the Radisson Moriah Plaza Tiberias Hotel in Tiberias, Israel, the myth of the Wild West is the motif of its recently opened Texas Bar Restaurant:

> [T]he 140-seat conversion is bedecked in weathered pine and exposed-brick with swinging doors, guns, saddles and other paraphernalia. When they are not dishing up steaks imported from the U.S., burgers and chili, servers in cowboy outfits entertain the crowds with songs and mock shoot-outs. A country-Western band plays nightly, too.
>
> General Manager Danny Alkalay, who worked on the concept for a year, says he wanted something that would make all his international guests feel comfortable. "It's unique in Israel, and so far it has been packed," he says. "People are excited because they don't expect to find this kind of restaurant in a 5-star hotel."[26]

Frequent-dining clubs are becoming more prevalent among upscale and luxury hotels in the 1990s to help boost business from the local market in particular. An annual fee is usually charged, ranging from $50 to $200 in exchange for discounts on food items on the menu (but not beverage). Some clubs have a slightly different twist. The Jaxx restaurant at the Park Hyatt Chicago offers preferred seating to club members and a free bottle of wine with the first dinner visit. The Ritz-Carlton in Cleveland, Ohio, gives a complimentary overnight stay or a Sunday brunch after 10 visits to "The Restaurant."

In both the midscale and the upscale lodging sectors, hotels are offering pantries, kiosks, and self-service coffee bistros to the busy traveler. From a hotel management perspective, they are more cost-effective than the labor-intensive room service venue. In-house guests appreciate the fact that, in most instances, the cost savings are passed on to the customer; especially when all they have really wanted was a reasonably priced cup of coffee and muffin on the run.

Many hotels are leasing, outsourcing, and/or developing partnerships with restaurant chains or independent operators for their food and beverage services. The idea is not new. Trader Vic's, a 57-year-old Polynesian/Asian themed restaurant chain, has 21 units, 19 of which are located in upscale hotels including Hilton, Westin, and New Otani. More recently, management of the luxury class Grosvenor House Hotel in London, England, has turned over its fine-dining restaurant (with a five-year contract agreement) to Michelin Star Chef Nico Ladenis. Ruth's Chris Steak House operates one of its units in the Crowne Plaza Suites Hotel in Birmingham, Alabama. Baskin-Robbins ice cream stores can be found at a number of Hilton International properties worldwide.

As well stated in a recent issue of the *International Journal of Hospitality Management*, "[h]otels around the world are rethinking the ways they operate and deliver their food and beverage. From limited service budget hotels to the luxury full-service five star hotels, increasingly establishments are looking to outside operators or proven franchise concepts to enhance customers' perceptions and to help profitability."[27] The growth phenomenon of these partnerships is expected to continue and the subject is revisited in more depth in Chapter 12.

Catering

We define catering in this text as the planning, preparation, and delivery of food and beverage services for a group event. The principal players include caterers, hotels, restaurants, and private recreational clubs such as golf clubs, tennis clubs, and yacht clubs. We are referring here to clubs that have the physical capacity to handle catered events. Table 4.6 gives a summary of this scenario and following is a more detailed look at suppliers in the catering business.

Caterers are companies whose primary business is that of catering. These firms have their own facilities to house an event and/or the capability to cater an event off-premise. For example, you may be planning a 75-person wedding to be "catered" at your parents' home and hire a catering firm to handle all of the food and beverage logistics for the event. Or, a business

---

TABLE 4.6 *Catering, Catering Suppliers, and Sampling of Catered Events*

Catering

The planning, preparation, and delivery of food and beverage services for a group event

Catering Suppliers

Catering companies
Hotels
Restaurants
Clubs

Examples of Catered Events

Weddings
Bar mitzvahs
Convention banquets
Social events
Retirement parties
Charity balls

---

may be planning an employee Christmas party and book a "catering house" or a "catering hall" where the event will take place. In other words, some catered events are held "on premise," that is, at the caterer's establishment. Many catered events take place elsewhere, such as a pavilion at a park or, as in the example given previously, at someone's home. For these kinds of events, a caterer has the responsibility of preparing, delivering, and serving the meal where the customer arranged for the event to be held.

In Washington, DC, for instance, caterers abound. Ridgewell's, for example, is a caterer that targets the many politicians and lobbyists in this town who often hold business-related catered events at their homes. Ridgewell's caters over a thousand events a year in the nation's capital.

Hotels are very much in the catering business. Many have catering departments responsible for the sales solicitation of local events such as weddings, local business functions, social events, charity balls, and so forth. Catering managers in these departments also handle the food and beverage aspects of conferences and conventions booked by the sales department of the hotel. These include banquets, receptions, and refreshment breaks held throughout the duration of the conference.

Catering revenues in hotels can be as high as 40 to 50 percent of total food and beverage revenues. Profit margins are typically higher than that of hotel restaurant and room service revenues as well. This is largely because forecasting attendance for catered events is usually more accurate than for restaurant or room service sales. Good forecasting makes food purchasing, food preparation, and labor scheduling more controllable and, thus, less costly.

Restaurants are often in the catering business, too. The Hilltop Steak House recently ventured into on-premise catering in addition to its restaurant business. Major renovations were made to create function rooms to accommodate large group events. This operation now has a catering sales department that is busy booking banquet functions for up to 400 persons. As commented by Hilltop's former catering director, "we go after both the social and corporate markets and business is flourishing."

During holiday periods such as Easter, Mother's Day, and New Year's Eve, the catering business is typically slow. At Hilltop, during these periods, the function rooms are temporarily reconfigured to a restaurant dining arrangement. The 700-seat restaurant becomes a sold-out 1200-seat restaurant for these busy holiday periods. Thus far, the two-product-line approach of offering both restaurant and catering services to the general public at the Hilltop Steak House is working out quite well.

Clubs, such as golf or country clubs, that have the physical facilities frequently host catered events, especially weddings, bridge club luncheons, retirement parties, and so on. Larger clubs often have a fully staffed catering department whose primary responsibility is to sell and service these kinds of events. They compete directly with caterers, restaurants, and hotels for this business. A distinguishing feature that private clubs can offer and their competitors cannot is exclusivity. One typically has to be a member of the club to book the event. This feeling of prestige can be important to some potential customers in that it has the appeal of being able to say, "I booked it at the club."

Contract Foodservices

Contract foodservice companies are firms that provide food and beverage management for organizations, especially institutional organizations. These companies are sometimes referred to as foodservice or contract management companies. Contracting out or outsourcing is big business. As noted in Van Nostrand–Reinhold's *Encyclopedia of Hospitality and Tourism*, "contract management companies are a major force in the institutional foodservice segment. They are expected to continue as such and grow substantially as more and more businesses and institutions contract out various services that are supplemental to their primary mission."[28] For example, almost half of college and university campuses in the United States utilize contract foodservice companies. These educational institutions are in the business of education. The provision of foodservice is a necessity of the institution but not its primary mission.

Daka International is in the contract foodservice business, managing the food and beverage operations at over 600 universities, hospitals, and corporations in the United States. Over half of its clientele are large colleges and universities such as the University of Florida and Northeastern University. Daka is also the contract foodservice company for the Smithsonian Institute in Washington, DC, serving thousands of customers a day.

Prisons are correctional institutions that have a captive audience who need to be housed and fed. Service America, another institutional foodservice contractor, was one of three foodservice exhibitors at a recent American Correctional Association (ACA) conference held in Dallas, Texas. Although prisons are only just beginning to contract out their food operations, Service America is betting that it is a new growth opportunity. The number of prisoners in state and federal correctional facilities currently exceeds one million. Dial soap, also an exhibitor at the ACA conference, was in the negotiation stage with the Texas Department of Corrections A contract "could place Dial soap—perhaps exclusively—in the hands of about 75,000 state prisoners [!]"[29]

Restaurants, catering, and contract foodservices are all commercial enterprises on the foodservice side of the hospitality industry. They each require sales management to augment the marketing efforts to get and keep a customer. Restaurants target individual and small group patronage. Catering is specific to organized group events requiring food and beverage services. Contract foodservice management focuses on the institutional market. All continuously seek to satisfy the ever-changing needs and wants of clients and customers alike.

SUMMARY

This chapter looked at the lodging and foodservice side of the hospitality industry. For lodging, the focus was on hotels, resorts, and conference centers. The foodservice discussion included restaurants, catering, and contract foodservices.

Hotels are typically categorized by type, size, and location. This is referred to as product segmentation. Property types include budget/economy, mid-market, upscale/first-class, and luxury. Location product segmentation categories include downtown, suburban, highway, airport, and resort. Size categories are typically defined as under 75 rooms, 75 to 150 rooms, 150 to 300 rooms, 300 to 500 rooms, and over 500 rooms. Convention hotels are large, first-class operations catering to the needs of the association and convention markets.

All-suite hotels and the extended-stay market represent a growth area in hospitality. This market is largely made up of businesspeople who stay at a lodging establishment five nights or longer.

Product-line development is practiced in the hospitality industry, especially on the lodging side of the business. Product-line development is when a company that is in a core business, such as lodging, develops product concepts that reach out to separate and distinct markets. Marriott is one such company that has several product concepts including Marriott Hotels, Resorts, and Suites, Courtyard by Marriott, and Residence Inn by Marriott.

Resorts are first-class hotels located in rural areas typically offering some type of outdoor recreational activity such as golf and tennis. Resorts target both the upscale leisure traveler and the meetings and conventions market. Resorts are owned and/or managed by both independent and chain-operated hotel companies.

Conference centers are lodging establishments specifically designed for small-to-medium-sized meetings averaging 20 to 50 attendees. The International Association of Conference Centers (IACC) has established criteria for official designation as a conference center. These criteria include climate control, upholstered armchairs, appropriate acoustics, and 24-hour access for all meeting rooms at the establishment. Many truly "dedicated" conference centers do not accept individual travel business.

Restaurants, catering, and contract foodservices are many and varied in the hospitality industry. Restaurants are independently owned or chain operated. Mid- to upscale hotels provide foodservice as well. The level of service varies tremendously in the restaurant business from fast food to family-style table service to fine dining. Home delivery is also an option offered by numerous restaurant establishments. In the United States, $.50 of every dollar spent on food is spent on restaurant foodservice purchases. It is a large and expanding industry. Chain-operated restaurants are major players in the United States and Canada, and have a growing presence in Europe.

Catering is the planning, preparation, and delivery of food and beverage service for group events. This is the primary business of catering companies. Caterers have their own facilities to house an event and/or have the capability to cater events off premise. Hotels, restaurants, and country clubs are in the catering business, too, although it is not normally their primary source of business. Catered events at these kinds of establishments are usually held on-premise.

Contract foodservice companies are firms that provide food and beverage management for organizations. Institutional organizations such as universities and hospitals often outsource their foodservice needs to contract management companies. These companies manage all aspects of on-premise food and beverage needs for their clients on a contractual basis. Similar to other segments of the foodservice industry, contract management is a growing business in hospitality. Hospitals are in the health care business. Universities are in the education business. For these organizations, it often makes sense to outsource their foodservice needs to professionals in the field.

DISCUSSION QUESTIONS

1. What is product segmentation?
2. Table 4.1 gives examples of product segmentation in the lodging industry. Discuss the characteristics of each property type and how they differ from each other.
3. All-suite hotels and the extended-stay market are growth areas in hospitality. Why?
4. What is product-line development? Suggest some hospitality examples to support your response.
5. Resorts, which have historically catered to the upscale leisure traveler on vacation, have diversified to also target the meetings and conventions market. Discuss.
6. Discuss the growth of conference centers and distinguish between the four basic types.
7. Compare and contrast restaurants, catering, and contract foodservices. How are they similar? How are they different?

NOTES

1. *The Random House Dictionary of the English Language*, 2nd ed., unabridged, Random House, New York, 1987.
2. Daniel C. Peek, "New Optimism in the Hotel Sector," *Wall Street Journal Europe*, November 17–18, 1985, p. 12.
3. Randell A. Smith, "Focus on the Economy/Budget Market," *Hotel & Resort Industry*, July 1994, p. 31.

4. Timothy N. Troy "Knights Hopes to Cash in with Credit Card Promo," *Hotel & Motel Management*, June 6, 1994, p. 19.

5. Randell A. Smith, "Focus on the Mid-Price Market," *Hotel & Resort Industry*, December 1994.

6. Robert A. Nozar, "Wingate Strives for Critical Mass," *Hotel & Motel Management*, February 5, 1996, p. 6.

7. Robert A. Nozar "AmericInn Chooses Goal," *Hotel & Motel Management*, May 6, 1996, p. 61.

8. Randell Smith and John D. Lesure, "Don't Shoot the Messenger— Forecasting Lodging Performance," *Cornell Quarterly*, February 1996.

9. "Opryland Hotel Convention Center" [advertising supplement], *Corporate Meetings & Incentives*, June 1996, p. 76.

10. Margery Stein "When Luxury Is a Necessity," *Corporate Meetings & Incentives*, July 1995, p. 29.

11. Ibid.

12. Randell A. Smith, "Focus on the All-Suite/Extended-Stay Market," *Hotel & Resort Industry*, October 1994, p. 20.

13. Helen Bond, "Suburban Hotels Must Match Location with Strategy," *Hotel & Motel Management*, January 22, 1996, p. 54.

14. Glenn Withiam, "Sheraton's New Mid-Market Entry," *Cornell Quarterly*, October 1995, p. 15.

15. "The Registry Resort" [advertising supplement], *Corporate Meetings & Incentives*, June 1996, p. 62.

16. Sam Haigh and Robert W. Hudson, "Understanding Conference Centers," International Association of Conference Centers, 1989, p. 5.

17. Ibid., p. 18.

18. David Ghitelman, "Conference Center Firms Plan Growth Spurt," *Meetings & Conventions*, June 1996, p. 29.

19. Ibid.

20. William P. Fisher, "The Restaurant and Foodservice Industry," in *VNR's Encyclopedia of Hospitality and Tourism*, Mahmood Khan, Michael Olsen, and Turgut Var, Eds., Van Nostrand–Reinhold, New York, 1992, p. 3.

21. Tom Powers, *Introduction to Management in the Hospitality Industry*, 4th ed., John Wiley, New York, 1992.

22. Christopher C. Muller and Robert H. Woods, "An Expanded Restaurant Typology," *Cornell Quarterly*, June 1994, p. 28.

23. Louise Kramer, "Home-Meal Replacement: Not a Fad," *Nation's Restaurant News*, March 18, 1996, p. 68.

24. Ibid.

25. Alan Liddle, "Menus Are Wrappin' to a New Beat," *Nation's Restaurant News*, March 18, 1996, p. 59.
26. Anne Spiselman, "Around the World with 8 New Concepts," *Hotels*, May 1996, pp. 73–74.
27. Gary Hallam and Tom Baum, "Contracting Out Food and Beverage Operations in Hotels: A Comparative Study of Practice in North America and the United Kingdom," *International Journal of Hospitality Management*, Vol. No.1, 1996 15 (1), p. 41.
28. Mickey Warner, "Institutional Foodservice Management," in *VNR's Encyclopedia of Hospitality and Tourism*, Mahmood Khan, Michael Olsen, and Turgut Var, Eds., Van Nostrand–Reinhold, New York, 1992, p. 249.
29. Kevin Helliker, "Expanding Prison Population Captivates Marketers," *Wall Street Journal*, January 19, 1995, p. B1.

Chapter 5

Hospitality Businesses: More Suppliers

LEARNING OBJECTIVES

1. *To become familiar with more players in the hospitality industry*
2. *To better understand these businesses, which include:*
   - *Convention centers*
   - *Casinos and gaming*
   - *Cruise lines*
   - *Timeshare and vacation ownership*
   - *Country inns and bed-and-breakfasts*
   - *Theme parks*
   - *Tourism destinations*

This chapter continues the discussion on hospitality suppliers. The previous chapter focused on the hotel and foodservice side of the business. This chapter takes a closer look at additional suppliers including convention centers, casinos and gaming, cruise lines, timeshare and vacation ownership, country inns and bed-and-breakfasts, theme parks, and tourism destinations. A more detailed discussion of each of these hospitality businesses follows.

CONVENTION CENTERS

Convention centers are exhibit halls providing large amounts of unobstructed space for exhibits and trade shows. As noted earlier in Chapter 3, trade shows require large amounts of space for exhibitors to display their wares and meet face to face with potential customers. Convention centers provide foodservice but not lodging accommodations. Exhibitors and attendees stay at nearby hotels for their overnight lodging needs.

Convention centers range in size from 75,000 to 1,000,000+ square feet. In comparison, a football field is 48,000 square feet (160 feet × 100 yards). Thus, the typical convention center could house at least two football fields. Following are some examples of how convention center sizes vary from locale to locale:

Atlantic City Convention Center (Atlantic City, New Jersey)	436,000 square feet
Baltimore Convention Center (Baltimore, Maryland)	115,000 square feet
McCormick Place Convention Center (Chicago, Illinois)	1,600,000 square feet
Ernest N. Morial Convention Center (New Orleans, Louisiana)	667,496 square feet
Orange County Convention Center (Orlando, Florida)	350,000

The preceding convention centers are expanding their facilities because of increased demand. Shown in Figure 5.1, Louisville's (Kentucky) Commonwealth Convention Center is expanding, too, and will be "featuring 285,000 square feet of extremely flexible space."

Associations are the major purchasers of exhibit and trade show space at convention centers, such as the American Academy of Ophthalmology and the American Society of Mechanical Engineers. Associations contract with the convention center for their anticipated exhibit space needs. This is usually

FIGURE 5.1 *Commonwealth Convention Center (Louisville, Kentucky) advertisement. (Courtesy of Louisville and Jefferson County Convention and Visitors Bureau. Reprinted with permission.)*

negotiated on a square footage basis. The association then sells space to exhibitors who are suppliers of various products and services to members of the association. In other words, the association members who are the attendees at the exhibit and trade show are customers or potential customers of the exhibitors.

Exhibitors display their wares in 8-by-10-feet or 10-by-10-feet booths. Some larger exhibitors secure several booths side by side. The booths are lined up in the main hall and put together by a setup crew hired by the convention center. Exhibitors setup their own displays within the booth (or booths) they are assigned. Corner and/or high-visibility booths are usually more expensive.

Function space for meeting activity is located on the periphery of the convention center. Figure 5.2 gives a diagram of the main hall and function space configuration for the Ocean City Convention Center in Maryland.

Most convention centers are owned and operated by state or local governments. Their organizational structure is similar to that of a hotel including a general manager, a sales and marketing department, an event services department, and an operations department that focuses on the physical maintenance of the complex. A department of public safety is another important division, especially for public facilities such as convention centers. Security is typically a high priority at exhibits and trade show events.

A growing trend is increased privatization of the management of publicly owned convention centers. As noted in the *Cornell Quarterly:*

> Private management of municipal entities is still a relatively new idea. But it is also a sign of the times—a sign that government can no longer afford *laissez-faire* management of public assets. Benign acceptance of public works that continually operate at a loss is becoming a thing of the past.[1]

Convention centers, in particular, often operate at a loss. In other words, revenues taken in each year rarely exceed the expenses incurred to operate the facility. Government-owned and-operated facilities are increasingly looking to the private sector for more efficient management. By the early 1990s, close to 20 percent of convention centers in the United States were managed by private companies.[2] This trend is expected to continue.

CASINOS AND GAMING

Casinos are in the gaming and entertainment business. Gaming provides the major source of revenue for casino operations. In the past decade, gaming has evolved into an industry of its own. There are traditional casinos, casino hotels and resorts, theme casinos, riverboat casinos, and casinos located on Native American lands.

Approved gaming is gaining momentum across districts and regions throughout the United States and Canada. "Previously restricted by government and frowned upon by citizens, gaming is winning a growing level of acceptance and is seen as an easy way to generate tax revenues, create jobs and enhance tourism."[3] Gaming markets are emerging in Europe and Asia. Roger Cline, a hospitality consultant with Andersen Consulting who follows this industry, "points to Greece, Tunisia, Australia, the Philippines and Eastern Bloc countries that are encouraging casino-resort development."[4] Monte Carlo, on the other hand, in Monaco near the southeast of France, has been a gaming resort for many, many years.

Polk County, Iowa, has bought into casino gaming to enhance its local economy.

> It is a local politician's dream. Polk County, Iowa, is taking in so much money that residents are fighting over how to spend it. . . .
>
> After the Prairie Meadows racetrack here stumbled into bankruptcy five years ago, officials in Iowa's biggest county played what many considered a long shot. They spent $26 million to convert the track clubhouse into a casino, installed 1,100 slots and became the only U.S. county to own a gambling hall.
>
> It was an instant winner. Prairie Meadows is tossing off nearly $5 million a month in profit to the county.[5]

Theme casino hotels and resorts continue to emerge in the marketplace, especially in Las Vegas. These are mega hotels that go beyond traditional hotels in terms of their size and product offering. They target multiple markets including singles, couples, families, conventions, exhibits and trade show events, and the mature market. Examples of these mega hotels include the Luxor with 2526 guest rooms, Treasure Island with 2900 guest rooms, and the MGM GRAND with 5005 guest rooms.

Gaming as entertainment has been the tradition of Las Vegas. Today, these types of hotels have redefined entertainment to include gaming, roller coasters, lagoons, pyramids, amusement parks, volcano replicas, upscale shopping and fine dining, and "pyrotechnic pirate ships."[6] At Circus Circus (3800 guest rooms), "the resort not only offers circus themed decor, but a genuine circus arena, complete with trapeze artists, acrobats, jugglers and clowns."[7] Indeed, at these mega casino hotels there is more than just gaming to appeal to diverse customer markets.

Conventions have long been attracted to casino hotels. The mega theme casino hotels are targeting this market, too. Figure 5.3 displays an advertisement announcing the opening of the MGM GRAND that is targeted at meet-

All-New Bayfront Multifunctional Space With the Style and Grace to Equal Your Event

Located within a reasonable drive for one-third of the nation's population, Ocean City Convention Center has a proven record as an attendance-boosting destination.

You're going to like our convention center with its new 50,000 sq. ft. exhibit hall, 25,000 sq. ft. renovated ballroom, 18,000 sq. ft. renovated exhibit hall, 28,000 sq. ft. of new and renovated breakout rooms, and 61,200 sq. ft. of pre-function space.

Couple our new center with 9,500 hotel rooms, 22,000 restaurant seats, a nearby airport and you begin to understand why so many groups like the Mid-Atlantic Food Dealers, the Greater Washington-Maryland Service Station & Automotive Repair Association, the American Rental Association, and the Maryland State Dental Association keep coming back for more. Call now. The best dates at the Mid-Atlantic's best beach are going fast.

Third Floor

Room 305 overlooks the Grand Ballroom. Room 301 is outfitted as a Board Room. Two elevators service the Third Floor.

MEETING ROOM	SQUARE FEET	THEATRE CAPACITY
301	725	Board Room
302	200	Board Room
303	365	Office
304	545	50

Second Floor

This level is created for larger meetings and events requiring numerous breakout rooms. The Grand Ballroom's flexible partitions allow three simultaneous large meetings up to 1,600 in the morning — followed by an afternoon meeting of 2,400+.

Suites 210 - 213 overlook the first floor's larger exhibit hall providing the ideal headquarters for any event in the main exhibit hall.

* 209 and 214 feature deluxe appointments and finishes suitable for exclusive cocktail receptions or executive boardroom-style meetings.

MEETING ROOM	SQUARE FEET	THEATRE CAPACITY
Ballroom A	12,474	1,400
Ballroom B	4,736	530
Ballroom C	5,032	560
Ballroom ABC	22,242	2,490
201	1,702	190
202	1,426	160
203	1,518	170
204	1,426	160
205	1,426	160
206	1,518	170
207	1,152	130
208	1,872	210
*209	1,824	200
S210	1,200	135
S211	336	40
S212	416	45
S213	1,173	130
*214	825	Board Room
215	1,665	185
216	1,369	155
217	1,369	155
218	1,517	170

First Floor

Halls A and B feature columnless, 33-foot ceilings and telescoping seating for concerts and athletic events. A portable stage is available.

MEETING ROOM	SQUARE FEET	THEATRE CAPACITY
Exhibit Hall A	28,148	3,130
Exhibit Hall B	20,430	2,300
Exhibit Hall AB	48,578	5,430
Exhibit Hall C	17,700	N/A Exhibits Only
C101	864	100
C102	1,044	120
C103	792	90

Dimensions are approximate and subject to change.

FIGURE 5.2 *Ocean City Convention Center (Maryland) brochure excerpt. (Courtesy of Ocean City Convention and Visitors Bureau. Reprinted with permission.)*

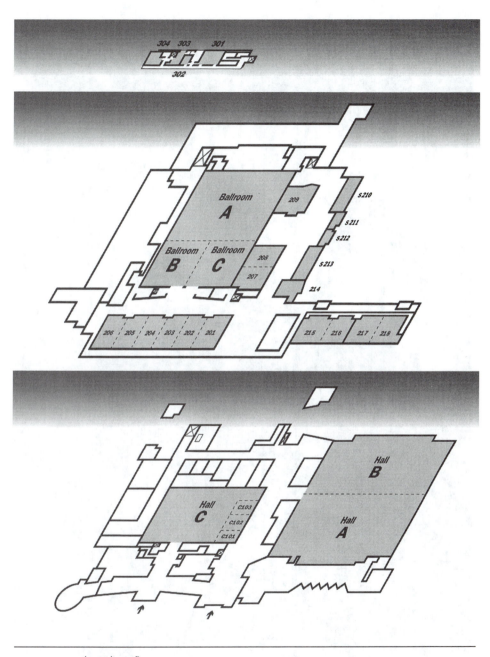

FIGURE 5.2 *(continued)*

FIGURE 5.3 *MGM GRAND advertisement. (Courtesy of MGM GRAND. Reprinted with permission.)*

ing and event planners. The 400,000 square feet of meeting space includes function rooms, ballrooms, and unobstructed space for exhibits and trade show events. This portion of the hotel is not surprisingly called the MGM GRAND Conference Center.

Riverboat casinos are "floating" casinos. They are literally housed on boats with most of them based on the Mississippi River and its tributaries in the United States. The largest concentration of riverboat casinos is in Illinois, Iowa, Louisiana, Mississippi, and Missouri. They are not hotels; there are no guest rooms provided for lodging accommodations. Many riverside municipalities prefer riverboat gaming in that it isolates the negative connotation associated with gambling.

Jurisdiction is still quite prohibitive for gaming establishments despite its recent growth. Only 10 states in the United States allow commercial gaming. (This excludes riverboat and Native American casinos.) Atlantic City, New Jersey, and Las Vegas, Nevada, still dominate the industry in North America. The obvious downside aspects of gaming are concerns about social impact, compulsive gambling, and propensity for crime. Religious groups, in particular, are strongly against casino gaming as a legal entity. Proponents argue that revenue generated for local communities through gaming outweighs the costs. Controversy continues on the pros and cons of legalized gaming at local, state, provincial, and federal levels.

CRUISE LINES

In many respects, **cruise lines** are floating resorts. Like resorts, passengers on a cruise are provided lodging, meals, and entertainment. It is the entertainment side that makes a cruise different. This includes both onboard and shore excursion activities. While onboard, large cruise ships offer a variety of entertainment options including pools, hot tubs, dancing, night clubs, theater, fitness centers, gaming, and dining. Lots of dining. As noted by Anthony Marshall, a frequent contributor to *Hotel & Motel Management*:

> People ask me, "What do you do on a cruise?" Answer: Eat! Food is served from 6:30 a.m. until one in the morning. Diets and health-food concerns are tossed overboard. For many passengers, a cruise is a continuous dining experience punctuated by a land tour to see something of interest.[8]

Passengers also have the option to relax, wind down, and enjoy private moments at sea.

Ports of call are what many travelers look forward to when taking a cruise vacation. These shore excursions can be a half day or several days, depending on the cruise line's itinerary. The ship pulls into harbor and passengers spend time on shore at their leisure. They are clearly notified of departure times when the ship will return to sea. Following is a sample nine-day Scandinavian cruise offered by Norwegian Cruise Lines:

Day	Port	Arrive	Depart
1	London (Dover), England	—	4:00P.M.
2	Amsterdam, The Netherlands	8:00 A.M.	11:00 P.M.
3	Cruise North Sea	—	—
4	Cruise Oslofjord	—	—
	Oslo, Norway	Noon	—
5	Oslo, Norway	—	4:00 P.M.
6	Helsingborg, Sweden	8:00 A.M.	4:00 P.M.
	Copenhagen, Denmark	8:00 P.M.	—
7	Copenhagen, Denmark	—	6:00 P.M.
8	Berlin (Warnemunde), Germany	7:00 A.M.	8:00 P.M.
9	Transit Kiel Canal	—	—
*	London (Dover), England	6:00 A.M.	—

*Disembarkment usually begins two hours after docking.

Typical cruise line itineraries vary from 3-to-4-day excursions to 9-to-12-day excursions. Prices vary depending on cabin type, cabin occupancy, time of year, type of ship, amenities offered, and duration of the cruise. Regardless, we are talking several thousand dollars even for a 7-to-10-day adventure. Round-trip airfare to get to the departure port may or may not be included in the price. Prices do include all meals and most entertainment while onboard.

Cruise line ships come in all shapes and sizes. They range from the *Hebridean Princess* (Hebridean Island Cruises) with a 49-passenger capacity to the *Carnival Destiny* (Carnival Cruise Lines) with a capacity of 2600. Others include Royal Caribbean's *Song of Norway* with a 1004-passenger capacity and Celebrity Cruise's *Mercury* with a 1870-passenger capacity. Even Walt Disney Co. is getting into the cruise line business with its 2400-passenger ship named *Disney Magic*. Mickey Mouse is waving his wand at the bow of the ship.

Mega cruise ships emerged on the scene in the 1990s. Although plagued by delays in the mid-1990s:

[There is] an unprecedented shipbuilding program by the cruise industry. In all, cruise companies are planning to launch 14 new ships in the next three years, at a total cost of more than $5 billion. But these are enormously large and complex boats, equipped with everything from wedding chapels to Broadway-style theatre.[9]

The *Grand Princess* of Princess cruises even has a basketball court for those rainy days at sea.

TIMESHARE AND VACATION OWNERSHIP

The concept of timeshare and **vacation ownership** first emerged in the French Alps in the 1960s. What this means is that vacationers own a block of time in an apartment unit, often in a resort-type location. "When you own a time-share it's much like owning a condo. One difference is that instead of buying it outright, you typically buy one week a year, or a 1/52 interest in it."[10] In other words, one has legal ownership of one week's worth of time in a unit. Sometimes two or three weeks are purchased, which may be in the same location or in several locations.

Timeshare or vacation ownership is essentially a multiyear prepaid vacation. The ownership contract can be anywhere from 7 to 30 years. The initial base price can vary from $6000 to $60,000 with the average in the $10,000 to $20,000 range. The actual price paid will depend on the time of year, number of weeks, and level of accommodations purchased. Added to the initial base price are annual maintenance fees.

Many timeshare owners want to vacation in different places each year.

> Trish and John Snider of Carlsbad, California, are time-share fans. They own three vacation weeks, one in Park City, Utah, another in Mazatlan, in Mexico, and the third accesses several resorts in Mexico. The Sniders have been to Utah only twice in ten years, but they've swapped the condo there for time in the Austrian Alps and extra weeks in Mexico.[11]

For vacation owners, there are exchange companies, or exchange networks as they are sometimes called, such as Resort Condominiums, Inc. (RCI), and Interval International (II). These are membership-based organizations that coordinate exchanges among timeshare owner members. Members pay an annual fee to belong to the organization plus additional fees for each exchange made. In other words, members "swap" their timeshare units and the exchange network acts as the agent to orchestrate and keep track of the numerous exchanges that take place. The authors know a couple who have never stayed at the timeshare unit they purchased in Vienna, Austria. Each year since they bought the unit, they have exercised the exchange option to travel elsewhere. "One of these days we will get there. But for now we are enjoying travel to other parts of the world."

Hotel chains such as Marriott, Hyatt, and Ritz-Carlton are getting into the vacation ownership game. "They're selling time-shares; they're converting entire floors into condominiums."[12] And, as noted by the director of brand advertising and communications for Marriott Vacation Club International, "[v]acation ownership is now a $6 billion industry and we're going to see more hotel companies enter the field."[13] There are more than 30 Marriott resorts where vacationers can purchase timeshare units. Marriott Vacation Club International currently has 80,000 vacation owners. Owners can exchange on a preferred basis at other Marriott Vacation Club International resorts or through Interval International at 1200 resorts worldwide.

The Disney Vacation Club is another major player in vacation ownership. In this organization, ownership is purchased in terms of points. The points represent overnight accommodations of varying types and time-of-year usage. For example, 250 points may be equivalent to 25 nights for a studio unit or 10 nights for a two-bedroom unit. The owner can return to the same unit each year or exchange points for alternative options such as another resort facility, a cruise, or a ski vacation in Vail, Colorado. A minimum number of points is required for the initial purchase, usually starting at 150 points. In the mid-1990s, 150 points had an approximate value of $10,000. Similar to other timeshare ownership arrangements, annual dues are paid each year. Other restrictions may apply as well.

Vacation ownership is gaining momentum in the leisure travel market. Many consider it a leading trend in hospitality. "The World Tourism Organization has called timeshares one of the fastest-growing sectors of the travel-and-tourism industry."[14] The exchange option is one of the main reasons for this trend. More and more, vacationers are looking for alternatives to the traditional annual vacation in the same location. Being able to "own" your vacation spot yet not be locked in, so to speak, is appealing.

COUNTRY INNS AND BED-AND-BREAKFASTS

Country inns and bed-and-breakfasts (B&Bs) are small, unique lodging establishments. They range in size from 3 to 30 rooms. Even 30 rooms is considered a large country inn. Most are independently owned and operated by an innkeeper, not by a general manager in the more traditional sense. In other words, they are typically family run and often the family lives on the premises.

Though similar in many respects, country inns tend to be larger than B&Bs and normally have a restaurant facility serving breakfast, lunch, and dinner. People from the local and surrounding community often dine at country inn restaurant establishments. B&Bs rarely have restaurant facilities. Breakfast is simply prepared and served in the owner's home. The host commonly sits down and joins guests for the breakfast meal. B&Bs, for the most part, are private homes with family guest room(s) made available to the public for overnight accommodations. They are businesses, albeit small, that must comply with local city ordinances. "Although most innkeepers enter the business primarily to meet people and entertain, in all but the smallest residential B&Bs they must meet the legal requirements of a fully licensed lodging business."[15]

Country inns are often of historic interest. The White Hart is one such inn, located in Wiltshire, England. The original building was reputedly built in 1553. Constructed of stone and situated alongside the ByBrook River, its exterior was used for one of the scenes in the film *Dr. Dolittle*. The White Hart is a 90-minute drive from London, England. The price for overnight accommodations ranges from $85 to $100.

Country inns can also be expensive. At the Post Ranch Inn, overlooking the Pacific Ocean in the Big Sur region of California (just south of San Francisco), the price ranges from $365 to $645 for a one-night stay. The Stonepine Inn, near Monterey, California, attracts the rich and famous.

> Andre Agassi and Brooke Shields were married at Stonepine last summer. Politicians Sam Nunn and Pete Wilson are repeat guests. Prices range from $275 to $1,200 per night, and for a small supplement, persons so famous that they want to avoid the media can get transportation from nearby Monterey Airport by helicopter.[16]

If one wants complete privacy, the entire facility can be reserved for $10,000.

Numerous guidebooks are published describing country inns and bed-and-breakfasts. Two examples are *Best Places to Stay in New England* (The Harvard Common Press) and *The Great Little Country Inns of Southern Ontario* (Deneau Publishers). These books are frequently used by travelers to select a country inn or B&B when putting together a travel itinerary. A brief description of selected establishments and their surrounding areas is included in the publication. Today, Web sites are used by many travelers as well. A guidebook to Ontario's finest country inns can be found at www.innbook.com, which is the Internet address for North America's Most Prestigious Guest Accommodations.

THEME PARKS

Theme parks provide entertainment for people of all ages and have become destinations in themselves. Who has not gone or not wanted to go to Walt Disney World? Universal Studios Florida is another major player. Legoland theme park recently opened in Windsor, England. They are more than just amusement parks. Today's theme parks have brought a new dimension to hospitality. Following is more detailed discussion on developments in the world of theme parks.

Disneyland is renowned as the first major theme park to open its doors in 1955 in Anaheim, California. Since that time, Walt Disney Co. has developed Walt Disney World in Orlando, Florida, Disneyland Paris in France, and Tokyo Disneyland in Japan. Orlando is the largest park with 30,000 acres. The Paris park covers 5000 acres, Tokyo has 400 acres, and Anaheim has 330 acres.[17] No matter how you look at it, these are large theme parks.

Attractions at Walt Disney World include the well-known Magic Kingdom, Epcot Center, and Disney–MGM Studios. Visitors enjoy the entertainment of Mainstreet, Frontierland, Fantasyland, Future World, and tours of movie-making demonstrations for full-length feature movies. Each of these attractions is a park within the theme park and each offers a host of eating facilities. Just in Disney–MGM Studios alone, there are over 20 facilities at which to grab a bite to eat. Disney World's latest additions include the opening of Animal Kingdom and the Wide World of Sports complex. The 200-acre sports complex includes a 9500-capacity stadium and is the new home to the Harlem Globetrotters. An estimated 35 million people a year visit one or more of the many attractions at Walt Disney World, Florida.

Sea World is another major player in the theme park business. Locals and tourists alike enjoy watching Shamu do her tricks. The famous water ski shows are popular, too. Sea World's latest addition—Journey to Atlantis—opened in 1998. This roller coaster and water ride attraction:

> [F]ollows an elaborate, fast-paced script with a heavy emphasis on special effects. The story begins with the ancient city having re-emerged from the sea and continues by sending visitors into a battle between good and evil within the city's walls.
>
> The ride's vehicles—designed to look like rickety fishing boats—careen and splash their way through the city's interior, eventually reaching speeds of nearly 50 mph and sending riders on two 60-foot plunges.[18]

Sea World is also initiating a dolphin interaction program. Visitors can get in the water with the dolphins under the supervision of trainers.

Not to be outdone, Universal Studios Florida is also adding new attractions. "Twister," based on the 1996 blockbuster movie, opened in 1998. Billed as a close encounter with a tornado, the new attraction "will break new ground in its use of special effects and technology that will simulate the sights, sounds and feel of a tornado."[19] Islands of Adventure is scheduled to open in 1999. This 90-acre "mini" park consists of five artificial islands in a lagoon setting. Features will include an Incredible Hulk roller coaster ride, Dr. Seuss characters throughout the park, and a Spiderman thrill ride.

Europe, too, is expanding its theme parks. There have been several major openings since the early 1990s, including Disneyland Paris in 1992; Port Aventura near Barcelona, Spain, in 1995; Warner Brothers Movie World in

Germany in 1996; and Legoland in Windsor, England, in 1996. Warner Brothers Movie World is planning to open another similar theme park in the United Kingdom in 1999. Baby boomer families are increasingly seeking family entertainment in Europe as they are in North America.

Most theme parks charge entrance fees on a per person, day-to-day basis. Discounts are usually given to children and seniors. At Disney World, a one-day adult pass was $42 (child $33) per theme park in 1997. One could purchase a four-day park hopper at $159 for adults and $127 for children. The "hopper" pass allows access to all three park attractions including the Magic Kingdom, Epcot Center, and Disney–MGM Studios. One can easily spend four days exploring all three parks.

Theme parks have sales managers similar to hotels, conference centers, and convention centers. These sales personnel actively seek group business from both the leisure and the convention markets. Universal Studios Florida, for example, has sales managers based at its headquarters in Orlando, as well as in Boston, New York, Philadelphia, Chicago, Dallas, and Toronto. Entrance fees are negotiated with each group. Fees will vary depending on the size of the group, length of stay, and time of year the group plans to visit the park.

TOURISM DESTINATIONS

In this text, we define **tourism destinations** as geographic areas or regions that have multiple hospitality product offerings for the leisure traveler. In many respects, a tourism destination is a product in itself. "The tourism product is a combination of all the various supplier entities that provide the tourist with the total travel experience and satisfaction."[20] The supplier entities are lodging, foodservice, transportation, and entertainment such as nightclubs, festivals, golf courses, wilderness, and beaches. Cities, counties, states, provinces, regions, and countries often market themselves as tourism destinations. State parks and theme parks are considered by many to be tourism destinations, too. Following are examples of a state, regional, and country tourism destination.

The state of Florida actively promotes tourism. Its climate and numerous attractions including state parks, theme parks, sandy beaches, and the Everglades make it particularly attractive to tourists. Florida targets multiple markets and has sales teams who aggressively seek these markets. For example, there is a Director Marketing—Canada for the Florida Tourism Industry Marketing Corporation. This sales and marketing position is one of several for Florida Tourism. The Director Marketing—Canada is responsible for all of Canada. Canadians, in particular, frequently head south in the winter to take a break from the colder climate of the north.

Iles d'Or is a region of three small islands—Porquerolles, Port-Cros, and Ile du Levant—off the coast of southern France. It has come to be known as the "Golden Isles of the Riviera."[21] Quite different from the attraction of Florida, these islands "are, in the opinion of many, the last refuge on the Riviera, their quiet and unspoiled beauty a welcome antidote to the noise and congestion of the mainland."[22] There are several small hotels and restaurants on the islands, and numerous beaches and biking trails. Yet, to the authors' knowledge, there is no active tourism sales promotions for the region. Given its natural beauty and unpretentious character, one can understand why. It is really not needed.

Costa Rica is a developing country starting to promote tourism. It is located in Central America between the Caribbean Sea and the Pacific Ocean. One of the authors took a 10-day trek traveling through Costa Rica with a guide and one other couple. The trip was organized by Coast to Coast Adventures, a small, young San Jose–based tour company. No theme parks, no golf courses, no four-star hotels. Instead, there was biking, hiking, rafting, and kayaking. Overnight accommodations were modest lodging facilities or camping. Hot showers were rare. A day-to-day itinerary of the trip is shown in Table 5.1. Costa Rica is an example of a tourism destination for the adventurous traveler who wants to "get away from it all."

The preceding examples demonstrate how varied and diverse tourism destinations can be. As described in Chapter 3, there are many types of travelers looking for different kinds of hospitality experiences. Children, young adults, families, businesspeople, seniors—they all have vacation needs. Researching tourism destination possibilities is where many of these travelers start when looking for the "ideal" spot to meet their needs and wants.

SUMMARY

This chapter discussed suppliers in the hospitality industry including convention centers, casinos and gaming, cruise lines, timeshare and vacation ownership, country inns and bed-and-breakfasts, theme parks, and tourism destinations. It was a continuation of the previous chapter, which focused on the hotel and foodservice side of the business.

Convention centers are exhibit halls providing large amounts of unobstructed space for exhibits and trade shows. They range in size from 75,000 to 1,000,000+ square feet of space. Convention centers provide foodservice but not lodging accommodations. Function space is often located on the periphery of convention centers. Most convention centers are owned and operated by local state or governments.

Casinos are in the gaming business, which is the major source of reve-

TABLE 5.1 *Itinerary for Costa Rica Coast to Coast*

The Coast to Coast Trip (C2C)—Trip notes

The company is named after this trip because it is unique. It is definitely the most exciting and challenging trip that we offer. There are a large variety of activities, and most people are usually not experienced in all three of the main sports. However, as long as participants are reasonably healthy and are willing to learn, we will do the rest. The trip is not advisable for children under 14 years of age, people with a medical condition for which strenuous physical exercise is not recommended, or those who will be upset if they get sweaty, wet, or dirty.

Day	Activity	Kms	Place	Details	Lodging
1	Arrival in Costa Rica		San Jose	C to C representative will meet guest(s) at the airport—transfer to hotel in San Jose—short evening group talk on details for following day.	Hotel in San Jose
2	Flight to Quepos		Manuel Antonio	Morning flight to Quepos—time to explore Manuel Antonio and get to know other members of the group—afternoon overview of the trip. **B, D**	Hotel in San Jose
3	Biking (25 kms) Hiking (14 kms)	39 KM	Pacific Slopes	4:30 AM departure from the beach—approx. 2 hours of biking then breakfast—4–5 hours of hiking—great spot for camping in the mountains. **B, L, D**	Camping
4	Hiking (7 kms)	7 KM	Los Santos	The day is basically one big climb (Cemetery Hill)—great swimming holes along the way—Afternoon free to explore the area. **B, L, D**	Camping
5	Hiking (6 kms) Biking (13 kms)	19 KM	Santa Maria de Dota	3 hours of hiking—3 hours of biking—lunch in the town of San Marcos—early arrival to the town of Santa Maria—time to walk around and enjoy the local color. **B, L, D**	Hotel in Santa Maria
6	Biking (46 kms)	46 KM	Continental Divide	Hardest day of the trip—4:30 AM departure—14 km climb before breakast—great mountain biking on roads and trails the rest of the day—8–10 hr. day. **B, L, D**	Cabins in the Orosi Valley

TABLE 5.1 *(Continued)*

Day	Activity	Kms	Place	Details	Lodging
7	Free Day		Orosi Valley	Free day to recover, relax and explore the area.	Cabins in the Orosi Valley
8	Biking (9 kms) Hiking (13 kms)	22 KM	Tapanti	Easy biking through coffee plantations—relaxing breakfast before the start of the hike—4 hrs. of hiking without packs—camping near a river. **B, L, D**	Camping
9	Biking (6 kms) Rafting (10 kms) Biking (3 kms)	19 KM	Pejibaye River	A little bit of everything— biking along the Pejibaye River—first day of rafting (inflatable kayaking in low water)—long day, but easy going—last 3 km is a steep up-hill climb. **B, L, D**	Hotel in Turrialba area
10	Biking (18 kms) Rafting (8 kms)	26 KM	Pacuare River	3 hrs of biking on paved road—last 5 km on dirt road to Pacuare River put-in-1½–2 hours of rafting (10 km)—time at the camp to explore the area, hike to a nearby waterfall, play in the river, or relax in a hammock. **B, L, D**	Camping at El Nido del Tigre
11	Rafting (17 kms)	17 KM	Pacuare River	3–5 hr of rafting—time in the morning to enjoy the area— relaxing buffet breakast— lunch on the side of the river—side hike up a creek to great swimming hole. **B, L, D**	Camping or cabins
12	Rafting (40 kms)	40 KM	Caribbean	Ten-hour day of drifting and paddling (no rapids)—lots of bananas along the way— scorching sun—bubbly in the surf. **B, L, D**	Camping or cabins
13	R & R in Cahuita		Cahuita	Early morning motor boat ride to awaiting bus—1½ hr. drive to Cahuita. **B, L**	Hotel in Cahuita
14	R & R in Cahuita		Cahuita	Time to visit Cahuita National Park—afternoon ride back to San Jose (3 hrs.)	Hotel in San Jose
15	Departure		San Jose	Transfer to the airport. **B**	

Source: Coast to Coast Adventures. Reprinted with permission.

nue for casino operations. There are several types of casinos including traditional casinos, casino hotels and resorts, theme casinos, riverboat casinos, and casinos located on Native American lands. There has been recent growth in the gaming business yet jurisdiction is still quite prohibitive. Only 10 states in the United States allow commercial gaming. Nonetheless, worldwide growth of the gaming industry is expected to continue.

Cruise lines are like resorts in that they provide lodging, meals, and entertainment. Unlike resorts, however, cruise lines are at sea. Large cruise ships offer a variety of entertainment options including theater, fitness centers, pools, gaming, dancing, nightclubs, and dining. Many trips include ports of call. Ports of call are when the ship pulls into harbor at various points throughout the trip and passengers have the opportunity to spend time on shore at their leisure. Typical cruise line itineraries vary from 3-to-4-day to 9-to-12-day excursions.

Timeshare and vacation ownership is when vacationers own a block of time in an apartment unit usually in one-week intervals. Often two- or three-week intervals are purchased. Ownership contracts range from seven to 30 years. Many owners trade or "swap" their units and, thus, can experience new and different locations each year. These exchanges are often coordinated through membership organizations such as Resort Condominiums, Inc. (RCI), and Interval International (II). In essence, timeshare and vacation ownership is a multiyear prepaid vacation that offers the opportunity to explore new vacation "spots" each year.

Country inns and bed-and-breakfasts (B&Bs) are small, unique lodging establishments ranging in size from 3 to 30 rooms. Country inns tend to be larger than B&Bs and normally have a restaurant serving breakfast, lunch, and dinner. B&Bs rarely have restaurant facilities. Breakfast is served in the kitchen of the owner's home. B&Bs, for the most part, are private homes with family guest rooms open to the public for overnight accommodations.

Theme parks are large amusement parks that provide entertainment for people of all ages. Attractions include roller coasters, water rides, animal shows, movie-making demonstrations, cartoon and storybook characters, sports complexes, water ski shows, thrill rides, and so forth. Major players, such as Walt Disney World and Universal Studios Florida, continue to expand their facilities, periodically adding new attractions. Theme park entrance fees are usually charged on a day-to-day basis. Walt Disney World has an estimated 35 million visitors a year.

Tourism destinations are geographic areas or regions having multiple hospitality product offerings for the leisure traveler. A tourism destination is a product in itself. They typically include lodging, foodservice, transportation, and entertainment accommodations. Cities, counties, states, provinces, regions, and countries often market themselves as tourism destinations. Theme parks and state parks, too, are considered by many to be tourism destinations.

DISCUSSION QUESTIONS

1. What are convention centers and who are their target markets?
2. Briefly describe the various types of casino operations. How are they similar? How are they different?
3. Why are cruise lines like floating resorts?
4. What is vacation ownership? How do exchange companies such as RCI and Interval International come into play?
5. Discuss the similarities and differences between country inns and bed-and-breakfasts.
6. Describe some of the recent developments in the theme park business.
7. A tourism destination is a product in itself. Discuss.

NOTES

1. Marc Ackerman, "Privatization of Public-Assembly-Facility Management," *Cornell Quarterly*, April 1994, p. 73.
2. Ibid.
3. Jeff Weinstein, "Gaming Still Drives Worldwide Expansion," *Hotels*, August 1995, p. 17.
4. Ibid.
5. Richard Gibson, "Slot Machines Pay off Big for Iowa County Racetrack," *Wall Street Journal*, June 24, 1996, p. B1.
6. Maria Lenhart, "Veiled Vegas," *Meetings & Conventions*, June 1998, p. 65.
7. Ibid.
8. Anthony Marshall, "Resorts Can Learn Much from Cruise-Ship Colleagues," *Hotel & Motel Management*, February 19, 1996, p. 9.
9. Nancy Keates, "Cruise-Ship Delays Leave Guests High and Dry," *Wall Street Journal*, October 24, 1997, p. B1.
10. Leonard Novarro, "Own Your Own Vacation Spot," *Modern Maturity*, May/June 1998, p. 69.
11. Ibid.

12. Nancy Keates, "Elite Hotels Downgrade for the Masses," *Wall Street Journal*, February 21, 1997, p. B8.

13. Mike Sheridan, "Warming Up to Vacation Ownership," *Hotels*, March 1997, p. 67.

14. Mike Malley, "Timeshare Synergies," *Hotel & Motel Management*, March 17, 1997, p. 20.

15. Ali A. Poorani and David R. Smith, "Financial Characteristics of Bed-and-Breakfast Inns," *Cornell Quarterly*, October 1995, p. 58.

16. Bruce Schoenfeld, "California's Inn Places," *Bloomberg Personal Finance*, April 1998, p. 96.

17. Harold E. Lane and Denise Dupre, *Hospitality World!* Van Nostrand–Reinhold, New York, 1997.

18. Christine Shenot, "Journey to Atlantis Will Be a Wild Ride to Sea World Visitors," *Orlando Sentinel*, March 21, 1997, p. A-12.

19. Christine Shenot, "Universal Says You'll Be Blown Away," *Orlando Sentinel*, February 7, 1997, p. B-1.

20. Michael M. Coltman, *Introduction to Travel and Tourism*, Van Nostrand–Reinhold, New York, 1989, p. 88.

21. Roberta Kipp, "Golden Isles of the Riviera," *Globe and Mail*, May 21, 1994, p. F7.

22. Ibid.

PART THREE

Personal Selling and Sales Management

Chapter 6

Personal Selling: The Sales Process

LEARNING OBJECTIVES

1. *To better understand the sales process and how it works in hospitality sales*
2. *To become familiar with the various stages of the sales process, which include:*
   - *Prospecting and account qualification*
   - *Probing and solving customers' problems*
   - *Presentations, negotiations, and pricing*
   - *Overcoming objections and closing the sale*
   - *Contracts and letters of agreement*

In Chapter 2, we introduced the five-step process to personal selling (see Table 2.2). This chapter elaborates on the **sales process** which includes prospecting and qualifying accounts, probing and solving customers' problems, making presentations, negotiating, overcoming objections, closing the sale, and contracts and letters of agreement. Service delivery aspects of the sales process are addressed in Chapter 7.

The term **account** is commonly used in sales. It refers to a customer or a grouping of customers from an organization, such as a business enterprise or a professional trade association, that has ongoing needs for hospitality services. For example, a hotel sales manager may be assigned the "IBM account." An account such as this typically has multiple customers representing various divisions of the organization. These customers have differing needs and separate files are established for each. Several files may indeed be kept for just one customer who may have several purchase occasions with differing needs for each.

In other words, a customer is an individual who purchases your product. This customer may or may not be the end user of the product purchased. Regular customers are often referred to as **clients**, especially in the business market segment. Accounts are customers or a multiple number of customers from the same organization. Joe Smith and Donna Jones may each be a meeting planner for two separate divisions of General Electric (GE) who regularly schedule meetings at your establishment. They are both customers or clients and each is a part of the GE account.

PROSPECTING AND ACCOUNT QUALIFICATION

Prospecting is searching for new customers. It is the act of seeking new sources of business for your hospitality establishment. It is not good enough to wait for customers to walk in the door. Prospecting is essential to the short-run and long-run success of any business. That is, we prospect not only to find customers, we prospect to look for the best customer, too. A customer who simply walks in the door may or may not be the ideal customer for your business. Higher revenue generating customers and/or customers whose needs you can better match may be uncovered through prospecting. There are several ways to go about prospecting and the following discussion describes various approaches to this task.

Current Accounts

One of the best sources to uncover new business is within current accounts. Current accounts can harbor many sources of untapped business potential.

Prospecting for new customers within corporate and association accounts, in particular, should be conducted on a regular basis.

For example, consider Mr. Andrew Pond, director of sales training for ABC Pharmaceutical. He is a regular client who frequently books his one-week sales training seminars at your hotel. The hotel sales manager assigned this account routinely calls on Mr. Pond to learn of upcoming sales seminars for future booking possibilities. The opportunity from a prospecting perspective is to ask this client who *else* in the organization has lodging, banquet, and/or meeting needs. This could be other managers or directors within the sales division or possibly contacts in other divisions of ABC Pharmaceutical such as the human resources, marketing, and accounting departments, and so forth.

Current clients may know of potential customers outside their organization as well, that is, colleagues of theirs who hold similar positions in other organizations. The only way to find out, of course, is to ask. It is your job as sales manager to search for new customers through current customers and not simply expect these clients to produce names and contacts for you.

Leads and Referrals

Leads are potential customers with whom no contact has yet been made. Learning of potential customers from current customers as discussed previously is essentially developing leads for prospective customers. This type of lead is called a **referral**. Referrals are especially powerful when the source of the referral is a satisfied customer who is recommending your facility to future potential customers. Other sources for leads include convention and visitors bureaus, colleagues from the business community, local news coverage, and national sales offices of hospitality chain operations.

Convention and visitors bureaus (CVBs) are good sources for leads. These bureaus, which represent cities across the United States, regularly receive inquiries from potential customers asking about hotel and restaurant facilities, exhibition halls, air and ground transportation, and so forth. Most hospitality organizations are members of their local CVB. Inquiries are passed on as leads to paid members of the CVB. (Other activities of convention and visitors bureaus are discussed in more depth in Chapter 11, which addresses the subject of intermediaries.)

National sales offices of hospitality chain operations are set up, in part, to prospect and generate leads for unit-level operations. National sales account executives seek out potential customers in specifically assigned geographic areas and/or for specifically assigned national accounts. For example, this type of salesperson may be assigned association and corporate business accounts based in the Northeast. Say a lead is uncovered from a Connecticut-based corporate account for a three-day meeting scheduled to take place at one of several locations on the West Coast. In this situation, the national sales account executive will pass on this lead to all chain properties located on the West Coast that have the facilities and services to meet the needs of this potential customer.

Colleagues from the local business community (as well as friends and neighbors) can be excellent sources of new business. Being active with the local chamber of commerce, for example, keeps you abreast of new developments in your city or township. The chamber of commerce itself regularly schedules luncheons, board meetings, political events, Christmas parties, and so forth. The local newspaper is another a source of prospects. Who has recently been promoted? What company or corporation is moving into the area? Who has announced their wedding engagement? Are there upcoming events in the initial planning stages where organizers and/or participants are in need of overnight accommodations, catered functions, or other similar hospitality services?

Business directories, typically published by chambers of commerce, are another source to garner prospective leads. These directories commonly include the names of key management personnel, type of business, number of employees, and parent company (if applicable) of companies in the local community.

The Yellow Pages of the local phone book provide addresses and phone numbers of all the organizations in the local community. In the Greater Orlando Yellow Pages, for example, there are 155 groups listed in the association classification section (see Table 6.1). This section also references other sections in the phone book by specific category such as athletic organizations, business and trade organizations, religious organizations, and veteran and military organizations. This could be considered a grouping by market segment potential from a hospitality perspective.

Sources such as the Yellow Pages or business directories can be especially useful when starting a hospitality business such as opening a new catering service, a new restaurant, or a new hotel. Although specific names and contacts are not given, often times "cold calling" can be an appropriate means to prospect and generate leads.

Cold Calling

Cold calling is essentially "knocking on doors" and its use in hospitality sales is controversial. Some suggest it is an outdated and inefficient means of prospecting. For many sales professionals, cold calling was replaced with

TABLE 6.1   *Excerpts from the Greater Orlando Yellow Pages: Association Section*

Air Conditioning Contractors Association of Central Florida 315 Melody Lane Casselberry	260-2206
Aluminum Association of Florida Inc 3319 Maguire Blvd Orlando	898-9287
Alzheimer's Association Greater Orlando Chapter 2010 Mizell Ave Winter Park	628-0088
American Association of Homes and Services for the Aging SE Regional Office 50 S Lucerne Cir W Orlando	246-0062
American Biofeedback Council 282 Short Ave Longwood	331-8776
American Culinary Federation Chapter of Central Florida 2900 W Oak Ridge Rd Orlando	826-8908
American Diabetes Association 1101 N Lake Destiny Dr Maitland	660-1926
Marine Marketing to Women 200 W Welbourne Ave Winter Park	629-4941
Medical Eye Bank of Florida Suite 104/22 W Lake Beauty Dr Orlando	422-2020
Meeting Professionals Int'l Greater Orlando Chapter 45 N Magnolia Ave Orlando	420-5900
Mended Hearts Chapter No 66 1641 N Hastings St Orlando	295-4075
Mid Florida Utilities & Transportation Contractors Association 8708 Pine Barrens Dr Orlando	679-8477

telemarketing in the late 1970s and early 1980s. **Telemarketing** is the process of telephoning potential customers from lists such as the Orlando Yellow Pages discussed previously. Telemarketing, however, is really cold calling; only it is done by phone rather than by a personal visit to the office of a prospective customer. The objective is the same for both—learning of potential customer needs and wants and assessing whether your product or service can satisfy those needs and wants.

Many places of business have "No Soliciting" signs prominently displayed at the front entrance. No soliciting is a formal way of saying "No Cold Calling" on the premises for any salespeople including those in hospitality. In other words, unless you have a prearranged appointment with a prospect, you are not welcome. Nonetheless, the practice of cold calling is commonplace. As suggested by Jeffrey Gitomer, a sales professional and author of *The Sales Bible*:

> It seems every office building I go into the sign on the door says "No Soliciting." It has to be the funniest sign in sales. What a useless sign to post in front of a salesman. I'd like to have a dollar for every "No Soliciting" sign I've ignored. What is the purpose of the sign and who does it deter?

> . . . What do salespeople think of "No Soliciting" signs? I polled the "Early Risers Lead Club," the largest pure sales lead association in the Charlotte area, made up of entrepreneurs and salespeople. I asked how they felt and what they did when they encountered the dreaded sign.

> "I go in buildings so fast I don't see the signs," says Cindi Ballard, president of El El Interior Plantscapes; "I've been cold calling [for years] and I've never had a problem."

> "Once I was told 'No Soliciting' by a company," says Earl Coggins of Pony Express. "I said 'I'm just trying to save you some money. They said come right in'."

> "Most buildings are built with that sign on the door." says Richard Herd of Continental Advertising. "I feel like it's meant for other kinds of salesmen, not me. I ignore it and have never had a problem."

> "Everyone's got one; it doesn't affect me," says Ward Norris, president of Crown Resources. "If they tell me 'no soliciting', I say I was so focused on meeting you and learning your name, I must have missed the sign."

> "I cold call on the telephone. That way I can't see if there's a sign on the door," says Bob Dillard of Bob Dillard Sales.[1]

Telemarketing can be an efficient form of cold calling from a time and cost perspective; that is, it is easier and quicker to pick up the phone. However, a personal visit can often be more productive. For example, direct face-to-face contact with a receptionist may prove to be helpful for future calls should business potential result from the initial call. Human nature is such that one remembers a face-to-face conversation more readily than a phone conversation. And it is usually more difficult to turn away someone standing in front of you than to hang up on someone on the other end of the line.

The primary purpose of cold calling is to garner information on the hospitality service product needs of a potential customer, find out who the decision maker is, and, in turn, determine if a true prospect has been identified. This may be accomplished in one call, or it may take several follow-up calls to complete the task. It is important to remember that the objective of cold calling is *not* to make a sale. Rather, it is the business of searching for prospects and beginning a relationship once a prospect has been found.

It takes a great number of calls to uncover prospects, and it takes a great number of prospects to get only a few customers. Figure 6.1 illustrates this point—one moves from prospects to possibles to probables to customers. Customers do not materialize out of thin air. Widely known in professional selling and well stated by Howard Feiertag, a sales clinic columnist for *Hotel & Motel Management*, "out of every 10 leads, three turn into prospects, and one is likely to book some business with you."[2] A key word here is "likely." Likely does not mean yes. It simply means that there is a high probability that a sale can be made with a prospect that is well qualified and that a match potentially exists between prospective buyer and seller.

Account Qualification

Qualifying an account is an aspect of probing to identify the basic needs of the potential buyer. Whenever calls are made—whether with regular customers or when prospecting for potential customers—a sales call report is prepared by the sales account executive. Shown in Figure 6.2 is a sample sales call report. This example demonstrates what took place during a sales call with a current account. The director of sales, Sue McCutcheon, met with her client, Rob Lattuca of RCL Electronics, to discuss an upcoming meeting. (Follow-up action for this sample account will be described shortly.)

When prospecting, the sales call report is usually accompanied by a

FIGURE 6.1 *From prospects to customers.*

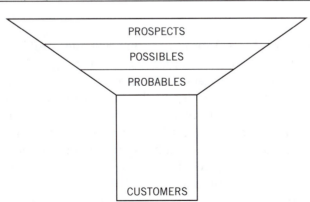

```
                    SALES CALL REPORT
File No. C9825                  Sales Manager S. McCutcheon
                                Date MAY 25, 1998

Organization: RCL Electronics

Contact: ROB LATTUCA              Title: MNGR-SALES PROMOTIONS
Address: 600 NORTH SHERMAN AVENUE
City: MIDTOWN, U.S.A.             Phone: (607) 273-8552

  • SHORT TERM BOOKING FOR NEXT AUGUST (SEE SPECS ATTACHED).
    AGREED ON SPECIAL FLAT RATE OF $102 SINGLE OR DOUBLE,
    MOSTLY SINGLES.

  • KNOWS HOTEL WELL, NO NEED FOR SITE INSPECTION

  • SIMILAR TO MEETING HELD HERE TWO YEARS AGO. GOOD GROUP,
    WELL ORGANIZED.

  • VERBAL DEFINITE. PUT TOGETHER LETTER OF AGREEMENT,
    HAND DELIVER.



                           Trace Date   JUNE 1, PICK-UP
                                        CONTRACT
```

FIGURE 6.2 *Sample sales call report.*

customer profile sheet (see Figure 6.3). This customer profile sheet outlines information on the customer with regard to market segment, industry and/or organization represented, general (or generic) customer needs, and sales implications. For instance, identifying the industry in which a prospective client operates can be very helpful. It is not unusual to have common features of customer needs in the same industry. For example, in the pharmaceutical industry, sales training meetings and heavy use of audiovisual equipment at these meetings are commonplace. This information can help streamline and/or better focus the probing process.

The sales implication section of a customer profile sheet should include

---

Customer Profile Sheet

(A) Market Segment: _____

(B) Customer Industry/Organization: _____

_____

(C) Customer Title (Job Function): _____

_____

(D) General Customer Needs (By Priority):

    1. _____

    2. _____

    3. _____

    4. _____

    5. _____

    6. _____

(E) Industry/Organization's Distinguishing Characteristics: _____

_____

_____

_____

_____

(F) Sales Implications: _____

_____

_____

_____

_____

FIGURE 6.3 *Sample customer profile sheet. (Courtesy of Marriott International. Reprinted with permission.)*

items specific to this potential account. These items typically include the degree of price sensitivity, the time of year that a purchase is required, the frequency of spouse programs, or any aspect of particular importance to the customer as it relates to his or her hospitality needs.

When prospecting for conference and convention business, a more detailed account qualification form is completed addressing specific issues typical for this market segment. Shown in Figure 6.4, these issues include such items as types of meetings, number of meetings, size of meetings, date or time of year preferred, and so forth. When possible, historical information on past meeting activity is included as part of the account qualification process.

Of importance when qualifying a prospect is identifying who specifically is the decision maker for the account. A principal contact for an account may or may not be the primary decision maker for the final purchase. For example, an executive secretary may be the main contact for a law firm that has incoming visitors on a regular basis. This secretary routinely makes the hotel and restaurant reservations for these out-of-town guests. However, the final decision on which hotel or which restaurant to book is made by a senior law partner. This senior law partner and the executive secretary are both customers, so are their guests. The secretary may be very influential in the decision, and the guest, of course, is the end user who ultimately needs to be satisfied. Presumably, a satisfied guest also satisfies the law firm and, thus, influences in a positive way future reservation decisions. Once the account is established, calls continue to be made by the sales account executive including courtesy calls to the executive secretary and attempts to establish a relationship with the senior partner. It is important to keep in mind and stay abreast of who makes the final decision. And these final decisions are often based on customer satisfaction of *all* customers of an account.

PROBING AND SOLVING CUSTOMERS' PROBLEMS

As we noted in Chapter 1, the essence of sales and marketing is finding ways to solve customers' problems. Without needs and problems, there are no opportunities for sales and marketing to pursue. In hospitality, as in all industries, an effective sales manager uses **probing** to learn of "problems" that a potential customer needs resolved.

Problems can be relatively simple such as a desire to go out for dinner to celebrate a special occasion and at issue is deciding where to dine. Should the answer be a favorite restaurant, management of the restaurant needs to learn which day and at what time a reservation is preferred. Getting a call from the prospective customer is the start of the sales process and initial probing begins by learning more about the reservation requirements. When the guests arrive, they are seated by the host or hostess and probing continues by the waitperson for menu selection, beverage selection, and so forth. Each step of the way is an opportunity to sell and, perhaps, even uncover needs and wants that customers did not know they had—such as a glass of

ACCOUNT QUALIFICATION FORM

Group Name: _____

Contact: _____ Title: _____

Address: _____

_____

Phone: _____ Fax: _____

Type of Company or Association: _____

What do they do? _____

Current Practices:

Number of Meetings: _____

   Types of Meetings: (Circle Appropriate Types)

Board Meeting	Incentive	Sales
Convention	Legislative	Seminar
Trade Show	Management	Training
Committee Meeting	New Product	Other: _____

Date or Time of Year Preferred: _____

Attendees: _____ # of Ppl: _____

# of Rooms: _____ Arr/Dep Pattern: _____

Budget: _____

Type of Hotel Preferred: _____

General Meeting Specs: _____

_____

General F&B Requirements: _____

_____

Historical Information:

Where have you met before? _____

When? _____ # of Rooms? _____

What budget historically do you set? _____

Marriott History: Where? _____ When? _____

# of Rooms? _____ Rate? _____

FIGURE 6.4 *Sample account qualification form. (Courtesy of Marriott International. Reprinted with permission.)*

wine, a favorite dessert, an espresso coffee. Some hoteliers and restaurateurs call this "upselling." More important, however, is to take a professional sales approach at the end of the meal and probe one step further by asking, "Did you enjoy your meal?" In other words, you are asking the customer, "Did we solve your problem?" The goal is a satisfied customer, and the best way to find out is to ask.

Probing is asking questions, lots of questions. The objective is to learn as much as you can about customer needs and wants. Some potential clients may articulate quite clearly what it is they are seeking. Others may be more nebulous. Some purchases are simple or fairly routine tasks such as the dinner reservation example noted previously. Complex purchases, on the other hand, require a lot of time and energy on the part of both buyer and seller. Continuous probing and questioning is often necessary to uncover what the potential customer is truly seeking.

Open-Ended Questioning

There are essentially two types of questions—open ended and close ended. Open-ended questioning is asking broad general questions coupled with listening. Subsequent questions follow and the process continues. The following example illustrates this point:

Sales Manager:	We look forward to the possibility of hosting your upcoming meeting. Could you tell me more about what you are looking for?
Customer:	Yes. We are planning a three-day meeting for roughly 25 people for late October. We will need a meeting room and lunch each day and overnight accommodations. [Silence]
Sales Manager:	What kind of meeting are you planning?
Customer:	This particular meeting is for our accounting and finance division. They need some time away from the office to review our current computer system, deliberate where the problems are for their division, and make recommendations for improvements. We are overdue for an upgraded system, especially for the accounting folks. [Silence]
Sales Manager:	Sounds like you might need a lot of table space to spread out papers, computer spreadsheets,

	and such. Do you have a particular setup in mind?
Customer:	Well, we have never had this kind of meeting before. Do you have any suggestions?

Note that thus far all questions from the sales manager have been open ended. Now that the prospective client has asked a question, the sales manager has an opportunity to recommend several alternatives and put the buyer back in a decision-making mode. One suggestion might be a "board-of-directors" style setup where all participants sit around one large table. The sales manager could additionally suggest a "classroom" or "schoolroom"-style setup where each participant sits behind a desklike table, making it easier to work in small groups should they wish to do so. (See Figure 6.5 for sample meeting room setups.) The main task at this point is to keep probing. Much more information is needed before the sales manager should try to close the sale and "book the business."

Open-ended questions are usually best for probing. They should be somewhat focused to help give direction to the prospective buyer for responding to the question. The sales manager's meeting room setup question in the previous scenario is a good example of an open, yet focused question.

"Loaded" or "leading" questions can be problematic. These are questions that are overly focused on the seller instead of the buyer. Referencing the preceding scenario, an example of a loaded question would be, "The classroom-style setup is much better suited for your meeting agenda, wouldn't you agree?" The sales manager, in this instance, is pushing the classroom-style setup because it takes up less function space than the board-of-directors style. A more objective and more customer-oriented question would be, "Classroom style or board-of-directors style are two possibilities that come to mind. Would you like to see a sample setup of each?" This question is much better and is also nonthreatening. Should the buyer not know the difference between the two setups, he or she is not put in a potentially embarrassing situation. This more "neutral" approach returns the focus to the needs and interests of the buyer. As noted by Mary Ann Oberhaus, author of *Professional Selling*:

> Neutral questions are objective and unbiased. Loaded questions, on the other hand, use judgmental language. Leading questions [can] imply that one answer is preferable to another. Both loaded and leading questions are typically closed. Because these types of questions are likely to trigger a defensive response, neutral questions are preferable.[3]

We concur. Neutral questions are preferable and can be open or closed as well.

MEETING & BANQUET FACILITIES

The DoubleTree Guest Suites in Vero Beach caters to small meetings from 5 to 50 people. At your service is a sales and catering staff to guide you with appropriate menus, breaks, theme dinner parties, and assure your company a successful meeting.

Seminole Suite

Executive Suite overlooking the Atlantic Ocean with a boardroom table seating 10 or director table seating 22.

Lanai Room *with attached Patio area*

Available after 10:30 a.m.
For private seminars, meetings, luncheons, dinners and receptions.
Lanai 1,000 square feet
Patio 500 square feet

Sit Down Dinner	*Buffet*	*Reception*	*Seminar*
60	*80*	*100*	*48*

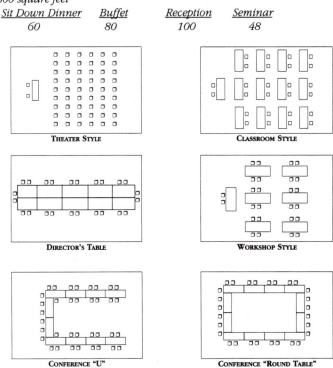

FIGURE 6.5 *Sample meeting room setups. (Courtesy of Promus Hotels, Inc. Reprinted with permission.)*

132

Closed-Ended Questioning

There are times in hospitality sales when a combination of open-and closed-ended questioning is appropriate. Often times clarification is needed. Should a prospect say, "Our closing banquet should be top of the line," do not assume a $50 per person dinner. Ask what price range or what budget the client has in mind. For some, $30 a plate may be considered a fancy meal; for others, it might be in the $75 range. Assumptions are dangerous when probing. Never assume, always ask.

For regularly scheduled events, such as an annual convention or a traditional year-end Christmas party, it is helpful to get a history of recent past events from the prospective buyer. Questions for this type of probing might be as follows:

- Where was this event most recently held?
- What was the attendance?
- Did you require overnight accommodations? How many singles? How many doubles? How many suites?
- What type of menu did you have? How many courses were served? Did you choose to offer wine?
- Did you require audiovisual equipment?
- Were there special spouse programs?
- How might your upcoming event be similar and/or different from previous events of this type?

Answers to these questions can be summarized in a sales call report and/or on an account qualification form. Some hospitality organizations have convention history report forms designed specifically for this type of query. An example for the RCL Electronics account introduced earlier is shown in Figure 6.6. As can be seen, this report gives a sales manager a detailed "picture" of what transpired in the recent past for a similar event. Should the potential client give slightly different facts and figures for the current event being planned, further probing is needed to find out *why.*

The convention history report ideally comes from a previous event held at the facility. For chain operations, a sister hotel, resort, or conference center is a good source as well. Sometimes, however, a competitor may have to be contacted to obtain this information. It is common practice in the hospitality industry for suppliers to share these types of facts and figures. Although an experienced meeting planner or corporate travel planner may have this information, it is best to verify it with the supplier of the most recent similar event.

Sometimes planners inflate these figures to ensure that they will not

CONVENTION HISTORY REPORT

Name of Group _____ RCL ELECTRONICS _____

Meeting Planner _____ ROB LATTUCA _____

Hotel _ REGAL CROWNE _____ City _ MIDTOWN, U.S.A. _____

Month _ JULY _____ Year _ 1996 _____ Att ____ 350 _____

Rates: Sgls $95 ____ Dbls $95 ____ Suites $125 _____

Day	S	M	T	W				
Date	7/21	7/22	7/23	7/24				
Room Block	150	325	150	40				
Reservations								
Actual Pick-up	151	290	140	30	(MOSTLY SINGLES)			
Singles								
Doubles								
Suites ⊛	1	3	3	1				

F & B Estimates: Banquet Food _____ HEAVY _____

Banquet Bev _____ MEDIUM _____

Restaurant _____ LIGHT _____

Bar _____ MEDIUM _____

General Comments: _____

_____ GOOD GROUP – NO PROBLEMS. BQT GUARANTEES LATE, HOWEVER. _____

_____ ROB LATTUCA, OVERALL, GOOD MEETING PLANNER. _____

_____

_____ ⊛ BOOKED AT LAST MINUTE, NOT ON ORIGINAL CONTRACT. _____

FIGURE 6.6 *Sample convention history report.*

encounter problems later on such as not enough guest rooms or attendees feeling cramped for space in a meeting room. Suppliers, however, need to ensure that they are not put in a position to oversell an account. In other words, inventory is precious. Should a buyer reserve 100 guest rooms and only 60 rooms are needed in the end, the remaining 40 rooms have the potential to go unsold. As noted in Chapter 1, this perishability aspect of the service product is a critical issue in hospitality. An unsold room cannot be resold at a later date. The lost revenue for that particular room on that particular night is lost forever.

PRESENTATIONS, NEGOTIATIONS, AND PRICING

Presentations are an integral part of the sales process. Upon completion of initial probing, the sales account executive should have enough information to "present the message." The message should essentially say to the prospective buyer, "I think I have a solution to your problem, and here it is." The message should be forthright and direct, and should keenly distinguish between the features and benefits of your product offering.

Features refer to the physical or tangible aspects of the product offering. Benefits refer to the customer's use of these features. A feature may be your newly renovated ballroom, which includes such amenities as a sound booth, VCR capabilities, spot lighting, recessed chandeliers, and rearview projection screens. These features could be of significant use and benefit to a meeting planner requiring a multitude of audiovisual and multimedia equipment. However, for a couple considering your ballroom for a wedding reception, they could probably care less about these "features." More important to them might be the spaciousness of the ballroom, quality of carpeting, type of table linen provided, placement of the dance floor, and the like. The features and related benefits of the honeymoon suite may be the most important of all. When presenting the message, it is the benefits derived from the features presented that are important to your potential customer, not the features themselves.

Personal Presentations

Presentations can be done in person, in writing, by video, on the Web, by CD-ROM, and on the phone. A combination of one or more of these is not uncommon. Which to use depends on the target audience and product offering. For complex purchases, such as group events, personal face-to-face presentations are best. Ideally, these are done on premise and are called "site inspections."

A **site inspection** is when a prospective client is brought on premise and given a tour of the facilities. Tours of this type can take anywhere from one to five hours to complete depending on the needs of the buyer. A potential buyer who is already familiar with your facilities may need only a quick look. Or, as is often the case for regular accounts, the site inspection may be skipped altogether. For new prospects not familiar with the property, time is needed for them to acquaint themselves with what you have to offer and how it will benefit them.

Some sales managers give tours of the "front of the house" as well as the "back of the house." Front of the house refers to facilities actually used by the customer such as guest rooms, restaurants, function rooms, public restrooms, cocktail lounges, registration areas, foyers, suites, and parking facilities. Back of the house refers to the kitchen area, housekeeping, receiving areas, loading docks, and equipment storage areas. An experienced purchaser of hospitality services, in particular, knows that a well-managed, clean back-of-the-house operation usually means a well-managed, clean front-of-the-house operation, too.

Throughout the site inspection and at its conclusion, the sales manager continuously presents the message of what his or her company can offer to meet the needs of the prospective buyer. Continuing with the three-day, late October meeting, following is an example of what may have transpired at the conclusion of the tour:

Sales Manager:	Now that you have seen our facilities, what do you think?
Customer:	I'm impressed. I'm still not sure which meeting room setup would be best for our meeting but overall the function rooms seem well equipped and in excellent condition. The guest room accommodations seem to suit our needs as well. [*Silence*]
Sales Manager:	Great. We do not need to make a decision regarding the specific meeting room setup right now. I would like to put together a formal proposal for you and your colleagues to review.
Customer:	That would be fine. Our guest room needs are doubles and we will need a closing dinner banquet as well. The other nights people will be on their own for supper. They may work late into the evening. Who knows? [*Silence*]
Sales Manager:	Would you like to see our banquet menus? Or

	meet with our catering director while you are here?
Customer:	No, not now. I'm late for an appointment downtown. Just include the menus in the package you send. [*Silence*]
Sales Manager:	No problem. Thank you for your time. I'll bring the menus and the proposal over to your office first thing in the morning. We look forward to doing business with you.

Although somewhat simplified, the sales presentation has now been made. A sales call report would be written up and a proposal would be developed and delivered to the client as promised.

A tentative booking entry is recorded internal to the operation when preliminary dates and space requirements are known. This keeps the entire sales team abreast of each sales manager's tentative booking activity. Figure 6.7 shows the tentative booking entry recorded by sales manager Sue McCutcheon for the RCL Electronics account.

Reservationists for hotels and restaurants also make personal presentations, albeit over the phone and not face to face. The process is still the same—probe, learn of customer needs, make a presentation, and ask for the business.

The use of a toll-free 800 number to a central reservation system (CRS) by prospective customers is commonplace. Holiday Inn (HI) has toll-free numbers around the world, including North America, Europe, the Middle East, Australia, and the Pacific Rim, where a customer can make an HI reservation worldwide at no cost. For example, a customer traveling in Belgium can make a reservation at the Holiday Inn in Sydney, Australia, through the use of the HI toll-free number.

Ruth's Chris Steak House has a toll-free number for customers to make a luncheon or dinner reservation at any of its 50+, restaurants across the United States and Canada (see Figure 6.8). Unlike a hotel chain CRS, customers are connected directly to the restaurant of their choice through a coding system that allows them to make the reservation. One of the authors experimented with this toll-free number for a reservation at Ruth's Chris Steak House in Miami, and was quite satisfied with the process.

Nonpersonal Presentations

Nonpersonal presentations support the personal selling effort. Introduced in Chapter 2 as part of the communication mix, these efforts include advertising,

BOOKING ENTRY

Sales Manager S. McCutcheon
Date 5/25/98

✓ Tentative _____ Definite _____ Meeting Dates ___August 3-7_____ Year _98_ Total Rooom Nights _710_

Name of Group ___RCL Electronics_____

Contact/Title ___Rob Latuca MNGR—Sales Promotions_____

Address/Phone ___600 North Sherman Avenue_____

___Midtown, U.S.A._____ (607) 273-8552

Day	SUN	MON	TUE	WED	THU	FRI	SAT	SUN	MON	TUE	WED	THU	FRI	SAT	RATES
Date	8/3	8/4	8/5	8/6											
Singles	170	350	170	20											$102
Doubles															$102
Suites															✕
Total	170	350	170	20											

Reservation Cut-off Date ___2 Weeks_____

Complimentary Accommodations ___(None)_____

Special Billing Instructions ___TBD (To Be Determined)_____

Comments/Specific Instructions ___Reservations ———➤ Tentatively block three suites @ $125

___Not requested yet, but typically do so at last minute.____

___We have verbal definite for this business._____

_____

_____

FIGURE 6.7 *Sample tentative booking form.*

direct mail, brochures, and merchandising. Other examples here include menus, videos, postcards, and promotions in books as well. Again, these support materials do not actually "close the sale," but they can help make the sale happen.

In the series of figures that follow are examples of nonpersonal presentations. They include the previously mentioned Ruth's Chris Steak House advertisement (Figure 6.8), an early-bird dinner special promotion for the Ebb Tide Restaurant of Cape Cod (Figure 6.9), postcard promotions of the Filet of Sole Restaurant of Toronto (Figures 6.10), and an excerpt from the Peter Graben Caterers brochure targeting the business market (Figure 6.11).

Videos have become commonplace in the 1990s to describe various hospitality products to prospective customers. Hotels, cruise lines, and tourism destinations, in particular, frequently use this tool to assist in their sales efforts. Videos are essentially brochures with sound and action. Developing a good video can be expensive and costs can reach the $25,000 mark. Nonetheless, they can be very effective when done well. As noted in a recent issue of the *HSMAI Marketing Review*, well-done videos focus on what is unique about the product, have good soundtracks, and use broadcast-quality tapes. In addition, keep it short—8 to 10 minutes is best—and whenever possible, hire a professional to get the job done right.[4]

Travel books of all types are growing in popularity and numerous prospective customers use these guides to obtain general and specific information when making travel plans. Having your hotel or restaurant highlighted in these books certainly gives a boost to sales. For example, Tim and Zina Zagat are authors of several restaurant books including *Zagat Restaurant Surveys* and *America's Top Restaurants*. In each of these books, restaurants are grouped by city. For restaurants picked to be included in the guide, a brief but fun description of each is given. Price estimates per meal (cost per person for dinner, one drink, and a tip) are given by dollar signs: $ = under $25, $$ = $25–$50, $$$ = over $50. *Successful Meetings* magazine featured a cover story on these two books by the Zagats. The publishers also asked the Zagats for their recommendations on the best spots for a small group of business colleagues "in a strange city . . . scratching their heads, wondering where to go for good food and a good time."[5] Their response for the Greater Boston area included Olives Restaurant:

> Olives [is] "a pretty serious place,". . . . Deemed the "hottest spot in town" by patrons, the former dance hall's wooden decor is awash in deep reds, browns, and golds, helping guests digest the hearty comforting dishes. The Northern Italian cuisine has been called "phenomenal," but it's the lamb alla pastore and honey-cured spit-roasted duckling that are the legends here. Make reservations—or eat somewhere else.[6]

 *Y*ears ago, nobody made an oven hot enough to broil my steaks perfectly and seal in the juices. So I designed my own. We still use those 1800-degree monsters to lock in the corn-fed flavor of our U.S. Prime Midwestern beef. That's why there's nothing like the taste of a sizzling Ruth's Chris steak. Come in soon. And come hungry.

For reservations at any Florida Ruth's Chris call toll free 1-800-544-0808. Enter the 2-digit code to be connected directly to the restaurant:

Ft. Lauderdale–10 N. Palm Beach–17
2525 N. Federal Hwy. 661 U.S. Hwy. 1

N. Miami Beach–25 Orlando–28 Tampa–53
3913 N.E. 163rd St. 999 Douglas Ave. 1700 N. Westshore Blvd.
In the Intracoastal Mall Interior Decor Center

©1996 RCSH

FIGURE 6.8 *Ruth's Chris Steak House advertisement. (Courtesy of Ruth's Chris Steak House. Reprinted with permission.)*

The Ebb Tide

Where Your Cape Cod Evening Begins
"TRADITIONAL NEW ENGLAND CUISINE"

EARLY EVENING DINNER SPECIALS
Available from 4:30 – Must be seated by 5:30
Featuring 18 entrees, choice of appetizer or salad, relish tray, homemade breads, choice of vegetable & potato, dessert & coffee

FULL DINNER MENU
Featuring local seafood, prime rib and Ebb Tide Signature Dinners
Available until closing

——— SAMPLING OF DINNER SPECIALS ———
• Seafarer's Sampler •
Scallops, scrod & shrimp baked in a sherry bread crumb dressing
• Prime Rib •
• Chicken Cape Cod •
Cranberry glazed boneless breast of chicken

Please Visit Our New Gift Shop

The Ebb Tide
38 years of quality, value and service

Chef-Owners
The
McCormick
Family

94 CHASE AVENUE • DENNISPORT • (508) 398-8733

FIGURE 6.9 *Ebb Tide Restaurant advertisement. (Courtesy of the Ebb Tide Restaurant. Reprinted with permission.)*

FIGURE 6.10   *Filet of Sole Restaurant postcard. (Courtesy of Filet of Sole Restaurant. Reprinted with permission.)*

Dear Patrons;

We have been serving our customers the freshest and finest fish and seafood for the past 11 years. We are now offering, additionally, the finest steaks money can buy in this continent.

Less than 2% of all beef production within the United States is classified as Prime grade. This quality grade beef evaluates the age of the meat, colour and the marbling within the meat. The Prime grade beef has the highest percentage of marbling and great texture resulting in a tender, juicy and flavourful steak.

To: OUR VALUED CUSTOMER

FROM: THE CHEF, FILET OF SOLE

SUBJECT: U.S.D.A. PRIME BEEF

Daily Luncheon & Dinner Specials, Lobsters, Oysters, Fresh Fish & Prime Steaks

Filet of Sole Restaurant, 11 Duncan Street, Toronto, Ontario M5H 3G6 • (416) 598-3256

FIGURE 6.10 *(Continued)*

Books and press coverage such as this help present the message for you. How do you get included in these publications? Have a topnotch product and lots of satisfied customers. An aggressive public relations agency helps, too.

Direct mail is another type of nonpersonal presentation. As noted in Chapter 2, it is a form of advertising and not face-to-face personal contact with a potential client. Once a prospect has been clearly identified, follow-up contact can be made with direct mail (see Figure 2.3). Direct mail can help present a message such as a special promotion or a new product offering. Nonetheless, a personal call (even by phone) is the most effective way to determine if you truly have an interested buyer. Direct mail cannot probe, a personal call can.

Negotiations

Much has been written over the years about negotiations in hospitality sales. "You Can Be a Powerful Negotiator,"[7], "Focus on Negotiating,"[8], "Negotiate

FIGURE 6.11 *Peter Graben Caterers brochure excerpt. (Courtesy of Peter Graben Caterers. Reprinted with permission.)*

Yourself into a Good Relationship,"[9], and "The Wind Has Shifted: A New Climate for Hotel Negotiations."[10]. Publications such as these, sales professionals, and buyers alike all have a similar message. The message is that when the needs of *both* buyer and seller are put on the table a more open and more positive relationship is developed. It is the job of the sales manager to find the "win–win" situation, that is, to find the best fit for both buyer and seller.

In hospitality sales, three key issues typically emerge—rates, dates, and space. What is the cost to the buyer or revenue to the seller? What are the preferred dates of the buyer or date availability of the seller? What are the space requirements of the buyer or the capacity of the seller? It goes back to the definition of marketing in that the customer is looking for the right product, at the right place, at the right time, and at the right price. In negotiations, we add the dimension of the seller. Partnerships. What is the win–win situation? Who is willing to trade X for Y? Y for Z? When both parties give and take, a solution can often be found.

If a customer is price sensitive and preferred dates are important, the amount of space requested may be an area of flexibility on the part of the buyer. Conversely, if a seller is in a high demand period and capturing high rates is important, the seller may be in a position to give away a little more space to secure the business. But, in this scenario, we are not yet in a win–win situation. Both buyer and seller are considering a trade-off on space, which doesn't leave much room for negotiations. But if the seller can suggest a lower rate for slightly different dates and the buyer can seriously consider this alternative, then a win–win situation could be in the making. The seller gives up preferred rates for dates and the buyer gives up dates for better rates. A partnership is starting to emerge.

Let us return to the three-day, late October, accounting and finance division meeting. Assume the dates are very important to the buyer, yet these dates are during a high-demand period for the supplier. In this case, the salesperson may suggest one of two alternatives: first, a higher room rate or, second, a smaller meeting room with limited capacity. This gives the choice of rates or space, if the buyer wishes to meet over his or her preferred dates. The buyer may decide to give up space; the seller would then give up rates.

This compromise creates a win–win situation. The buyer wins dates and rates; the seller wins space (which can then be sold to other potential clients). Indeed, some sales managers propose this very rates/dates/space issue directly to experienced buyers. They say to the buyers, "We are offering rates, dates, and space—you take two, I'll take the third." It's not always that easy, but sometimes it works.

For group business, planned meal functions can play an important part in the negotiation process. Should the hotel, resort, or conference center anticipate higher-than-usual food and beverage revenue from a particular group, the sales manager has more flexibility in negotiating room rates, dates, and/or space concessions. Savvy buyers are quite aware of this incremental revenue source for the supplier. They will push to get the best deal they can get. If it is a good piece of business, book it.

Pricing

One of the most ticklish areas in negotiations is pricing. The customer wants the lowest price possible and the the supplier wants the highest. The art of negotiation is finding the *best* price, that is, the price at which both buyer and seller are satisfied.

A helpful way to look at pricing is in terms of demand, competition, and cost. These three factors help set a conceptual framework for arriving at a fair price. As shown in Figure 6.12, demand sets the ceiling, supplier costs set the floor, and the level of competition determines where on the continuum the actual price will fall. Following is a more detailed discussion explaining the model.

The demand ceiling is "what the market will bear." It determines the highest point a price can go from the customer's perspective. Say a couple

FIGURE 6.12   *A conceptual framework for the pricing decision.*

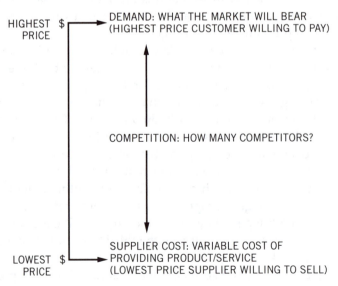

is planning to go out for dinner. They may set their budget at $50. Perhaps they would like to keep it to $40, but $50 is their upper limit. The ceiling has been set at $50. Restaurants perceived to be priced higher than this amount for a dinner for two will not be considered an alternative choice for this couple.

Costs refer to the costs of the seller. At a minimum, or the floor of the pricing continuum, is the variable costs of conducting business. If it costs a restaurant $15 to produce and service a dinner for two, then it doesn't make sense to price the dinner at less than that amount. The lowest possible price to offer is a minimum of $15 for this restaurant.

In all likelihood, the final price range will end up somewhere in between. This is largely due to the level of competition. How much competition? If there are a number of competitors in the same locale offering similar dining experiences, then the price could be forced down to the $25 to $35 range. Should competition be minimal and you have a good product offering, the price could end up in the $35 to $45 range.

For this restaurant scenario, the price range from which to make a pricing decision is $15 to $50. The degree of competition will be a major factor in the final menu price range decision. The following chart captures the essence of this example as it applies to the Figure 6.12 framework:

Price Level	Price Range	Degree of Competition
Highest	$40–$50	No competitors
High	$35–$45	Few competitors
Medium	$30–$40	Some competitors
Low	$25–$35	Number of competitors
Lowest	$20–$30	Many competitors

Price determination is all too often strictly cost driven by the supplier. In the end, the customer is the real decision maker in pricing decisions. He or she can simply say yes or no. Thus, the art of negotiation—or setting the menu price range as is the case in the preceding example—is finding out at what threshold the customer will say "yes." Again, demand sets the ceiling, costs set the floor, and the level of competition helps determine where the final price will be.

Single-Product and Bundle Pricing

Another aspect to pricing is the issue of single-product versus bundle or package pricing. **Single-product pricing** is when a basic price is set for the basic product. The price of a guest room at a mid-priced hotel may be $75.

If the customer wants additional services, say breakfast the following morning, a separate price is paid for this product offering.

Bundle pricing is when two or more aspects of a product or service are priced as one. Combo meals or value meals offered at many fast-food restaurants are examples of bundle pricing. Typically, they include the basic meal such as a cheeseburger or burrito combined with fries and a soft drink—all for one price.

Hotels often bundle price. Weekend packages targeted at the leisure market are typically priced in this fashion. Business travelers are starting to see bundle pricing, too. Many of today's individual business clientele have a preference for this simpler approach to pricing from a customer perspective. As recently noted in the *Cornell Quarterly*:

> The Miyako Hotel, located in San Francisco's Japantown, has announced that it will roll into its room rate the cost of a full American-style breakfast, local telephone calls, and incoming fax service.... The 218-room property, which offers Japanese futon rooms and deep Japanese-style bathtubs, is responding to a research study that found add-on charges are at the top of the list of irritations for frequent business travelers.
>
> Miyako general manager John Banta pointed to the comment of one traveler: "I have to budget for each expense and I don't want to be nickled and dimed to death."[11]

Conference centers (and increasingly hotels and resorts) often bundle price on a per person basis for meetings and conferences. Instead of having a separate price for guest rooms, meals, and coffee breaks, function rooms, and audiovisual equipment, a per person price for the entire event is quoted. Many attendees and meeting planners prefer this type of pricing for budgetary purposes.

Some hospitality establishments use a combination of single-product and bundle pricing. The Mr. Goodcents Subs and Pastas restaurant chain presents such a menu. As shown in Figure 6.13, the menu offers half and whole giant sub sandwich options, party trays, separate salad and side dishes, and all-inclusive Centsable™ meals. Note that the delivery charge is separate and not included in the price for food and beverage. Delivery is not the core product but the service is available for those who want this option. The restaurant concept and its menu presentation is fun, creative, and appealing to the target audience. The Mr. Goodcents menu is priced with a combination of single-product and bundle pricing options.

OVERCOMING OBJECTIONS AND CLOSING THE SALE

Thus far, we have looked at prospecting for new leads, probing to fully qualify leads and customers, presenting to demonstrate how we can meet the needs of the customer, and negotiating to search for a win–win solution. Each represents a stage of the sales process. A prospect has been found, the account has been qualified, the message has been presented, and initial negotiations have begun. Overcoming objections and closing the sale, which are closely related, are next. Following is a discussion of each.

Overcoming Objections

Rarely does a prospective buyer agree to all aspects of an initial proposal. Once again, rates/dates/space may surface as a source of potential conflict. Sometimes location turns out to be a major obstacle. Or, certain aspects of the product or service are simply not wanted or needed by the prospective client. Perhaps the amount of space desired by the buyer is not available during the preferred time period of the buyer. Or, the initial room rate quote was felt to be too high. In instances such as these, further probing is needed to look for opportunities and search for solutions.

A key point when handling objections is to have the prospective buyer prioritize (or reprioritize) his or her basic needs. It is important to know and/or clarify whether you are dealing with a "big" problem or a "small" problem. Having the buyer restate what is most important returns the focus to the buyer as well. For a meeting planner, for example, the number one priority may be a good rate to help meet budget constraints. Yet the major objection may be the small size of the guest rooms. First, the sales manager has the opportunity to query if the size of the guest rooms is really a critical factor to the overall success of the meeting. Additionally, the sales manager has the opportunity to reinforce the competitive rate already negotiated. Remember that a meeting planner's main goal is a well-run successful meeting. Reminding a planner of this objective is a positive way to help overcome objections. Your guest rooms may be small relative to the competition's, but they may also be bright, airy, well appointed, and not a deterrent to the success of the event.

On the other hand, close proximity to corporate headquarters may emerge as a top priority. If your establishment is just too far away, especially relative to competitors, then a win–win situation may be out of reach. Time spent on this potential account has not all been lost, however. A relationship has been developed, especially when dealing with new prospects. You have now started to build a rapport with a prospective client. Future business potential for other types of meetings and events, where priorities may be different, can be pursued at a future date.

It is important to remember when trying to overcome objections to always be positive. Never argue and do not be defensive. It is also good advice to not speak negatively about the competition. These tactics simply do not

MR. GOODCENTS.
— SUBS & PASTAS —

MR. GOODCENTS

PARTY TRAYS FROM MR. GOODCENTS.

...a welcome guest at any party!

THE CENTSATIONAL SUB TRAY

Choose from our variety of subs.
All subs are sliced and dressed to order.

15 Centsable People ------------- 3299 cents

THE DELI-SLICED MEAT TRAY

Your choice of Ham, Bologna, Salami, Pepperoni,
Roast Beef, Turkey, and Capicola.

14-18 Centsable People -------- 3499 cents
20-24 Centsable People -------- 4499 cents

THE INTERNATIONAL CHEESE TRAY

Your choice of Cheddar, Swiss, Mozzarella,
American, and Provolone.

14-18 Centsable People -------- 2799 cents
20-24 Centsable People -------- 3799 cents

THE OVEN-FRESH COOKIE TRAY

All cookies are freshly baked. Choose from
Chocolate Chip, Peanut Butter or a variety of both.

14-18 Centsable People -------- 1799 cents
20-24 Centsable People -------- 2199 cents

The Best Subs & Pastas in the Nation!

Bonner Springs
13021 Kansas Ave.(K-7 & Kansas Ave.)
Tel 441-4041 • Fax 422-1282

Kansas City, KS
8145 State Ave. (Westfield Center)
Tel 788-3800 • Fax 788-8889

Phone or Fax for Delivery!

Mr. Goodcents® ... Delivers!

13021 Kansas Ave
Tel 441-4041
Fax 422-1282

8145 State Ave.
Tel 788-3800
Fax 788-8889

Delivery charge of $1.00

M501 AGF 1/98
"Coca-Cola" and the Contour Bottle design are registered trademarks
of The Coca-Cola Company.

FIGURE 6.13 *Mr. Goodcents Subs and Pastas menu. (Courtesy of Mr. Goodcents Franchise Systems. Reprinted with permission.)*

GIANT SUB SANDWICHES

WHITE OR WHEAT BREAD

ORDER BY NUMBER, PLEASE	HALF	WHOLE	
1) Mr. Goodcents Combo™ ------------------	309	499	cents
(Ham, Bologna, Salami, Pepperoni)			
2) Centsable Sub™ --------------------------	274	429	cents
(Bologna, Ham, Cheese)			
3) Penny Club™ ------------------------------	309	489	cents
(Roast Beef, Turkey, Ham)			
4) Italian Combo ---------------------------	314	499	cents
(Capicola, Pepperoni, Salami)			
5) Ham & Cheese --------------------------	304	449	cents
6) Pepperoni & Cheese -------------------	304	449	cents
7) Salami -------------------------------------	304	449	cents
8) Roast Beef -------------------------------	309	479	cents
9) Turkey -------------------------------------	309	479	cents
10) Tunafish ---------------------------------	314	479	cents
11) Chicken Parmesan Sub ----------------	389	589	cents
12) Mr. Goodcents Steak Alfredo™ ---------	354	529	cents
with Green Peppers & Onions			
13) Meatball ---------------------------------	349	529	cents
14) Sausage ---------------------------------	364	529	cents
with Green Peppers & Onions			
15) Chicken Salad -------------------------	314	479	cents
16) Cheese Mix ----------------------------	309	469	cents
17) Seafood Sub ---------------------------	354	559	cents
Double Meat ------------------------------	100	200	cents
Cheese ------------------------------------	20	40	cents

CHEESES
Swiss, American, Mozzarella, Cheddar & Provolone

STANDARD DRESS
Lettuce, Tomato, Onion, Oregano, Salt, Pepper, Oil & Vinegar

ALSO AVAILABLE
Mustard, Mayonnaise, Pickles, Jalapenos, & Spicy Mustard

Good Food That Makes Good Sense!®

HOT PASTAS

CHOOSE EITHER CREAMY ALFREDO OR RED PASTA SAUCES

	Pasta	Meatballs	Sausage	
Spaghetti ---------------------	299	369	369	cents
Centsational™ Size ------	374	444	444	cents
Mostaccioli -----------------	299	369	369	cents
Centsational™ Size ------	374	444	444	cents
Rainbow Rotini -------------	299	369	369	cents
Centsational™ Size ------	374	444	444	cents
Lasagna --			399	cents
Alfredo Chicken Pasta ----------------------			399	cents
Centsational™ Size ---------------------			474	cents
Chicken Parmesan Pasta --------------------			399	cents
Centsational™ Size ---------------------			474	cents

PASTA SIDES

Pasta --	129	cents
Meatballs(2) ---------------------------------------	165	cents
Sausage(1) ---	165	cents
Bread Sticks(2) -----------------------------------	79	cents

CENTSABLE™ MEALS

The Penny -------------------------------------- **309 cents**
Pasta & Sauce, Bread Stick, & Reg. Drink

The Nickel -------------------------------------- **399 cents**
1/2 Ham & Cheese (#5) Sub, Chips, & Reg. Drink

The Dime --------------------------------------- **429 cents**
Chicken Parmesan Pasta, Bread Stick, & Reg. Drink

The Quarter ----------------------------------- **399 cents**
1/4 Sub, Soup or Side Salad, & Reg. Drink

The Penny, The Nickel, The Dime, The Quarter... CENTSATIONAL!!!

FIGURE 6.13 *(continued)*

work. An objection can be a positive sign. Why should prospective buyers take the trouble to object on certain issues unless they are seriously considering your product? If negotiations have come this far, a genuine interest in your product offering has clearly been demonstrated. Keep probing. The win–win situation could be close at hand.

Closing the Sale

Many sales are lost because the salesperson did not ask for the business. There comes a point when it is time to say; "We very much want your business. Will you book your meeting with us?" or "We want you as our customer. May I make the reservation for you?" Always ask for the business. Take the initiative to come to closure; do not wait for the buyer to do this for you.

Prospective buyers come in all shapes and sizes. Some are experienced in the purchase of hospitality product offerings and some are not. Some are decision-making oriented; others are indecisive. Some are aggressive and some are more laid back in their approach to conducting business. Some are just plain wheeler-dealers who enjoy being in charge and giving the sales manager a hard time. And, as suggested by the well-known marketing guru Theodore Levitt over 30 years ago, "consumers are unpredictable, varied, fickle, stupid, shortsighted, stubborn, and generally bothersome."[12] We have encountered them all.

There are several closing techniques from which to choose. Some are more appropriate than others depending on the level of experience, circumstances, and personality of the buyer, and the preference of the seller. They range from the "hard-sell" approach to the "soft-sell" approach; that is, some methods are more direct than others. No one way is best. It is a judgment call on the part of the sales account executive. Following is a description of each.

Direct Approach:	Restate points of agreement and ask for the business. This works best with an assertive, decision-oriented buyer ready to make a decision. The examples given previously illustrate this approach.
Trial Approach:	Ask if the buyer is ready to make a decision. This open-ended technique is particularly appropriate when more probing might be a possibility or when it is difficult to discern whether a buyer is ready to make a final de-

cision. The questioning should be nonthreatening, such as; "It is my understanding that your primary needs are A, B, and C. Is this correct? Do you agree we can best meet those needs?"

Assumptive Approach:
Similar to the direct approach yet presented in such a way that a "yes" response is encouraged. For example, the question might be phrased, "Then you will sign a contract with us for next July?" Note that this is a closed-ended question.

Alternative Choice Approach:
When negotiations have narrowed down to a few major decisions or choices that need to be made. An example would be, "Would you like to book your meeting with us in the first week of December or in the second week of December? Which is best for you?" This approach is similar to a trial closing, only it is more direct, closed-ended questioning.

Minor Decision Approach:
This closing technique is helpful for buyers who are indecisive and have difficulty making decisions. In this situation, small decisions are encouraged to be made throughout the negotiation process. For example, "Do you prefer the soft blue or the soft yellow table linen settings?" For some buyers, it is easier to make a major and/or final decision after several smaller decisions have already been dealt with.

Challenge Approach:
A dominant person wants challenge. "I know that you are able to make the decision, can you make it now?" Though somewhat risky, it puts this type of buyer under pressure to say "yes" or "no." If the answer is no, then ask "Why not? Is there an issue we have not addressed yet?" This technique is a trial approach, yet it is very direct and presumptive.

Negation Approach:
When a lack of urgency for making a decision is suspected of the buyer, sometimes

forcing the decision helps to close the sale. "Jack, October is a busy month. I want your business but I need to know now whether you are going to book with us." In other words, this technique puts pressure on the buyer to commit. Similar to the challenge approach, it is a bit risky and used when the sales manager is fairly confident that the buyer is able to make a decision and likely to purchase your product.

The preceding approaches to closing are not exhaustive but do capture the varying techniques that can be used to close a sale. Note that most are closed-ended questions. As commented earlier in this chapter, open-ended questions are usually best for the initial prospecting and probing stages of the sales process. As you approach the closing phase, closed-ended questions are usually more effective. They are direct, to the point, and offer a professional approach to asking for the business.

CONTRACTS AND LETTERS OF AGREEMENT

A sale is truly closed when a signed contract is in hand, that is, a document signed by both parties outlining pertinent details of the agreement. From a legal perspective, this document is considered legally binding. By signing a **binding contract,** each party has accepted the obligation to fulfill his or her part of the agreement. For complex events, such as conferences and conventions, contracts are essential. For more basic purchases, such as when making a hotel or restaurant reservation, a confirmation from the hospitality establishment is all that is needed. In restaurant sales, a verbal confirmation is normally accepted.

The terms confirmation, letter of agreement, and contract represent frequently used terminology in hospitality sales. They have slightly different meanings, however, which can vary with the type and circumstances of the hospitality purchase, and among hospitality organizations. Following is a discussion of each.

Confirmation

A **confirmation** gives details of what was agreed upon between two or more parties. Travel agents often act as a third party for the purchase of a hospitality product. An example of this type of confirmation is shown in Figure

6.14. Flight arrangements to and from Montego Bay in Jamaica are booked for Robert Lewis and confirmed by Frederick Travel. Note that there are no signatures. The actual price and signature agreement for these arrangements are on a separate "contract," in this case a good old-fashioned credit card called American Express.

Letter of Agreement

A **letter of agreement** is a formal document with space given at the end for each party to sign the agreement. When both signatures are secured, it then becomes binding. Figure 6.15 shows a sample letter of agreement for the RCL Electronics account. Signatures of both the buyer, Robert Lattuca of RCL Electronics, and the seller, Susan McCutcheon of the Regal Crowne Hotel, make this letter of agreement a contract.

Contracts

The confirmation and letter of agreement shown in Figures 6.14 and 6.15, respectively, are similar in that each is fairly clear on the agreement made. The difference in these contracts is the degree of formality and length of detail. The more complex the purchase, the more detailed and formal the contract becomes. Contracts can be six to eight pages in length, some even longer. And some can get cumbersome and a bit overdone.

Long, detailed contracts are not necessarily bad contracts. There are appropriate times when specific agreements need to be well articulated such that each party has a clear understanding of what is expected. This is especially true in convention sales. Two typical clauses included in these types of contracts are cutoff dates and rate confirmations. Each is described next.

Cutoff Dates

An association, for example, may book a convention and reserve, say, 250 rooms for arrival on Monday, May 1, with departure Thursday, May 4. The actual reservations, however, are normally booked by the association delegates planning to attend the convention (and not by the meeting planner). The contract will read such that the 250 rooms are reserved for this group up to three weeks prior to the arrival date. This would be referred to as a "three-week cutoff date." At this point, any rooms that have not been reserved by delegates are released from the original 250 room block. The clause gives the hotel the opportunity to resell unreserved rooms to the general

```
╔══════════════════════════════════════════════════════════════════════════════╗
║                                   871 Victoria Street North, Kitchener, Ontario N2B 3S4  (519) 745-1860  FAX (519) 745-6263
║   ▓▓▓ FREDERICK TRAVEL           987 Gordon Street, Guelph, Ontario N1H 6H9  (519) 836-0061  FAX (519) 821-9770
║                                   851 Fischer-Hallman Rd., Kitchener, Ontario N2M 5N8  (519) 579-5140  FAX (519) 570-4359
║   CLARE MILLAR TRAVEL            THE PEOPLE YOU CAN TRUST                         G.S.T. #12256066
╠══════════════════════════════════════════════════════════════════════════════╣
```

PNR LOC: 7QIIEG				DATE: 18 DEC 1996	
AGENT: 255H21				INVOICE: ITIN 9255	

```
    TO:                                FOR:
    LEWIS/ROBERT MR                    LEWIS/R MR
    RR 2                               SHAW/M MRS
    PUSLINCH ONTARIO
    N0B2J0
```

                              --ITINERARY--

FROM	TO	CARRIER	FLT/CL	DATE	DEP	ARR	ST
ORLANDO/INTL	MIAMI	AMERICAN	1483 V	08 MAR 97	913A	1013A	OK
NONSTOP						SATURDAY	
EQUIPMENT-DC-10 JET						FLYING TIME- 1:00	
			SEAT 33H33J				
MIAMI	MONTEGO BAY	AMERICAN	211 V	08 MAR 97	1110A	1250P	OK
NONSTOP	SNACK						
EQUIPMENT-AIRBUS A300 JET						FLYING TIME- 1:40	
			SEAT-33H33J				
MONTEGO BAY	MIAMI	AMERICAN	628 M	15 MAR 97	200P	339P	OK
NONSTOP	SNACK					SATURDAY	
EQUIPMENT-AIRBUS A300 JET						FLYING TIME- 1:39	
			SEAT-20H20J				
MIAMI	ORLANDO/INTL	AMERICAN	5837 M	15 MAR 97	530P	645P	OK
NONSTOP							
EQUIPMENT-TURBOPROP						FLYING TIME- 1:15	
OPERATED BY-FLAGSHIP AIRLINES			SEAT- 8A 8B				

FIGURE 6.14 *Sample confirmation. (Courtesy of Frederick Travel. Reprinted with permission.)*

public should the convention in the end not need the full 250-room allotment. Cutoff dates typically range from two weeks to 30 days prior to arrival.

Delegates who call or write to make their reservation *after* the cutoff date are not guaranteed a room will be available to reserve. The rooms are sold on what is called a "space available basis only." Sometimes the contract includes a clause that states any special rate considerations are no longer available after the cutoff date as well. Delegates will pay the "market rate."

REGAL CROWNE HOTEL

(SAMPLE)
LETTER OF AGREEMENT

May 27, 1998

ORGANIZATION: RCL Electronics

FILE NUMBER: C9825

FUNCTION NAME: 1998 SPP Meeting

CONTACT: Mr. Robert Lattuca, Manager-Sales Promotion
                     600 North Sherman Avenue
                     Midtown, USA

TELEPHONE: (617) 273-8552

FAX: (617) 272-8321

OFFICIAL DATES: August 3-7, 1998

GUEST ROOM   Sunday, August 3, 1998   170 Rooms
COMMITMENT: Monday, August 4, 1998   350 Rooms
                     Tuesday, August 5, 1998   170 Rooms
                     Wednesday, August 6, 1998   20 Rooms
                     Thursday, August 7, 1998   Departure

                     Before the cutoff date, we may review with
                     you and adjust your room block according to
                     the number of guest rooms actually occupied
                     at hotels where your functions of the same or
                     similar nature have been held in the recent
                     past.

ROOM RATES: It is our pleasure to confirm the following
                     special rates:

                         Single Occupancy - $102
                         Double Occupancy - $102

                     Please add the 3% city tax and 4% state tax
                     to the above net, noncommissionable rates.

RESERVATION   Rooming List
METHOD:

CUTOFF DATE: To ensure proper accommodations, we ask
                     that your rooming list be submitted to our
                     Reservations Department not later than July
                     20, 1998. At that time, the unsatisfied
                     portion of your guest room commitment will
                     be released for general sale to the public.
                     However, we will do our best to accommodate
                     room reservation requests received after
                     the designated cutoff date. These requests
                     will be accepted on a space available basis.

FIGURE 6.15 *Sample letter of agreement/contract. (Adapted from Doubletree Hotels. Courtesy of Doubletree Hotels.)*

CREDIT
ARRANGEMENTS:

Reserved rooms will be held until 6:00 PM on the day of arrival unless the reservation request is accompanied by a one night's deposit or assured by a major credit card or guaranteed by RCL Electronics.

Check-out time is 12:00 Noon on the day of departure and check-in time is 3:00 PM on the day of arrival. We will try to accommodate those guests arriving earlier in the day on a space available basis.

Individuals will be responsible for their own room, tax, and incidental charges in accordance with our standard credit procedures.

As requested, a master account will be established upon approval by our Credit Manager for all group food and beverage functions as well as any other authorized charges.

We request that you set aside sufficient time following the close of your convention to review all master account charges with a member of our Convention Services and Accounting Departments.

MEETING AND
FUNCTION SPACE
REQUIREMENTS

The following sets forth your preliminary meeting and function room requirement. We understand that you will provide us with the final day-by-day program not later than June 15, 1998. There will be no meeting and function space rental charges based on your scheduled food and beverage functions and your guest room commitment.

Day/Date	Time	Function (# of Guests)
Sun, Aug 3	Evening	Reception (200 pp)
	Evening	Dinner (200 pp)
Mon, Aug 4	9AM–5PM	General Session (200 pp)
	NOON	Luncheon (200 pp)
	Evening	Reception (350 pp)
	Evening	Dinner (350 pp)
Tues, Aug 5	9AM–5PM	Seminars (6 @ 50 ea, 300 pp)
	NOON	Luncheon (350 pp)
	Evening	Reception (200 pp)
	Evening	Dinner (200 pp)
Wed, Aug 6	8AM–9AM	Breakfast (150 pp)
	9AM–NOON	General Session (150 pp)
	NOON	Luncheon (150 pp)

FIGURE 6.15 *(continued)*

FOOD & BEVERAGE:	For your information, our ''current'' banquet menus are enclosed.
	We are pleased to confirm banquet prices three months prior to your actual convention dates. Please bear in mind that our attempt to confirm a price structure six months in advance is done so with the full knowledge and understanding that percentage food and beverage escalation factors are not included in the estimate.
	A guarantee of the number of persons attending each group food and beverage function will be given to the hotel at least 72 hours in advance of the function. The Regal Crowne agrees to set and prepare 5% over your guarantee for each function.
LIQUOR POLICY:	The sale and service of alcoholic beverages are regulated by the State Liquor Commission. The Regal Crowne as a licensee is responsible for the administration of these regulations. It is policy, therefore, that liquor cannot be brought into the hotel from outside sources.
CONVENTION SERVICES:	The Regal Crowne uses the Convention Services concept in handling all conventions. Our Convention Services Manager will be contacting you approximately six months prior to your convention to begin finalizing your program details. all applicable department heads will be available for a pre-convention meeting at your convenience. At that time, we will discuss any special requirements you need, as well as review the program details one last time. This will also enable you and your staff to meet the department heads who will be servicing your group throughout the course of the convention.
ATTRITION CLAUSE:	At this time, the Regal Crowne is holding 710 room-nights for your use over the above dates, totaling revenues of $72,420. Planned food and beverage revenues are estimated at $82,000. All revenue figures are net and not inclusive of taxes and service charges. We agree to allow for a 10% reduction in these figures. Should actual revenues fall below these figures, the difference will be posted to your Master Account.
CANCELLATION CLAUSE:	Should your entire program cancel, a cancellation fee of $150,000 will be assessed.

FIGURE 6.15 *(continued)*

DECISION DATE:

Regal Crowne agrees to reserve rooms, function space, and/or provide services for you as indicated in this Agreement, provided that you sign and regurn this Agreement to us no later than June 5, 1998. Without your signed confirmation of these arrangements, availability cannot be guaranteed after this date.

ACCEPTANCE:

Your signature on this agreement establishes this program on ''definite'' basis and represents your firm commitment to hold this program at the Regal Crowne in accordance with terms of this agreement.

SIGNATURES:

Robert Lattuca   6/1/98

Robert Lattuca   Date
Manager–Sales Promotions
RCL Electronics
Midtown, USA

Susan McCutcheon   5/27/98

Susan McCutcheon   Date
Director of Sales
Regal Crowne Hotel
Midtown, USA

FIGURE 6.15 *(continued)*

Cutoff date determination and related rate considerations are often very much a part of the negotiation process.

Rate Confirmation

Conventions are typically booked far in advance. It is not unusual to book three to five years prior to the actual dates that an event is scheduled to take place. Hotel room rates (and food and beverage prices) can rarely be confirmed that far ahead. Nonetheless, a meeting planner needs to know when the rates will be confirmed and what the rate range will be. The contract should state when the rate will be confirmed—which is normally one year in advance. The rate range should also be in the contract and is often stated in terms of current convention rates during a similar time of year. For example, a contract might read as follows:

> Our current convention rates during the May period are $125–$140 single occupancy and $145–$160 double occupancy. We offer a similar range of rates for your convention in 19XX not to exceed 10% of the above stated rates. Final rate quotations for your convention will be confirmed one year in advance of the scheduled arrival date. Food and beverage prices for catered events will be confirmed six months in advance.

Food and beverage costs fluctuate to a greater degree than the variable costs associated with an occupied guest room. Thus, a shorter lead time for confirmation of food and beverage prices in convention contracts is commonplace.

The preceding example demonstrates what might be included in a typical convention contract. It captures the essence of what the hotel and meeting planner have agreed to regarding specific aspects of the purchase agreement. The items may at first seem overly detailed. However, for complex events such as conventions, it is important that items such as these be clearly spelled out. When it comes to delivery what is most important to both buyer and seller is *no surprises!*

SUMMARY

The sales process includes prospecting and qualifying accounts, probing and solving customers' problems, making presentations, negotiating, overcoming objections, closing the sale, and contracts and letters of agreement.

Prospecting is looking for new customers. There are several ways to uncover new business. These include searching out new customer opportunities from current accounts, leads and referrals, and cold calling. Although cold calling is considered by some to be outdated and inefficient, others use cold calling techniques on a regular basis. Telemarketing is a form of cold calling and practiced by many in hospitality.

Account qualification is identifying the basic needs of a potential customer to ensure a potential fit indeed exists. Customer profiles are developed as a result. Of importance when qualifying a prospect is learning who specifically is the decision maker for the business. A principal contact for an account may or may not be the primary decision maker for the final purchase.

Probing is asking questions, lots of questions. It is a process of learning the specific needs of a potential client. There are two types of questioning techniques—open ended and closed ended. Open-ended questioning is asking broad general questions, listening, asking subsequent questions, and so forth. Closed-ended questioning is asking for detailed information that requires a specific response such as preferred meeting room setups, billing instructions, VIPs attending an event, and so on. In essence, probing is finding out a prospect's "problems" and searching for ways to resolve them.

Upon completion of initial probing, the sales account executive then presents to the prospective customer "solutions to his or her problems." These are ideally done in person on-premise after a site visitation, especially for group business. Rates, dates, and space are presented along with other details specific to customers' needs, wants, and preferences. Nonpersonal presentations can be done in writing, over the telephone, by video, by CD-ROM, and on the Web.

Rarely does a prospective buyer agree to all aspects of an initial proposal. Objections will surface and it is the job of the sales account executive to overcome these objections. Rates may be considered too high, dates may not be ideal, and/function space may be considered confining. A successful sales manager keeps probing to find out the "big" problem or problems. Often times there are only small concerns that can be worked out. The trick is to keep probing, always searching for the win–win solution. The goal is to reach a point where both parties feel good about the final solution.

Closing techniques include several approaches—direct, trial, assumptive, alternative choice, minor decision, challenge, and negation. Each entails closed-ended questions. The main issue when trying to close a sale is to ask for the business. Many sales are lost because the sales account executive did not ask for the business. Take the initiative to come to closure; do not wait for the buyer to do so. It may never come.

A sale is truly closed when a signed contract is in hand. A contract is a document signed by both buyer and seller. It is often a letter of agreement outlining pertinent details of the agreement. Once signed, it is considered legally binding. Binding means that each party has accepted the obligation to fulfill his or her part of the agreement. Complex events, such as conferences and conventions, require a contract. For more basic purchases, such as a reservation at a hotel or restaurant, a confirmation is all that is needed. In restaurant sales, a verbal confirmation is the norm.

The sales process, start to finish, can take anywhere from hours to months to complete. This varies depending on the complexity of the purchase. Nonetheless, the process is the same—open, probe, present, overcome objections, and close. Delivery is the final step of the sales process and is the subject of the next chapter.

DISCUSSION QUESTIONS

1. What is prospecting? Discuss several ways in which a sales manager can go about prospecting.
2. What is cold calling? What is its purpose? Some consider cold calling inefficient and outdated. Discuss.
3. Compare and contrast open-ended and closed-ended questioning. Are there stages in the sales process where one of these questioning techniques is more effective than the other?
4. Discuss the issue of rates/dates/space as it relates to negotiations in the hospitality sales process.
5. What are site inspections? Are they important in helping to close a sale?
6. A helpful way to look at the issue of pricing is in terms of demand, competition, and cost. Discuss.
7. Compare and contrast single-product pricing with bundle pricing. Is one more effective than the other?
8. Briefly describe various approaches to closing a sale. How does a sales manager choose which approach is best?
9. What is a letter of agreement? At what point is it considered legally binding?

NOTES

1. Jeffrey H. Gitomer, *The Sales Bible*, William Morrow, New York, 1994.
2. Howard Feiertag, "Focus on the Customer: Referrals to Boost Sales-Leads Potential," *Hotel & Motel Management*, May 20, 1996, p. 15.
3. Mary Ann Oberhaus, Sharon Ratcliffe, and Vernon Stauble, *Professional Selling*, 2nd ed. Dryden Press–Harcourt Brace College Publishers, Fort Worth, TX, 1995.
4. Laura Powell, "Video 101: Creating a Successful Marketing Video," *HSMAI Marketing Review*, Winter 1996, pp. 18–20.

5. Robert Carey, "Bon Appetit," *Successful Meetings*, May 1993, p. 46.
6. Ibid., pp. 46–47.
7. Roger Dawson, "You Can Be a Powerful Negotiator," *HSMAI Marketing Review*, Fall 1988, pp. 21–22.
8. Julie R. Ritzer, "Focus on Negotiating," *Corporate Travel*, June 1989, pp. 17–18.
9. Doris Sklar, "Negotiate Yourself into a Good Relationship," *Successful Meetings*, May 1986, pp. 127–128.
10. Rayna Skolnik, "The Wind Has Shifted: A New Climate for Hotel Negotiation," *Corporate Meetings & Incentives*, July 1995, pp. 23–26.
11. "Bed and Breakfast (and Phone and Fax)," *Cornell Quarterly*, December 1994, p. 15.
12. Theodore Levitt, Ed., "Marketing Myopia," in *The Marketing Imagination*, Free Press, New York, 1960, 1986, p. 162.

Personal Selling: The Delivery

Closing the sale is half the battle. What the customer is really buying is service delivery—be it the meeting room setup done correctly, the Big Mac served hot, the main course served promptly, guest registration done efficiently, or a final billing that is timely and accurate. Each of these, and many more, are affectionately known as "moments of truth" in hospitality. As stated by Jan Carlzon, renowned for his expertise in service delivery, "[w]e have 50,000 moments of truth out there every day."[1] Jan Carlzon, then president of Scandinavian Airlines (SAS), was reponsible for the successful turnaround of the struggling airline in the early 1980s. By "moments of truth," he was referring to the many and varied encounters their customers had with the airline on a daily basis. He embarked on a service delivery campaign throughout the entire organization of 20,000+ managers and employees. Highlighted by Karl Albrecht and Ron Zemke in their well-known and widely read publication, *Service America!*:

> What was not readily visible to the casual observer was that Carlzon had evolved, largely in an intuitive way, a unique approach to the company's management. This approach was characterized by an almost obsessive commitment to *managing the customer's experience* at all points of the service cycle. . . .
>
> A *moment of truth* by Carlzon's definition, is an episode in which a customer comes into contact with any aspect of the company, however remote, and thereby has an opportunity to form an impression. . . .
>
> Since managers cannot be there to influence the quality of so many moments of truth, they must learn to manage them indirectly, that is, by creating a customer-oriented organization, a customer-friendly system as well as a work environment that reinforces the idea of putting the customer first.[2]

Jan Carlzon, first and foremost, was marketing minded. His vision and self-initiated mandate was to move the company from a product-driven focus to a customer-driven focus, with special emphasis given to service delivery.

Sales and marketing is getting and keeping a customer. Opening, probing, presenting, negotiating, and closing a sale is getting a customer. Good service delivery is keeping that customer. It is the building of a positive long-term buyer–seller relationship. How one goes about measuring customer satisfaction is part of the process, too. This chapter focuses on the delivery and the measurement of customer satisfaction aspects of the sales process. Delivery, in hospitality, is often referred to as servicing the account.

SERVICING THE ACCOUNT

For hotels, conference centers, resorts, and convention centers that cater to the meetings and conventions market, there is typically a conference or convention services department devoted to the job of servicing the account. In smaller operations and/or for customers who have smaller meeting needs, this is sometimes done directly by the sales account executive who booked the account. For major food and beverage bookings, such as banquets and wedding functions, a catering services manager is normally given the assignment. For tour groups, it is common to have a sales manager handle all aspects of the sales process including the solicitation, booking, and servicing of the account. In some larger hotels, however, the service aspect for tour (and convention) guest room accommodations is assigned to a specific individual or department within the hotel's organizational setup. And, in some instances, certain services are performed by a service firm external to the organization. Following is a more detailed discussion of each of the preceding approaches to service delivery in hospitality.

Conference and Convention Services

In some operations, once an account is booked by a sales account executive, the detailed job of servicing the account is turned over to a **conference or convention services manager (CSM)**. This person is responsible for coordinating the many details that need to be pulled together to ensure a successful event. These details include such items as function room assignments, meeting room setups, VIP lists, refreshment breaks, audiovisual requirements, billing instructions, and so forth. In the ideal situation, the CSM works one on one with the meeting planner or association executive planning the event.

Catering aspects of a meeting or convention are sometimes handled by the CSM, as is done at Hyatt Hotels. At Hyatt, the department is appropriately called the catering and convention services department. In other hospitality organizations, such as Marriott, food and beverage aspects are handled separately by the catering department, albeit in close contact with the CSM. In either case, what is important is that a specific task is assigned to an individual in the hospitality organization to get the job done efficiently and effectively. Meeting planners and association executives, in particular, want to deal with as few people as possible. The fewer people responsible for various aspects of an event means the less likelihood for problems to surface because of miscommunication. Thus, the emerging CSM position in hospitality management is gaining momentum, regardless of the size of the hospitality establishment. As noted in the *Cornell Quarterly*, "[t]oday, virtually every major convention hotel has a CSM, and many smaller hotels, resorts, and other lodging and meeting locations such as conference centers have at least one individual who holds that title."[3]

Shown in Figure 7.1 is a sample organization chart of a convention services department. In this example, there is a director who coordinates all

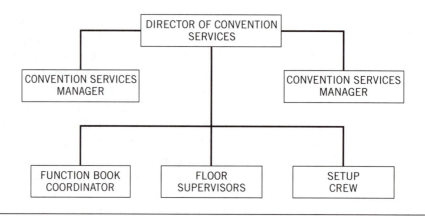

FIGURE 7.1 *Organization chart of a convention services department.*

activities of the department. Within the department, there are convention services managers, a function book coordinator, floor supervisors, and a setup crew. The **function book coordinator** oversees which group is assigned to which function room. **Floor supervisors** manage the setup crew. Setups for each function are explicitly laid out on a function room setup sheet, as shown in Figure 7.2. It is not unusual to have non–English speaking setup crews. Thus, pictures and diagrams help immensely to illustrate the desired layout. Getting the function room setup exactly as requested by the client is only one of the many details for which the CSM has ultimate responsibility.

One of the main tasks of the CSM is preparing the **convention resume**. This document details all aspects of the event and is sent to all departments. A sample convention resume is shown in Figure 7.3. (Note that this is the convention resume for the RCL Electronics booking described in the previous chapter.) It is normally distributed five to ten days in advance of the event and is the basis for the agenda of the preconvention meeting.

Preconvention meetings are typically held for large conventions, that is, 200 or more delegates registered for an event. In attendance at these meetings (often referred to as the precon meeting) are key personnel of the host facility and key members of the planning committee putting on the event. Each item on the convention resume is reviewed in detail including updated attendance figures, any changes in the scheduling of functions throughout the event, rooming list adjustments, and special or unusual aspects of the convention. In the convention business, in particular, last minute changes are inevitable. The preconvention meeting is one avenue to ensure that the latest facts and figures are conveyed to all those involved with the success of the event.

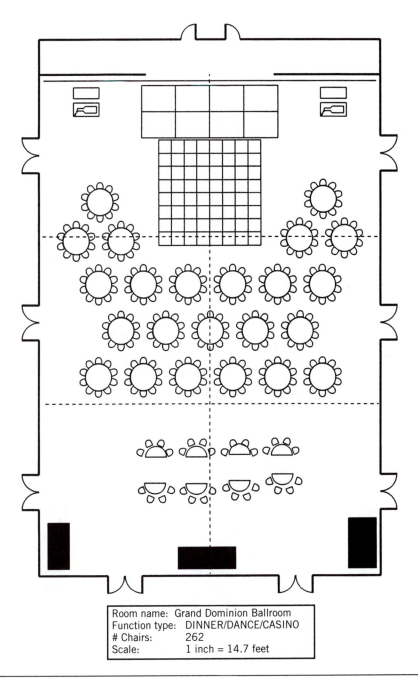

Room name: Grand Dominion Ballroom
Function type: DINNER/DANCE/CASINO
Chairs: 262
Scale: 1 inch = 14.7 feet

FIGURE 7.2 *Sample function room setup diagram. (Courtesy of Marriott International. Reprinted with permission.)*

REGAL CROWNE HOTEL

CONVENTION RESUME

DATE: July 25, 1998

TO: All Concerned

FROM: Charles ''Chip'' Newell
                   Director of Convention Services

PRECONVENTION   Friday, August 1, 1998
MEETING: 2:00PM Salon B

GROUP: RCL ELECTRONICS

CONTACT: Robert Lattuca, Barbara Hawthorne

TELEPHONE: (617) 273-8552 FAX: (617) 272-8321

SALES: Susan McCutcheon, Director of Sales

CATERING: Jill Doyle, Director of Catering

FILE: C9825

DATES: August 3-7, 1998

RATES: $102 single/double

PICK-UP: Saturday, August 2   15 rooms
                   Sunday, August 3   150   "
                   Monday, August 4   300   "
                   Tuesday, August 5   185   "
                   Wednesday, August 6   25   "
                   Thursday, August 7   All Depart

ACCOUNTING,   The Master Account should be set as follows:
FRONT OFFICE,
RESERVATIONS: RCL Electronics
                     Attn: Robert Lattuca
                     600 N. Sherman Avenue
                     Midtown, USA

                   Master Account largely covers receptions,
                   banquets, refreshment breaks, and the
                   Lattuca and Hawthorne suites.

AUTHORIZED   Robert Lattuca, Barbara Hawthorne
SIGNATURES:
                   Individuals are responsible for their own
                   charges, all guaranteed by RCL Electronics.
                   All rooms should be preregistered. The
                   following should be billed directly to the
                   Master Account:

                   1. R. Lattuca   Exec. Suite arr 8/2
                   2. B. Hawthorne   Exec. Suite arr 8/2

FIGURE 7.3 *Sample convention resume.*

| ARRIVAL/
DEPARTURES: | Major arrivals August 3 and 4, late morning and early afternoon. Major departure August 5 and 6, mid-afternoon. No late check-out charges until after 4:00PM | | | |

★ ★ ★   PROGRAM   ★ ★ ★

SATURDAY, AUGUST 2, 1998

24 Hours	Office	Salon A	Set up operating office. Four rented desks, copier being delivered. Bringing own computer equipment. Hook up phone, X-2400
8:00AM	Coffee	Salon A	See BEO
3:00PM	Coffee	Salon A	See BEO

SUNDAY, AUGUST 3, 1998

24 Hours	Office	Salon A	Same set; refresh
8:00AM	Coffee	Salon A	See BEO
2:00PM– 5:00PM	General Session	Regal A & B	200 pp. theater style, headtable 4
6:00PM– 7:00PM	Reception	Prince Hall	200 pp, see BEO
7:00PM– 10:00PM	Dinner	Regal C & D	200 pp, see BEO

MONDAY, AUGUST 4, 1998

24 Hours	Office	Salon A	Same set; refresh
9:00AM– 6:00PM	General Session	Regal A & B	200 pp, theater style, headtable 6
10:15AM– 10:45AM	Refreshment Break	Prince Hall	See BEO
12:30PM– 2:00PM	Luncheon	Regal C & D	200 pp, see BEO
3:45PM– 4:15PM	Refreshment Break	Prince Hall	See BEO
7:00PM– 8:00PM	Reception	Prince Hall	350 pp, see BEO
8:00PM– 11:00PM	Dinner	Regal C & D	350 pp, see BEO

FIGURE 7.3 *(continued)*

TUESDAY, AUGUST 5, 1998

24 Hours	Office	Salon A	Same set; refresh
8:30AM–NOON	Seminars	Palace A Palace B Palace C Palace D Palace E Palace F	500 pp each, school-room style, headtable 4
10:00AM–10:30AM	Refreshment Break	Prince Hall	See BEO
12:30PM–2:00PM	Luncheon	Regal C & D	350 pp, see BEO
2:30PM–5:30PM	Seminars	Palace A Palace B Palace C	50 pp each, school-room style, headtable 2
3:45PM–4:15PM	Refreshment Break	Palace A Palace B Palace C	50 pp each, serve in back of room, see BEO
6:30PM–7:30PM	Reception	Prince Hall	180 pp, see BEO
7:30PM–10:00PM	Dinner	Regal C & D	180 pp, see BEO

WEDNESDAY, AUGUST 6, 1998

24 Hours	Office	Salon A	Same set; refresh
8:00AM–8:45AM	Breakfast	Regal C & D	150 pp, see BEO
9:00AM–12:30PM	General Session	Regal A & B	150 pp, theater style, headtable 4
10:30AM–11:00AM	Refreshment Break	Prince Hall	See BEO
1:00PM–2:30PM	Closing Luncheon	Regal C & D	150 pp, see BEO

*   *   *

Reminder: Expect mid-afternoon check-outs both Tuesday and Wednesday, August 5 and 6, immediately following luncheons. No late check-out charges until after 4:00PM.

FIGURE 7.3 *(continued)*

Catering Services

Catering departments solicit as well as service foodservice functions. **Catering sales managers** solicit local banquet business such as weddings, Rotary Club luncheons, retirement parties, and other events. Once booked, the servicing of these functions may be handled by the catering sales manager who booked the event or it may be handled by a **catering service manager**. The actual organizational setup, similar to convention services, varies among hospitality organizations. The catering services manager attends to the specific details once an event has been booked.

Shown in Figure 7.4 is a sample organization chart of a catering department. It includes a director of catering, catering sales managers, a catering services manager, banquet managers, waitstaff, and a setup crew. A catering sales manager, for example, may have recently booked a local two-day meeting not requiring overnight accommodations. A catering services manager may be assigned the function which requires a meeting room and breakfast, lunch, and dinner each day. Menu details, specific timing, meeting room setup, banquet room setup, refreshment breaks, and so forth, are put together by the catering services manager. **Banquet managers** will then be assigned to specific meals of this booking to supervise when the actual meals and refreshment breaks take place. The banquet managers typically work from banquet event orders (BEOs). An example is shown in Figure 7.5. These are

FIGURE 7.4 *Organization chart of a catering department.*

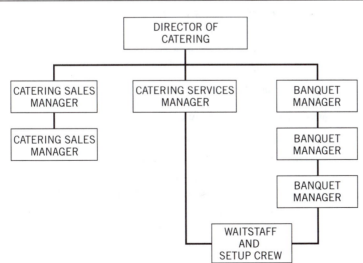

BANQUET EVENT ORDER
MARRIOTT HOTEL

PAGE#: 1
BEO#:
FILE#:
FOLIO#:

FUNCTION DAY/DATE:
ORGANIZATION:

POST AS:
MAILING ADDRESS:
BILLING ADDRESS:

CUSTOMER:
PHONE:
FAX:
IN-HOUSE CONTACT:

MANAGER:
DATE PRINTED:

*** GUARANTEE OF ATTENDANCE IS REQUIRED 72 HOURS (3 WORKING DAYS)
PRIOR TO FUNCTION, OTHERWISE, EXPECTED WILL BECOME THE GUARANTEE ***
*** FINAL ROOM ASSIGNMENT IS SUBJECT TO CHANGE ***

TIME	FUNCTION	LOCATION	ATTENDANCE EXP	GTD	SET
7:30PM–10:00PM	PRIVATE DINNER	Washingtonian II	64		

7:30PM   GOLD STANDARD PREMIUM   WASHINGTONIAN II

Cordial Cart/By the drink

Amaretto, 1 Each at $6.00

Bailey's Irish Cream, 1 Each at $6.00

Courvoisier VSOP, 1 Each at $8.00

Drambuie, 1 Each at $6.00

Frangelico, 1 Each at $6.00

Kahlua, 1 Each at $6.00

Sambuca, 1 Each at $6.00

Grand Marnier, 1 Each at $6.00

7:30PM   DINNER BUFFET   WASHINGTONIAN II

DINNER BUFFET

Homebaked Soft Rolls and Creamy Butter

International Cheese Selection
Danish Blue Cheese, French Brie cheese, Jarlsberg and English Cheddar

Exotic Field Greens Salad

FIGURE 7.5 *Sample banquet event order (BEO). (Courtesy of Marriott International. Reprinted with permission.)*

BANQUET EVENT ORDER
MARRIOTT HOTEL

PAGE#: 2
BEO#:
FILE#:
FOLIO#:

FUNCTION DAY/DATE:
ORGANIZATION:

Bleu Cheese Dressing
Fat-Free French Dressing
Creamy Herb Dressing
Tomato Shallot Dressing

SPECIALTY SALADS
Chicken Lo Mein Salad
Marinated Vegetable Salad
Blue Crab and Pasta Salad
Fresh Fruit Ambrosia Salad

Seared Tenderloin Medallion with Exotic Mushroom Demi Glaze
Breast of Chicken Piccata with Lemon Beurre Blanc
Grilled Canadian Salmon with Pineapple-Cucumber Relish

ACCOMPANIMENTS
Garden Medley Vegetables
Oven Roasted New Potatoes

DESSERTS
Baked Lemon Pudding Cake (Served Warm)
German Chocolate Tart
White Chocolate Cheesecake with Berry Coulis

BEVERAGE SERVICE
Iced Tea
$22.00 per person

7:30PM   PRIVATE DINNER ARRANGEMENTS   WASHINGTONIAN II

(1) Rosemount Estates Chardonnay $34.00 per bottle

(1) Rosemount Merlot $32.00 per bottle

ALL DEPARTMENTS

1. Note there will be no service charge for this group, guaranteeing under 75 guests.

ATTENTION MAITRE D'

Please Wine Service with dinner. After dinner cordial cart.

ROOM SETUP

(8) rounds of 8
Ashtrays and Matches

BANQUET SERVICES

Mirrors and Votive Candles
House Bud Vases set as a Complimentary Centerpiece with
Seasonal Flowers
White Tablecloths
White Napkins

Please Note: All Prices are Subject to 18% Taxable Service Charge and 4.5% Sales Tax.

prepared by the catering services manager for each meal to be serviced. They are similar to convention resumes, but normally not as lengthy. Indeed, convention resumes will often refer to BEOs for details of a meal function (see Figure 7.3).

As with convention services, what is important in catering services is that specific tasks be explicitly assigned so there is no guesswork as to who is going to do what. When problems emerge in hospitality service delivery, it is usually because someone thought that someone else was responsible for the task at hand.

Tour Group Sales and Service

Servicing tour group bookings is handled by the sales manager who booked the account or by an individual assigned this specific responsibility. In some lodging establishments that book a fair amount of tour group (and convention) business, there is a designated department that handles the guest room service details for such accounts. The Chateau Lake Louise is one such establishment.

The Chateau Lake Louise is a resort located in the heart of the Canadian Rocky Mountains and is part of the Canadian Pacific Hotels (CP) chain. It is a 500-room hotel that caters extensively to the group tour and convention markets. At this particular CP hotel, all guest room service aspects of tour and convention bookings are the responsibility of the group services supervisor. This individual manages a staff of five who attend to the front-office tasks of group accounts. These responsibilities include obtaining deposits and rooming lists for tour bookings, getting detailed guest room billing instructions for convention bookings, and dealing with special instructions such as VIP lists, adjoining guest room requests, hotel suite assignments, and so on. For convention bookings, in particular, the group services supervisor works closely with the CSM. A more detailed job description of the group services supervisor position at Chateau Lake Louise is shown in Table 7.1.

External Service Delivery

Service delivery is sometimes handled by a third party. In other words, the supplier of a basic hospitality product offering uses an outside firm to assist in service delivery. This is true for both the hotel and the restaurant side of the business.

At convention hotels, the delivery and setup of audiovisual equipment is often handled by an outside firm. Hotels will contract with a local audiovisual company to service the specific needs of individual clients. At many

---

TABLE 7.1   *Job Description of Group Services Supervisor*

The group services supervisor (GSS) at the Chateau Lake Louise has several responsibilities. The following highlights some of these job responsibilities, which entail the basic duties of this department at this hotel.

Group Tour Contracts

Review and double-check all group tour bookings including room block size, negotiated rate, rooming lists, complimentary accommodations (where applicable), special requests. Accuracy and detail very important.

Group Tour Billings

Prepare group tour billing sheet, credit deposits, check for (Canadian) GST tax exemptions, process cancellation fees where appropriate, attend to special requests.

Advisor Meetings

The GSS meets monthly with each member of the staff to discuss various aspects of the job including specific assignments, goals, special projects, motivational issues.

Monthly Staff Meetings

Agenda for this meeting typically includes team-building exercises, review of standards and mission statement, review of monthly planner and scheduling.

Monthly Planner and Scheduling

Typically includes hotel committee meetings to attend, group arrivals and departures, staff scheduling (including vacations), advisor meetings, preconvention meetings.

Leadership

The GSS "should be organized, motivated, knowledgeable, empathetic, understanding, diplomatic, assertive, supportive, approachable, confident, accurate, honest, and above all this leader should know how to fix the printer!"

Source: Adapted from Group Services Supervisor Standards, Chateau Lake Louise, 1997. Developed by Wendy Bennen, GSS. Courtesy of Canadian Pacific Hotels.

---

hotels, these companies will actually be based at the hotel, provide their own service personnel, and store most or all of their equipment on premise. Thus, the equipment is available at a moment's notice.

Not all hotel chains subscribe to the idea of outsourcing audiovisual services. Marriott, for one, has its own audiovisual division, with equipment and specialized staff to see to the needs of its clients.

In the restaurant business, Takeout Taxi, for example, is a service firm that delivers restaurant meals to residential homes in major cities across the United States. It is similar to pizza home delivery that is regularly done by pizza establishments such as Domino's, Pizza Hut, and Kelsey's Pizzeria. The major difference, however, is that Takeout Taxi is *not* a restaurant. It is a pure service delivery firm. It does not prepare the meal; it simply picks up and delivers the meal.

In Orlando, Florida, Takeout Taxi sells and delivers restaurant meals for Hooters, Grady's American Grill, Chili's Grill and Bar, Bono's Pit Bar-B-Q, the Black-Eyed Pea, and other restaurants in the area. The Takeout Taxi "menu" is essentially a brochure that includes all the menus of the restaurants it services. For the Orlando operation, the price of this service is not unreasonable. There is a $3.00 delivery fee per restaurant, a $10.00 minimum food purchase, optional driver gratuity for orders under $50, and a 15 percent gratuity added to the bill for orders of $50 or more.

Takeout Taxi has a 200,000+ customer database nationwide. That is a lot of customers for a foodservice delivery firm. Not surprisingly, restaurant meal home delivery is on the rise. Today's dual career couples and fast-paced young professionals increasingly want good-quality meals prepared by someone else yet eaten in the privacy of their homes.

MEASURING CUSTOMER SATISFACTION

Are your guests satisfied? Did you meet their expectations? Did you exceed their expectations? If you did meet guest expectations, why? If you did not, why not? Answers to these questions are important and essential to successful hospitality management. We need to know if we solved our customers' problems. We need to know why we did or did not get the job done right.

There are several ways to measure customer satisfaction in hospitality. These include comment cards, conversations with customers, guest surveys, customer complaints, and mystery shopper programs. Each of these approaches is discussed next.

Comment Cards

Probably the best known and most widely used approach to measuring customer satisfaction is the use of comment cards. These cards are prominently displayed on tables and at host stands in restaurants and in guest rooms and at front desks in hotels. Sample comment cards for Starbucks Coffee Company, Shells restaurants, and JHM Enterprises (a hotel management company) are shown in Figures 7.6 to 7.8.

Note that each has questions on the quality of the product/service offerings, cleanliness of the facilities, and attitude and/or friendliness of the staff. These are common areas of importance to all customers. Each of the cards also gives the customer the option of leaving the completed card at the

STORE #: ....

BUSINESS REPLY MAIL
FIRST CLASS MAIL   PERMIT NO 75396   SEATTLE, WA

POSTAGE WILL BE PAID BY ADDRESSEE

Starbucks Coffee Company
PO Box 3717
SEATTLE WA 98124-8878

MOISTEN, FOLD AND SEAL

HOW ARE WE DOING?

At Starbucks, we work passionately to bring you an enjoyable experience and want to know if we are meeting your expectations. Please take a few moments to share your thoughts with us. Your feedback will help us serve you better.

SKU 144494

CUSTOMER SERVICE

The quality of service at the register was:
Disappointing 1 2 3 4 5 Outstanding

The quality of service at the espresso bar was:
Disappointing 1 2 3 4 5 Outstanding

I was served in a timely manner:
☐ Yes   ☐ No

CLEANLINESS

The outside of the store was clean:
☐ Yes   ☐ No

The inside of the store was clean:
☐ Yes   ☐ No

SPECIFICS ABOUT YOUR VISIT

Which store(s) are you referring to? _____

What was the date of your visit? ____ MM ____ DD ____ YR

What time of day did you visit us?
☐ Morning   ☐ Afternoon   ☐ Evening

PLEASE SHARE YOUR COMMENTS WITH US: _____
_____
_____
_____

Our partners (employees) are here to help.
If for any reason you are not satisfied, please let them know.

PRODUCT QUALITY

The quality of my food item was:
Disappointing 1 2 3 4 5 Outstanding

The quality of my beverage was:
Disappointing 1 2 3 4 5 Outstanding

My questions about merchandise and products were answered to my satisfaction:
☐ Yes   ☐ No

OVERALL EXPERIENCE

I would recommend this Starbucks to a friend:
☐ Yes   ☐ No

Based on this experience, I will visit Starbucks:
☐ Less Often   ☐ As Often   ☐ More Often

MAILING INFORMATION

Name _____
Address _____
City _____
State/Province _____
Zip/Postal Code _____
Telephone (____) _____

Thanks for your time!

FIGURE 7.6 *Starbucks Coffee comment card. (Courtesy of Starbucks Coffee Company. © 1998 Starbucks Coffee Company. All rights reserved. Reprinted with permission.)*

179

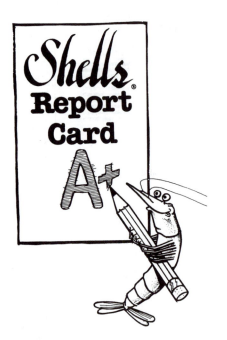

Dear Guest:

At SHELLS, our goal is to be your favorite seafood restaurant. To do this we know we must give you a variety of great tasting, quality seafoods, served by a knowledgeable friendly staff, at dockside prices, every time you visit.

Please let us know how we've done today, and give us your suggestions on how we can do even better.

Thanks for coming!

Bill Hattaway

Bill Hattaway

President

Please tear along perforation and mail

SHELLS Location _____

	Excellent	Good	Avg	Fair	Poor
Overall Experience	E	G	A	F	P
Food Quality	E	G	A	F	P
Portion Size	E	G	A	F	P
Service	E	G	A	F	P
Value for price	E	G	A	F	P
Cleanliness	E	G	A	F	P
Attitude of staff	E	G	A	F	P

in party _____ Food items ordered _____

_____

_____

Would you order the same foods again? _____

Did a manager visit your table?   yes   no

Would you recommend SHELLS to a friend?   yes   no

# of visits to SHELLS in the last 3 months
0   1–3   4–8   9+   First time

Age   1–17   18–25   26–45   46–55   56–65   65+

Bill, since you asked my opinion, to make my visit to SHELLS better I'd like to see you: _____

_____

_____

_____

Date _____ Time _____ am/pm Day _____

Servers name _____

Your name _____

Address _____

City _____ State _____ Zip _____

Telephone # (_____) _____

Please place in the mail – No postage required

FIGURE 7.7 *Shells Seafood Restaurants comment card. (Courtesy of Shells Seafood Restaurants. Reprinted with permission.)*

hospitality establishment or returning it by mail postage free at a later date. Some customers prefer to reflect on their experience prior to rating a restaurant meal or hotel stay. And some customers, satisfied or dissatisfied, ignore this form of customer feedback altogether.

JHM and Shells comment cards ask for ratings on price/value, an important consideration for today's value-conscious consumer. They both ask customer profile questions, too. This helps management spot trends of satisfaction or dissatisfaction among customer groupings such as age range, frequency of patronage, and business or leisure purchase purposes. Shells and Starbucks cards leave room for open-ended responses. Comment cards cannot possibly cover all aspects of a hospitality purchase. Thus, customers who wish to comment on a specific item (or items) can do so in the space provided. The pictorial humor presented on the JHM card, "Help Us Keep Our Ducks in a Row," can also be an effective way to capture the attention of hospitality customers, encouraging them to respond.

Comment cards are helpful tools to analyze customer response to hospitality product offerings. Research has shown, however, that two major problems emerge. First, many customers simply do not take the time or do not have the inclination to complete the cards. And, second, those that do tend to be highly satisfied or highly dissatisfied customers. It is important to get feedback from those customers who are "somewhere in the middle." One way this can be accomplished is through one-on-one direct conversations with customers while they are still on the premises.

Conversations with Customers

There are many opportunities to meet and talk informally with customers in the hospitality business. Conversing with customers is a less formal yet more personalized approach to obtain customer feedback. It is an especially good way to learn more from customers who do not fill out the comment cards.

At hotels, departmental managers often take turns standing in the lobby meeting and greeting guests. For those who are checking out, it is easy to open a conversation by saying, "Hello, I am one of the managers here and we hope you enjoyed your stay with us." In most instances, this manager would learn very quickly whether the guest overall had a good experience or not. If not, then there is the opportunity to, at a minimum, listen and hopefully be able to resolve what went wrong.

At the Marriott Toronto Airport Hotel, the general manager (GM) regularly visits the lobby on a daily basis. He also tours the VIP club floor lounge

NO POSTAGE
NECESSARY
IF MAILED
IN THE
UNITED STATES

BUSINESS REPLY MAIL

FIRST CLASS   PERMIT NO 159   GREENVILLE, SC

POSTAGE WILL BE PAID BY ADDRESSEE

JHM Enterprises, Inc.
P.O. Box 8375, Station A
Greenville, SC 29604

FIGURE 7.8 *JHM Enterprises comment card. (Courtesy of JHM Enterprises. Reprinted with permission.)*

Thank You!

We are pleased to be your host, and sincerely appreciate the opportunity to be of service to you.

It is our desire to serve you in the most comfortable, pleasant, and professional manner possible. Only you can determine if we are successful.

Please take a moment to complete this survey which will help us further improve our product and performance.

Again, thanks for staying with us!

How did you make your reservation?

☐ Directly with hotel
☐ Travel Agent
☐ By another JHM hotel
☐ AAA Directory
☐ 1-800-Toll-Free
☐ Other: _____

Hotel Name_____   City_____

How did you become aware of this hotel?

☐ Billboard
☐ Other Advertising
☐ Word of Mouth
☐ Sales call
☐ Referred by other hotel
☐ Appearance of hotel
☐ Other _____

Room Number _____
Arrival Date _____

How was your room?

	Excellent	Good	Fair	Poor
Price/Value	☐	☐	☐	☐
Attractiveness	☐	☐	☐	☐
Cleanliness	☐	☐	☐	☐
General Physical Condition	☐	☐	☐	☐
Bedding	☐	☐	☐	☐
Heating/Air Cond.	☐	☐	☐	☐
Television	☐	☐	☐	☐

Additional comments, if any: _____

How do you rate our services and facilities? (Please respond in all categories that apply.)

	Excellent	Good	Fair	Poor
Wake up calls, messages	☐	☐	☐	☐
Pool	☐	☐	☐	☐
Exercise room	☐	☐	☐	☐
Parking/grounds	☐	☐	☐	☐
Restaurant/Lounge				
Food quality	☐	☐	☐	☐
Cleanliness-restaurant/bar	☐	☐	☐	☐
Cleanliness-restrooms	☐	☐	☐	☐
Speed and efficiency	☐	☐	☐	☐
Friendliness, courtesy	☐	☐	☐	☐

If members of our staff were especially helpful, please tell us so that we may show them our appreciation:

Name/Position: _____
Comments: _____
_____
_____
_____
_____
_____
_____
_____
_____
_____
_____
_____
_____
_____
_____
_____
_____
_____
_____

And your bathroom?

	Excellent	Good	Fair	Poor
Cleanliness	☐	☐	☐	☐
Physical condition	☐	☐	☐	☐
Adequacy of supplies	☐	☐	☐	☐

Additional comments, if any _____
_____
_____
_____

If you return to this area, will you stay with us again?

☐ Definitely   ☐ Probably   ☐ Maybe
☐ Probably Not   ☐ Definitely Not

Did our Front Desk Personnel ask if they could assist you in making advanced room reservations?

☐ Yes ☐ No

How were you treated by our Front Desk Personnel?

Check In:
Speed & Efficiency   ☐ ☐ ☐ ☐

Check Out:
Speed & Efficiency   ☐ ☐ ☐ ☐
Friendliness / Courtesy   ☐ ☐ ☐ ☐

Additional Comments If Any: _____
_____
_____
_____

Would you consider yourself a frequent guest at our hotel?

☐ Yes ☐ No

What is the purpose of your trip/stay at our hotel?

☐ Business ☐ Leisure ☐ Business & Leisure

Your name and address (optional)

Name _____

Street _____

City/State Zip _____

_____

Company/Organization _____

_____

JHM
"The Hospitality Group"

Corporate Office:
PO Box 8375, Station A
Greenville, SC 29604

Was your room reservation in order at check-in?

☐ Yes ☐ No

PLEASE FOLD, SEAL, AND DROP IN THE MAIL. POSTAGE IS PRE-PAID.

FIGURE 7.8 *(continued)*

and habitually makes hallway walks throughout the hotel. This gives the GM a chance to meet and greet guests in various settings and the opportunity to talk informally with staff as well.

Managers in better restaurants routinely visit tables and ask patrons if they are enjoying their meal. Indeed, the Shells comment card asks this very question, "Did a manager visit your table"? (See Figure 7.7.) Senior management of this central Florida hospitality organization wants to know how frequently (or infrequently) unit-level management practices this approach to garner customer feedback. Again, so much can be learned by simply reaching out and giving customers a chance to express their satisfaction or concerns about their hospitality purchase.

Meeting planners can give tremendous feedback in that they see and experience so many aspects of the operation. The CSM, general manager, and sales account executive often conduct postmeeting evaluation sessions with these planners immediately following a scheduled event. At these sessions, there is open discussion on what went right, what went wrong, why, and how to improve for future events. For example, management may learn from these meetings that the food and beverage service is excellent but the area of housekeeping has room for improvement. These postmeeting evaluations can also help develop long-run rapport with clients. As noted in the *HSMAI Marketing Review*:

> Suppliers need this feedback to learn from the planners what they do well and in what areas they need to improve. Understanding good service delivery from a meeting planner's perspective brings good client relationships and repeat business.[4]

Planners respond positively when asked their input on suggestions and recommendations to enhance operations. And who knows better than customers where improvements can be made.

Guest Surveys

Guest surveys are questionnaires sent to selected customers after the purchase occasion. The selection of customers for these mailings is often done randomly. The survey may be general questions similar to those asked on comment cards. Or, in some instances, it may be detailed questions on a particular aspect of a product offering, such as the front office and guest registration, new product offerings, convention services, and so forth. Many hospitality organizations conduct this more formal and more sophisticated type of research.

Large hospitality chains do this kind of consumer research on a regular basis. These companies include Starwood Hotels & Resorts, Bass Hotels & Resorts, and Marriott from the hotel sector and the Darden Group (owners of the Olive Garden and Red Lobster) from the restaurant sector. As shown in Figure 7.9, Marriott lets its customers know in advance that a customer satisfaction survey questionnaire may be sent to them shortly after their stay. Although not all customers will receive the survey, it certainly conveys to guests that this kind of customer satisfaction research is routinely being conducted.

FIGURE 7.9 *Sample Marriott presurvey letter to guests. (Courtesy of Marriott International. Reprinted with permission.)*

Dear Valued Guest,

Welcome to the Marriott. We are glad you are here and hope your stay with us is enjoyable.

Please refer to the guest service directory in your room for information about our hotel and some of the local attractions. If we can be of further assistance, please call our front desk at extension 7100 or 7101.

Your opinion is important to us. Each month, Marriott International randomly sends surveys to our guests in order to produce a ''report card'' on how we are doing. In the next two weeks you may receive one of these questionnaires. Please take a few moments to complete this survey. The results of your comments are recorded and sent back to us so we may continuously strive for excellence.

We strive for a perfect ''10'' score for overall satisfaction. Should you have a problem, please call me at extension 55 so that I may immediately take corrective measures to ensure your comfort during your stay.

Thank you for allowing us the opportunity to be of service and we hope you enjoy your stay with us.

We look forward to seeing you again soon!

Sincerely,

General Manager

Sometimes hospitality organizations hire an outside research firm to conduct the surveys for them. Organizations such as Smith Travel Research and PriceWaterhouseCoopers are in the business of monitoring and researching the hospitality industry. They compile statistics and track trends on suppliers as well as buyers of hospitality. Many faculty at schools of hotel and restaurant management regularly conduct customer satisfaction research, too.

For example, a research study carried out at the University of Massachusetts focused on measuring meeting planner satisfaction with hotel convention services.[5] Meeting planner clients of a 900-room convention hotel were surveyed to learn of their level of satisfaction with the convention services department of this hotel. Participants were asked to rate several aspects of service including the preconvention meeting, setups on time, billing accuracy, audiovisual equipment, and the like.

The questionnaire was designed using the Likert scale technique. This technique asks participants to indicate the extent of their agreement or disagreement with a statement. For this study, a five-point scale was used, ranging from 1 = strongly disagree to 5 = strongly agree. Typical statements included "Coffee breaks were set up on time" and "Convention services managers (CSMs) were easily accessible." The closing statement was, "Overall, I was very satisfied with the convention services department at the hotel." A complete listing of the statements used in this study is shown in Table 7.2.

Clients that had held a meeting or convention at this hotel over a four-year period were sent the questionnaire. Table 7.3 shows the results of the responses to this survey. Following is a summary explanation of these results.

Overall, meeting planner clients of this hotel were quite satisfied. A mean rating of 4.5 out of 5.0 for the overall satisfaction statement is quite good. CSM accessibility and responsiveness, CSM preliminary planning, and setups on time also received good ratings in the 4.5 to 4.6 range. Lower ratings in the 4.0 to 4.2 range included billing procedures, audiovisual equipment, and soundproofing of function rooms.

Results of survey questionnaires such as this help management better assess its operation. Continuing with the previous example, billing procedures initially appeared to be problematic in convention services. Upon closer examination, however, the overall satisfaction and expectations fulfilled ratings were still high. Thus, as summarized by the researchers who conducted the study:

Our recommendation to the convention services department of this hotel is keep doing what you are doing, you are doing an excellent job. Do see

---

TABLE 7.2   *Listing of Statements for Convention Services Satisfaction Survey*

1. I was pleased with the preliminary planning that took place with the convention coordinator prior to the conference.
2. The preconvention meeting was productive.
3. Meeting rooms were set up on time.
4. Meeting rooms were free from noise.
5. Coffee breaks were set up on time.
6. Floor managers were available.
7. Convention services managers (CSMs) were easily accessible.
8. My audiovisual needs were met with dependable equipment.
9. Meeting rooms were refreshed after breaks.
10. The billing process was timely.
11. The billing statement was easy to understand.
12. The billing statement was accurate.
13. The convention services managers (CSMs) were responsive to unexpected problems that surfaced during the meeting.
14. My expectations of the convention services department at the hotel were fulfilled.
15. Overall, I was very satisfied with the convention services department at the hotel.

Source: M. Shaw, R. C. Lewis, and A. Khorey, "Measuring Meeting Planner Satisfaction with Hotel Convention Services: A Multivariate Approach," *International Journal of Hospitality Management,* Vol. 10, No. 2, 1991, pp. 137–146. Reprinted with permission of Elsevier Science.

TABLE 7.3   *Preliminary Results of Convention Services Satisfaction Survey*

Key Words for Attributes Rated	All Respondents	
	Mean	Standard Deviation
1. Preliminary planning	4.5	0.71
2. Preconvention meeting	4.4	0.82
3. Setups on time	4.6	0.72
4. Rooms free from noise	4.2	1.11
5. Coffee breaks on time	4.6	0.66
6. Available floor managers	4.4	0.79
7. CSM easily accessible	4.5	0.86
8. Audiovisual equipment	4.2	1.05
9. Meeting rooms refreshed	4.3	0.87
10. Billing timely	4.2	0.95
11. Billing readable	4.2	0.91
12. Billing accurate	4.0	0.97
13. CSM responsiveness	4.5	0.90
14. Expectations fulfilled	4.5	0.97
15. Overall satisfaction	4.5	0.91

Source: M. Shaw, R. C. Lewis, and A. Khorey, "Measuring Meeting Planner Satisfaction with Hotel Convention Services: A Multivariate Approach," *International Journal of Hospitality Management,* Vol. 10, No. 2, 1991, pp. 137–146. Reprinted with permission of Elsevier Science.

what you can do about your billing procedures, there appears to be room for improvement here.[6]

(For the interested reader, more detailed discussion of this study can be found in the *International Journal of Hospitality Management* and in the *HSMAI Marketing Review.*)

Customer Complaints

In many hospitality organizations, the dreaded customer complaint is a signal of failure. If a customer complains that he or she is unhappy about something, then he or she is a dissatisfied customer. But smart managers view complaints as positive. The customer is speaking up! The worst complaint of all is the one you never hear. No organization is perfect; no customer is perfect. Problems are always going to surface and are often the result of miscommunication and/or misunderstanding.

We always thought it a bit odd that some organizations have a customer complaint department. First, it signifies that complaints are normal, expected, and that a system is in place to handle complaints in a routine, matter-of-fact fashion. Second, and perhaps more important, the existence of a complaint department suggests that management at the source of the complaint is incapable of resolving the issue. Customer complaints, whenever possible, are best handled on the spot, especially in hospitality.

Empowerment, although controversial, has emerged in hospitality to address this very issue. Empowerment essentially means that an employee has the authority to correct a situation, within limits, without the approval of management or an immediate supervisor. For example, assume a hotel customer is checking out and upon reviewing the bill discovers that an erroneous $7 in-room movie charge is included in the bill. When the customer candidly "complains" that he or she did not view the movie, for goodness sake simply apologize and remove the charge from the bill. All too often, the front-office cashier has to seek advice from an immediate supervisor and/or the front-office manager to deal with the situation at hand. It can cost so little to resolve so many moments of truth in the hospitality business with a simple and honest "I am sorry for the error. We will correct it right away."

There was an instance similar to the preceding at a resort hotel on Cape Cod in Massachusetts. The guest disputed a $12 long-distance phone charge. Apparently, it took the involvement of the front-office manager, the resident manager, and, finally, the general manager who removed the charge. How much was the total bill for this guest and his family upon checking out after a two-week vacation? Reportedly, $5850!

At Ritz-Carlton hotels, employees can incur up to $2000 to resolve a complaint and/or satisfy a customer without the approval of management. This is not necessarily restricted to removing contested items from a bill when a customer is departing. If a customer is feeling ill, for example, and needs a particular over-the-counter drug from a pharmacy, an employee is "empowered" to simply jump in a taxi, go to a pharmacy, purchase the item, return, and deliver it to the guest. No charge. And no preapproval required from management to take the initiative to perform the task and to satisfy a guest—perhaps beyond expectations.

Customer complaints often come in by letter after a guest has departed. Complimentary letters are written to management, too. Both are important sources of feedback and need to be handled effectively. In a study conducted for a Canadian hospitality company, 50 percent of letters received by selected hotels and corporate headquarters were complaint letters, 20 percent complimentary, and 30 percent a combination of both.[7] When letters of complaint come in, what is important is to respond immediately, objectively, and by all means not defensively. Similar to the closing of a sale, being overly defensive when overcoming objections can be dangerous. Be straightforward, to the point, and if the hospitality organization honestly made a mistake, say so. Sometimes a monetary or similar incentive such as a complimentary meal on a future visit is an appropriate response as well.

In hospitality buyer publications, such as *Meetings & Conventions*, articles are often written suggesting to readers how to go about writing a letter of complaint. Interesting. A recent article entitled "Complaint Letters That Sing (and Sting)" offered the following advice to business travelers:

- Keep the letter short (one page), sweet (no venom or whining) and concise. Document the problem. Include names, dates, times, flight/room numbers and what happened. Back it up with photocopies of tickets, bills, receipts. Even if asked, don't send originals. Avoid rambling five- and six-page treatises. . . .
- Be reasonable. If your baggage was lost for two days, don't ask for a free first-class round-the-world ticket. . . .
- Wait for a response to your letter from the airline, hotel or car rental company. Ask its customer service department about turnaround time. If the matter has to be investigated, it could take two weeks. Expect a letter acknowledging your complaint. . . .
- Ask your travel agent for help. The agent who booked your itinerary may be willing to write your complaint letter, says Susan Dushane, travel consultant with Travel by Greta in Northridge, Calif., and a senior vice president for the Southern California chapter of the American Society of Travel Agents. "I'll write the letter expressing my displeasure at the way my client was treated," she says. "If they ignore me

and it's a hotel, I really go after them, wanting free room nights and upgrades and a letter of apology."....

• Don't cry wolf. As tempting as it may be, do not view airlines or hotels as plump geese waiting to be plucked. Every passenger complaint and the compensation paid is programmed into the computer and tracked. Airline security staff work together to spot abusers.[8]

Consumers are getting all kinds of advice on how to make effective complaints. They are getting fairly savvy and adept at it, too. It is our job as hospitality practitioners to learn how to better respond to honest and sincere complaints. The answer is be positive. Accept the customer feedback as helping you to improve your product, and not as an excuse to say, "oh, those stupid customers." The job of sales and marketing is getting and keeping customers. The effective handling of consumer complaints helps keep good customers returning again and again. A constructive response to guest complaints can also enhance positive word of mouth. Hopefully, renewed customers will bring back their friends and colleagues, too.

Mystery Shopper Programs

A way to monitor service delivery is through the use of mystery shoppers. These are people who are, in effect, "hired" to be customers who observe, take notes, and report back to management their impressions of various aspects of the hospitality service delivery. They are normally "incognito"; that is, service personnel are not aware that their performance is being judged by someone other than management or "real" customers. Personnel are advised (or should be advised) that mystery shopper programs are conducted at the establishment from time to time.

Mystery shoppers are typically given checklists of particular items for which management would like feedback. Some mystery shopper programs include actual surveys asking participants to rate on a scale, such as "1" for low to "5" for high, on how well service personnel performed in a certain area. Ratings on more tangible items, such as cleanliness of facilities and food quality, are commonly included also.

One of the authors had an opportunity to be a mystery shopper at the Epcot Center theme park for Walt Disney World in Orlando, Florida. This mystery shopper program is called the Epcot Guest Satisfaction Assessment Program. It is done periodically throughout the year to assess various aspects of service delivery at the park. Although details of the program are confidential, we can safely say it is hard work! There was a two-hour training session prior to the mystery shopping activity. This was followed by six to eight hours of moving through preassinged areas to act as regular customers throughout the rest of the day.

At Epcot, mystery shoppers who agree to the task are given a one-day free pass for a future visit to the theme park. They are also reimbursed for food purchases made as part of the assignment. At some hospitality establishments, professional firms are hired to develop and conduct the mystery shopper program. This is especially true for the lodging side of the business. As reported in the *HSMAI Marketing Review*:

> With the increased emphasis on sales training and development, many companies are utilizing "mystery shopper" call evaluation programs. While some produce the reports internally, the vast majority use one of the many vendors that provide this service to the hotel industry.[9]

Results of mystery shopping programs, when done effectively, can be a valuable tool and helpful to management and staff alike. Results are shared with service personnel, who are often rewarded for excellent ratings. When problems or areas for improvement are identified, more coaching and training are implemented. Thus, the outcome of mystery shopping programs is twofold. First, customer satisfaction on various aspects of service delivery are measured and evaluated. Second, enhanced training and development opportunities emerge. Both are important to successful hospitality sales and marketing.

SUMMARY

Service delivery is what the customer is truly buying. There are many "moments of truth" in service delivery. Moments of truth are the many and varied encounters customers have with a hospitality establishment. Service delivery is managing the customers' experience. Waitstaff at restaurants provide service delivery, chefs in the kitchen provide service delivery, and front-office guest services agents at hotels provide service delivery.

In lodging, conference services departments orchestrate the delivery process for meetings and convention business. The conference services manager, or CSM, coordinates these efforts. This job entails pulling together the many details that need to be addressed including function room assignments, meeting room setups, and audiovisual requirements. The CSM is also responsible for the convention resume, the preconvention meeting, and daily contact with the meeting planner throughout the event to ensure that all runs smoothly. Some catering and front-office departments have similar personnel who form like tasks.

Hospitality establishments also outsource various aspects of service delivery. At some hotels, audiovisual requests are handled by an outside firm. On the foodservice side, there are service firms that deliver restaurant meals to homes and offices. These companies are not truly in the hospitality business; they are in the business of service delivery.

Measuring customer satisfaction is an important aspect of service delivery. Did we meet and/or exceed customer expectations? If so, why? If not, why not? There are several ways to measure customer satisfaction. These include comment cards, conversations with customers, guest surveys, letters of customer complaints and compliments. Consumers even get professional advice on how to write an effective letter of complaint to a hospitality establishment.

Mystery shopper programs are another avenue to assess customer satisfaction. Mystery shoppers are not "real" customers. They are persons hired by a hospitality firm to act as customers and then report back to management on various aspects of service delivery they encountered. Service personnel are not aware that their performance is being judged by someone other than management or "real" customers. Personnel are advised, however, that from time to time mystery shopper programs are conducted at the hospitality establishment.

The job of sales and marketing is to get and keep a customer. Service delivery focuses on the keeping of that customer.

DISCUSSION QUESTIONS

1. How does good service delivery relate to the sales and marketing goal of getting and keeping a customer?
2. Can we really manage "moments of truth"?
3. What is the job of the conference services manager?
4. How does an external service delivery firm, such as Takeout Taxi, impact the hospitality industry?
5. Although comment cards are helpful in analyzing customer feedback, what are some disadvantages to this method of measuring customer satisfaction?
6. Are conversations with customers really a good way to measure customer satisfaction?
7. Who are mystery shoppers? Are mystery shopper programs an effective way to measure customer satisfaction?

NOTES

1. Karl Albrecht and Ron Zemke, *Service America!* Dow Jones–Irwin, Homewood, IL, 1985, p. 26.
2. Ibid., p. 27.
3. Rhonda J. Montgomery and Denney G. Rutherford, "A Profile of Convention-Services Professionals," *Cornell Quarterly*, December 1994, p. 48.
4. Laura Sims and Margaret Shaw, "Current Perspectives and Practices in Meeting Planning," *HSMAI Marketing Review*, Fall 1994, p. 48.
5. Margaret, Shaw, Robert C. Lewis, and Ann Khorey, "Measuring Meeting Planner Satisfaction with Hotel Convention Services: A Multivariate Approach," *International Journal of Hospitality Management*, Vol. 10, No. 2, 1991, pp. 137–146.
6. Ibid., p. 145.
7. Susan Morris, "Relationship Between Company Complaint Handling and Consumer Behavior," Master's Thesis, School of Hotel, Restaurant, and Travel Administration, University of Massachusets, Amherst, 1985.
8. Chris Barnett, "Complaint Letters That Sing (and Sting)," *Meetings & Conventions*, September 1996, p. 43.
9. Douglas Kennedy, "Mastering Your 'Mystery' Caller Evaluation Program," *HSMAI Marketing Review*, Spring 1997, p. 35.

Chapter 8

Sales Management

LEARNING OBJECTIVES

1. To understand what is meant by sales management from a hospitality perspective
2. To become familiar with various aspects of sales management, which include:
   - Sales organization
   - Sales account management
   - Recruitment
   - Training and development
   - Goal setting
   - Performance appraisals

Sales management is effectively directing the personal selling efforts of a hospitality establishment. It involves managing the sales process from both an individual and a team perspective. In other words, sales management addresses the logistics of sales solicitation and the development of sales account executives to enhance sales productivity. Sales account executives need to manage their day-to-day activities, sales teams need to coordinate their efforts, and customers need to feel that they are working with a professional and well-managed organization.

There are several components to hospitality sales management. These include sales organization, sales account management, recruitment, training and development, goal setting, and performance appraisals. Sales organization refers to departmental and individual organizational issues and inventory management. Sales account management addresses the specific issue of managing customer accounts—both current and prospective accounts. Recruitment of the sales force deals with the hiring of sales personnel. Training and development is concerned with the professional growth of these individuals. Goal setting is establishing goals and objectives for individual and team selling efforts and providing incentives to encourage the attainment of these goals. Performance appraisals are evaluations of sales account executives. This chapter focuses on each of these aspects of hospitality sales management.

SALES ORGANIZATION

Sales organization can be viewed from three perspectives. These include departmental organization, individual planning of sales activity, and inventory management. A sales department needs to be organized and sales managers within that organizational setup need to coordinate their efforts. Sales managers need to plan or "organize" their individual activities on a daily, weekly, and monthly basis. Allocating the sale of inventory to various customer segments needs to be managed as well. These are important issues in hospitality sales management and following is a more detailed discussion of each.

Departmental Organization

Organizing a sales department means determining who is going to do what. Sales solicitation needs to take place, administrative tasks need to be completed, and managerial decisions need to be made on a regular basis. In medium-to-large-sized hospitality establishments, a director of sales and/or a director of marketing coordinates these efforts. In smaller operations, it is not unusual to have one individual responsible for all of these tasks. For most bed-and-breakfast operations in the United States and Canada and the small boutique hotels in Europe, for example, sales activities are typically handled by the owner and/or manager of the establishment.

Shown in Figure 8.1 is a sample sales organizational setup for a midsized urban hotel targeting business clientele. The sales managers in this example are organized by target market and by geographic territory. Sales manager 1 is responsible for corporate accounts located in the immediate downtown and surrounding area. Sales manager 2 is responsible for national corporate accounts. This refers to companies based in other areas that conduct business or have the potential to conduct business at the hotel. Both of these sales managers solicit group and transient business from their account base.

Sales manager 3 targets meetings and convention business from national association accounts. This business may include executive board meetings, committee meetings, regional conferences, and annual conventions.

In this example, once group events have been booked they are turned over to the conference services department for service delivery. Both the sales managers and the director of conference services report to the director of sales and marketing. The sales team meets weekly to discuss issues pertinent to achieving the department's sales objectives.

FIGURE 8.1 *Organizational sales setup of a midsized hotel located in an urban setting.*

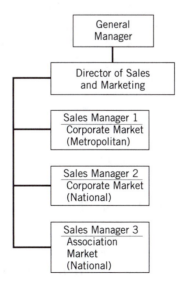

Weekly sales meetings are very much a part of a sales department's organizational structure, be it a sales force of two or twelve sales account executives. They are critical for effective communication within the department. At these meetings, each team member highlights his or her weekly activity with regard to new prospects uncovered, tentative bookings, "verbal" definites, cancellations, and so forth. (Verbal definites are bookings where clients have verbally committed their meeting or function to the facility but a signed contract is not yet in hand.) In other words, sales managers share with each other progress reports on various accounts they are currently working on. Thus, each team member gets an up-to-date informal report on the status of all current sales activities.

For example, one sales manager may be working on a tentative booking but considers it weak because of strong competition for this particular account. Call this Group A. Another sales manager may have a new prospect with similar space requirements interested in the same dates. Call this Group B. Assume, however, that the property has the capability of booking only Group A or Group B over the same dates because of space limitations. When these types of issues surface at sales meetings (which they frequently do), discussion will occur raising the following types of questions:

- What is the likelihood that either group will eventually book their business at the property?
- What is the estimated profitability and/or contribution margin for each group?
- Is either group a regular client?
- What is the likelihood of repeat business from either group? In other words, what is the long-term profitability for each?
- Can either group consider alternative dates? (A *very* important question.) What would encourage them to move dates?
- Do convention history reports match their current space allocation requests?

These are just a sampling of the questions that need to be raised and answered. It is a never-ending process in hospitality sales management to search for the best fit for both the buyer and the seller.

Individual Organizational Planning

Good sales managers in any industry plan their daily, weekly, and monthly activities. The same holds true for hospitality sales managers, too. A sales manager in hospitality handles anywhere from 50 to 150 accounts. Each account has one or more customers, all with business in varying stages of the sales process. One cannot call on 100+ accounts a day. And calling on just one or two customers a day is inefficient and not conducive to successful selling. Time needs to be set aside and scheduled for prospecting for new customers, too. How is all this accomplished? Through careful planning and sticking to that plan regardless of unforeseen obstacles that inevitably emerge.

Figure 8.2 shows a sample weekly planner for a sales manager. Space is allocated to schedule sales calls, sales meetings, travel itineraries, trade show attendance, and so on. Note that space is available to record regular accounts versus new accounts and/or prospecting sales activity. Space is also given to record personal sales calls versus telephone sales solicitation. Weekly planners serve as a way to track various types of sales activities to ensure, for example, that one is not spending too much time on regular accounts and not enough time prospecting for new accounts. There is also a checklist to ensure that a sales manager's time is appropriately spent with clients and prospective clients and not an inordinate amount of time is spent on administrative tasks such as filing reports and attending meetings.

Trace systems, or "tickler" files as they are sometimes called, help a salesperson stay organized. A trace system is setting a date when a customer account next needs to be reviewed and acted upon. In other words, one "traces" an account file to be pulled on a specific date for planned follow-up action. At the end of a sales call report, there is often space for a trace date and follow-up action to be taken on that date.

For example, say a sales manager has just completed a sales call with a regular account. Assume it was learned that a new product introduction meeting may be scheduled for late November but that the decision on whether to schedule that meeting would not be made until mid-September. The sales manager would then "trace" this account for mid-September to find out what decision was made. In the meantime, immediately after the initial sales call, a follow-up letter expressing interest in hosting the meeting and thanking the client for his or her time should be sent. Not a long letter, just a note saying, "Thank you for your time. You are a valued customer and we look forward to doing business with you soon." The next follow-up will be the trace date in mid-September.

In both of the authors' sales experience, they found the trace system absolutely essential in helping them to keep organized and to better manage 100+ customer accounts. One cannot possibly keep track of this number of customers in one's head. Trace dates are so simple yet so important to successful selling. *Every* customer account should have a trace date, without exception.

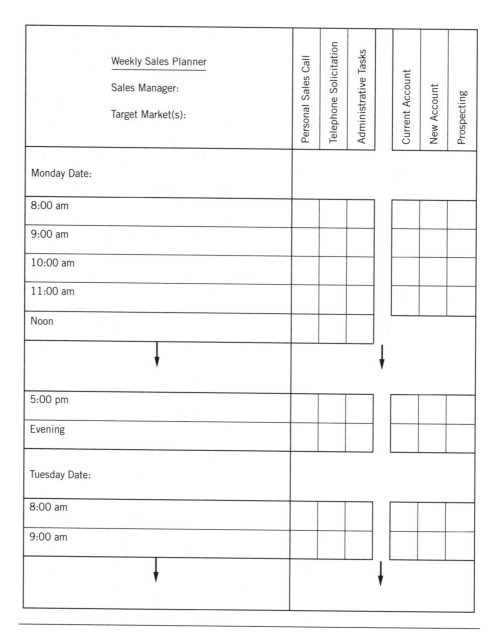

FIGURE 8.2 *Weekly sales planner sample.*

Inventory Management

Inventory management (sometimes referred to as inventory control) is essential in hospitality. We are dealing with a very perishable product and it needs to be handled with "kid gloves," so to speak. If we have a booking and it cancels at the last minute, the sale of that space is potentially lost forever. In other words, if a restaurant table, a theme park pass, or a hotel guest room reservation gets cancelled, and it is not resold for that day, the revenue from that sale is gone. Inventory management helps reduce the possibility (or probability) of lost revenue. Following are two hospitality examples to further explain this concept. A restaurant example is illustrated first, followed by a lodging example.

In table service restaurants, a host or hostess keeps track of inventory in a logbook. As reservations come in, they are recorded by date, size of party, and time preference for the reservation request. As reservation requests become tight for specific times and/or dates, management has the option to turn down reservation requests, continue accepting reservation requests, or suggest alternative time/date possibilities for the prospective customer to consider. These three approaches, in effect, are inventory management. The first takes the risk of not selling a "full house"; that is, tables will go empty. The second takes the risk of too many customers at the same time, which, in turn, means potential disgruntled customers. The third is attempting to match demand with available supply.

This third approach is the best way to deal with inventory management for restaurants, especially in high-demand periods. It does not always work, but an attempt should always be made to "smooth out" demand when periods of high customer counts are anticipated. The common practice of offering "early bird" specials is an example of proactive inventory management. More price conscious consumers often opt to eat slightly earlier than their normal routine to take advantage of price discounts. Management is trying to effectively smooth out demand and satisfy varying segments of customers at the same time.

Inventory management at hotels, in principle, is the same as for restaurants, yet is done in a slightly different manner. It is more complex and the following example illustrates how inventory management works in midsized lodging establishments.

Blocks of guest rooms are typically "reserved" or set aside for group and individual transient business. Groups tend to book further in advance than individual travelers; thus, space needs to be protected for the individual traveler market. A typical time frame for individuals to make their hotel reservations is three days to three weeks in advance. Groups normally book anywhere from one month to two years in advance. For periods of strong group demand, all guest rooms could be sold out to groups before the transient individual has arranged his or her travel itinerary. Many hotels target both group and individual business. Thus, by reserving or holding on to guest rooms for the individual traveler, inventory is protected to meet the shorter planning horizons of this market segment.

For example, a 300 room hotel may do 40 percent of its business with individual transient accounts and 60 percent with group accounts (see Table 8.1). Thus, 120 rooms are set aside for individual reservation requests and 180 rooms are set aside for group bookings. Sales account executives calling on group accounts have a 180-room allotment to sell to groups, not 300. The remaining 120 rooms are held exclusively for the individual travel market. Note in Table 8.1 that different blocks are held for peak and off-peak periods. Demand fluctuates by time of the year and day of the week for varying customer segments. In this example, more rooms are held for the typically higher-rated transient business in peak periods of demand.

Once the general parameters are set for inventory room blocks, tentative and definite bookings within the group room block are monitored on a regular basis. Shown in Table 8.2 is a sample inventory management report for the hypothetical McDonald Stewart Resort Hotel. The report (produced in April) shows the status of tentative and definite group bookings for an 11-day period for the following August. Also given are the previous year's occupancy statistics for the same period and average group and transient demand figures.

A preliminary review of this report shows that August 3–4 is weak in group bookings, both tentatives and definites, compared to average group demand. Conversely, August 8–9 presents the opposite problem. Should Walsh Associates become a definite booking, there is a strong potential to displace transient business over this period. The director of sales and mar-

TABLE 8.1 *Group and Transient Guest Room Inventory Allocation Example for a 300-Room Hotel*

Demand Period	Market Segment	Guest Room Inventory Allocation
Peak[a]	Group market	180
	Transient market	120
	Total room inventory	300
Off peak[b]	Group market	240
	Transient market	60
	Total room inventory	300

[a] Peak-period guest room inventory allocation is 60% group and 40% transient.
[b] Off-peak-period guest room inventory allocation is 80% group and 20% transient.

TABLE 8.2 *Sample Inventory Management Report*

Rooms Inventory Report 4/23/98	August 2–12, 1998						McDonald Stewart Resort Hotel (300 Rooms)				
Day of Week Date	S 2	M 3	T 4	W 5	Th 6	F 7	S 8	S 9	M 10	T 11	W 12
Definite group rooms	130	20	30	50	50	100	120	120	70	70	70
Tentative group rooms	10	10	0	40	40	40	75	105	50	50	0
1997 occupancy	100%	80%	70%	50%	50%	95%	90%	90%	70%	50%	50%
AVG group demand	140	120	105	60	55	140	115	120	90	65	60
AVG transient demand	150	120	105	90	95	145	155	150	120	85	85
Definite Bookings:											
HAFA Alumni	110										
Pickworth Co-op			10	50	50						
CIBC–Toronto						100	120	120			
CFSEA									70	70	70
MacLaurin & Co.	20	20	20								
Tentative Bookings:											
LLBO								30	50	50	
Subden Wineries	10	10									
University of Victoria				40	40	40					
Walsh Associates							75	75			

keting would review these figures at the weekly sales meeting. More group business is clearly needed for the August 3–4 period. Discussion would also take place on the Walsh account. Has a contract gone out? Could this group move to different dates? A move to August 3–4 would be ideal. What incentives could be given to this group to make this move?

In summary, the inventory management report gives an up-to-date status of group rooms definitely booked, tentatively booked, and those still yet unsold. It gives the sales team direction as to where efforts should be made for group sales booking activity. The preceding example focused only on the month of August. At weekly sales meetings, inventory management reports are often reviewed for three months to three years in advance depending on the circumstances for each period in question. The director of sales and marketing reviews these reports on a regular basis, almost daily.

SALES ACCOUNT MANAGEMENT

Sales account management involves developing, maintaining, and enhancing customer relationships. It does not mean customer manipulation. Sales account management is an approach to managing customer relationships that *benefits* customers and does not control them. It is especially effective in chain hospitality organizations where multiple properties seek business from the same customer accounts. A brief history of sales account management will help better explain what has evolved into today's approach to managing customer relationships.

The concept first emerged in the early 1970s (see Table 8.3). Sales managers started to develop expertise with specific market segments such as the corporate market, the association market, or the group travel industry market. Instead of calling on customers randomly, or responding to phone calls from prospective clients in a haphazard manner, the concept of sales account management emerged. Sales managers were assigned specific market segments—one became a specialist in anticipating the specific needs and wants of a targeted audience.

By the mid-1980s, sales managers further honed their skills to become knowledgeable on specific industries and/or professions. In the hotel business, for example, a sales manager might become a specialist in the sports market—professional sports, amateur sports, team sports, tournament sports, and companies that produce equipment and uniforms for the world of sports. Others developed expertise in, say, the health care field, the banking industry, the legal profession, the pharmaceutical industry, and so forth.

At the start of the 1990s, specialization became even more pronounced. National sales managers in many chain hotel organizations were now assigned specific customer accounts to call on for potential business. As noted earlier, a national sales account executive for Marriott International, for example, is assigned one account to solicit business—namely IBM. A very large

TABLE 8.3 *Evolution of Sales Account Management*

Decade	Approach to Account Management
1970s	Sales managers assigned specific market segments to solicit business such as corporate meetings, association conventions, social functions, or group travel industry sales.
1980s	Sales managers assigned specific industries and/or professions within an identified market segment such as the banking industry, pharmaceutical companies, insurance companies, the legal profession.
1990s	Sales managers assigned specific customer accounts within an identified industry and/or profession such as IBM, Ford Motors, Federal Express, American Society of Engineers.

account. Her job is to solicit IBM business worldwide for all Marriott brand hotels, not just one individual property. Why? Simple. An IBM client has only to deal with one sales representative and not hundreds throughout the chain for his or her hospitality lodging needs. It makes life a lot easier for a Marriott customer to have a direct link or direct line to one national sales account executive who represents all Marriott lodging establishments. This sales account executive, needless to say, works very closely with sales managers at property-level hotels regarding the specific needs and wants of each individual client. This particular account at Marriott has developed into a client base of 850 customers including meeting planners, corporate travel managers, managers, and administrative assistants throughout the IBM corporation. IBM books upwards of 1000 meetings a year at Marriott alone. Managing this account, as one could imagine, is no small task. Marriott has over 60 national account executives in these types of positions. They are assisted daily by hotel-based or regional sales associates who work hand in hand with the national account executives. Their direct-sales efforts are supported by telemarketing, direct mail, Internet sales, and other marketing programs.

Hyatt Hotels is another hotel chain that restructured its sales force to an account management–based system. As noted in *Business Travel News:* in the mid-1990s,

> Hyatt Hotels Corp. plans . . . to begin converting the sales forces at its individual properties to a new structure—with reps dedicated to specific accounts rather than market segments—after doing the same with its national sales staff over the past two years.
>
> It will be a more ambitious undertaking this time in one sense, given that there are 540 property salespeople, compared with 60 national reps.
>
> Where hotel chains traditionally have allocated their sales staff to corporate transient, group, incentive and leisure sales, Hyatt assigns each salesperson a group of accounts (between four and about 40), with responsibility for tracking, servicing and forecasting all of their travel needs. Thus, a travel manager deals with only one Hyatt account representative, rather than several.[1]

At Holiday Inn, the account management structure has been revamped, too. National sales managers no longer have "territories" such as the Northeast, the Midwest, or the West Coast. Rather, each now has the title "Director, Key Account Sales." Directors each have 15 to 20 accounts nationwide and they travel to wherever customers of these accounts are located to solicit business and build relationships. Many of these accounts are corporate accounts. However, several directors are also assigned, for example, tour wholesale accounts and state and federal government agency accounts. Key accounts at Holiday Inn produce up to 80 percent of the business for its U.S.-based properties.

National sales directors at Holiday Inn are also assigned "prospective key accounts." These are accounts that do business with Holiday Inn but are not yet major producers of business. These prospective accounts have been identified as having the potential to do so, however. Again, keeping a balance of calling on regular accounts and calling on prospective accounts is very much a part of what successful selling is all about.

Radisson SAS is an international hospitality organization based in Brussels, Belgium. It, too, actively uses the customer account management approach to personal selling. Newly formed in 1994, this organization is a strategic alliance between SAS Hotels, a Scandinavian-based hotel firm, and Radisson Hotels, a U.S.-based hotel firm. Radisson SAS manages and/or franchises this chain of hotels throughout Western Europe, Eastern Europe, the Middle East, and North Africa. It currently operates more than 80 hotels in these regions and plans to grow to 200 hotels by the year 2000.

Shown in Figure 8.3 is an overview of its account management structure. For each Radisson SAS company account, there is a director of worldwide accounts to coordinate sales activities with the travel manager of a client

FIGURE 8.3 *Account management structure of Radisson SAS Hotels. (Courtesy of Radisson SAS Hotels Worldwide. Reprinted with permission.)*

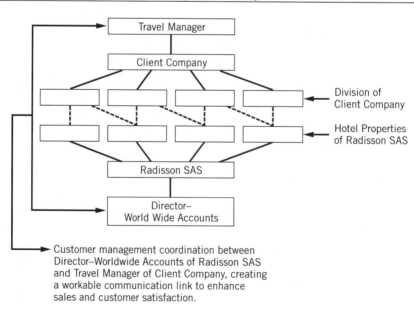

company. These accounts include such companies as Credit Lyonnais of France (a major European bank), Volvo of Sweden (an international automobile manufacturer), and Gucci of Italy (a world-renowned fashion designer). Companies such as these have a number of executives traveling on international business across the globe. This may be individual business travel or travel to group events such as corporate meetings or trade show exhibitions.

The travel managers at these client companies negotiate directly with the Radisson SAS director of worldwide accounts assigned the account for sales activities for all Radisson SAS hotels in the region. This is in close coordination with sales account executives at the property level. At Radisson SAS, there are currently 10 directors of worldwide accounts. They report to the vice president of sales and marketing who is based at the Brussels corporate headquarters.

Travel managers of client companies often work directly with travel agents. In these instances, the Radisson SAS director of worldwide accounts works closely with the travel agent, seeking a win–win situation for all three parties involved. Travel agency involvement in hotel sales in Europe, as in North America, is becoming prominent. Travel agents are customers, too, and they are discussed in more depth in Chapter 11.

RECRUITMENT: HIRING THE SALES FORCE

Hiring a good sales team takes time and effort. Many people apply for sales positions but sales is not for everyone. Thus, recruiters need to have good interviewing skills to uncover the best candidates in the hiring process. As stated in *Hotel & Resort Industry:*

> Have you spent thousands of dollars in search fees, hundreds of hours interviewing and mega-funds in training, and still only field an average sales team? Do you have one star performer, several average performers and one or two underachievers? Well, then it's time to look at your interviewing skills.[2]

A key component of good interviewing skills is listening. Give candidates an opportunity to let you know who they are, why they are interested in the job, and what skills they feel are important to successful selling. Then, listen to learn if they possess these skills *and* possess the skills that you are looking for as well. Common traits among successful sales account executives include self-confidence, high energy, empathy, honesty, stamina, enthusiasm, drive, patience, determination, a sense of humor, and a sense of self-worth. Empathy, in particular, is a characteristic shared by many top sales performers. Empathy is the capacity to share in the feelings or ideas of others. In sales, the "other," of course, is the customer. To truly understand customers is to "empathize" with their needs and wants as if they were your own.

The preceding skills are important for a lot of different types of jobs, but they are especially important for sales. Continuing with the publication noted previously:

> Hiring well in the first place [for a sales organization] eliminates a lot of problems down the line. There are several important characteristics to look for in a candidate:
> 1. Confidence. Someone who enjoys competition and knows how to prepare for challenge—in short, a winner;
> 2. Quickness of mind. Someone who can think on his or her feet, a constructive, conceptual thinker who can respond to virtually any situation instantaneously;
> 3. A sense of humor. Someone who can maintain perspective in this demanding business;
> 4. Boldness. Someone who is prepared to take calculated risks; and
> 5. Integrity.[3]

We concur that these are strong personal characteristics from which to launch a successful career in professional selling.

Announcing a sales position opening is typically done both within and outside the organization. Table 8.4 shows an excerpt from an internal posting for an entry-level sales position at Marriott Hotels, Resorts, and Suites. This job profile includes previous position specifications, technical skills, managerial skills, and academic requirements. Many of the skills desired for this position reflect those highlighted previously. College degrees are typically preferred by most hospitality organizations for entry-level sales.

There are several ways to uncover potential candidates in addition to internal job postings. One is through advertising in the print media. The Internet is increasingly being used as a means of finding and offering sales opportunities. Another way is to monitor your competition. That is, are there potential candidates on the sales force of your strongest competitor? Or, challenge your sales team to identify individuals with whom they come up against most frequently when competing for business. Hiring from the competition brings the benefits of competitive knowledge and established relationships with similar customers. This is not only a fair tactic for recruitment in hospitality sales, it is also common practice.

TRAINING AND DEVELOPMENT

Once recruited, both experienced and inexperienced sales managers need training and development. Experienced sales managers may need training in

---

TABLE 8.4   *Internal Posting for Entry-Level Sales Position*

Previous Position Requirements

- Eighteen months management or supervisory experience, or
- Two years hourly experience as a catering or sales assistant, or
- Two years outside catering/sales management experience, or
- Eighteen months Marriott experience as a reservation sales agent, or
- Two- or four-year college degree and completion of a Marriott Sales Internship

Technical Skill Requirements

- Prompt handling and follow-up of all inquiries to include customer follow-up and communications of group details to service department to ensure proper handling of meetings
- Utilizing selling skills to book all aspects of the meeting
- Maximizing revenue by selling creative food and beverage functions
- Familiarity with need periods and effective positioning of business to maximize profitability
- Understanding and achievement of individual room-night goals, catering goals, referral goals, and hotel goals
- Solicitation of accounts and markets based on direction of director of sales

Managerial Skills Requirements

- Provides constructive coaching and counseling to associates
- Actively supports the development, training, and mentoring of associates
- Knows how and when to impose deadlines and delegate tasks
- Motivates and provides a work environment in which associates are productive
- Demonstrates self-confidence, energy, and enthusiasm
- Presents ideas, expectations, and information in a concise, well-organized way
- Uses effective listening skills
- Manages group or interpersonal conflict situations effectively
- Understands how to manage in a culturally diverse work environment
- Uses problem-solving methodology for decision making and follow-up
- Has personal integrity, manages time well, is highly visible in areas of responsibility

Academic Requirements

- High school diploma or equivalent
- College degree preferred

Source: Adapted from Marriott International. Courtesy of Marriott International.

particular areas such as computer literacy skills and/or development in working with a new target market assignment. Inexperienced sales managers need "grass roots" training in the sales process and in sales management practices presented thus far in the text. If a recently hired sales manager is new to the organization, training is also required for systems and protocol particular to the organization.

People enter an organization with different skill sets and learn new skills at different paces. People already on the job get new assignments, promotions, and so forth. Both new hires and current personnel have strengths and weaknesses. Strengths need to be enhanced; weaknesses need to be strengthened. Thus, training and development needs vary considerably. It is the job of the director of sales and marketing to identify, evaluate, and act on the specific needs for each individual member of the sales team on an ongoing basis.

Looking at areas for potential needs, there are various sources for training. Following are some examples:

Example 1

Need area:	Sales process skills development
Skills required:	Ability to prospect, build relationships, make presentations, overcome objections, negotiate, close the sale, ensure service delivery
Sources for training and development:	Internal and/or external sales training seminars, mentoring with a senior sales manager, regular readership of trade publications

Example 2

Need area:	Time management skills development
Skills required:	Ability to organize and prioritize activities
Sources for training and development:	Internal and/or external time management seminars, coaching by a senior sales manager, provision of applicable time management tools such as daily planners and/or software programs

Example 3

Need area:	Computer literacy skills development
Skills required:	Ability to communicate internally within the organization and externally with the customer through technology
Sources for training and development:	Software programs, course offerings through local computer stores and/or local college or university, internal training

For sales process skills development, in particular, there are a number of different areas in which training may be warranted. One source may be more appropriate than another depending on the specific skill(s) that needs to be developed. You may turn to the supplier of your sales software program (to be discussed shortly in the next chapter) to develop or assist in developing training seminars. Annual sales conferences held by many hospitality organizations often include training and development as part of the agenda. Professional associations, such as the Hospitality Sales and Marketing Association International (HSMAI) or the American Hotel & Motel Association (AH&MA), frequently conduct conferences specific to skill development. This is done at both the regional and the national levels.

The use of internal or external sources, or a combination of both, for training and development is the decision of the director of sales and marketing. Much depends on the level of skill development needed, the number of sales managers involved, internal resources available, budgetary issues, and the size of the hospitality establishment. Even large firms, such as Sheraton, Hyatt, Holiday Inn, and Marriott, often outsource some of their sales training needs.

GOAL SETTING

The setting of sales goals and objectives is done in all industries, including hospitality. To be successful, you have to set expectations and state goals clearly. Success in achieving set goals should be recognized and rewarded.

Effective recognition can be accomplished in several ways and does not have to be elaborate. Some sales offices have a bell in a central area that is rung every time a sales manager closes a sale. The instant recognition and satisfaction of ringing that bell is a great motivator. Other sales offices use a mascot that rotates from one sales office to the next recognizing, for example, a sales manager who had the highest revenue generation in bookings over a given period of time. Other nonmonetary forms of recognition include celebrity lunches and award plaques such as "sales manager of the quarter." Recognition is brought to the attention of one's peers, upper management, and customers. Yes, customers feel good about working with an "award winning" sales account executive.

Monetary awards are customary, too. The most favored are end-of-the-year cash bonus awards and incentive travel awards. Recognition and awards, both monetary and nonmonetary, are based on achieving and/or exceeding set goals.

Goals can be established in a number of ways. These include setting revenue goals, high-versus-low-demand-period booking goals, current account versus new account booking goals, and market share and RevPAR (revenue per available room) goal attainment. Each is a common goal parameter in hospitality and often more than one is part of the overall goal-setting structure. That is, sales managers may have multiple goals to attain. Time frames are also given for each goal, typically on a monthly and/or annual basis. Individual and team goals are often set, too. Following is more detailed discussion of each of these.

Revenue Goals

Revenue-focused goals are probably the most widely used parameter for goal setting in hospitality. For hotels, this includes rooms as well as food and beverage revenue objectives. Often sales managers develop their own revenue goals and then meet with the director of sales and marketing for approval. Setting one's own objectives and then achieving those objectives instills pride and professionalism.

Room-nights booked and average daily rate (ADR) per booking are also sometimes used as a means to measure productivity. Nonetheless, room-nights booked × average rate estimates equals revenue. So we are still looking at revenue. Thus, today, more and more goals are set in terms of overall revenue generated with less emphasis on individual booking activity. Instead of having sales managers focus primarily on large bookings and high-average-rate business, more emphasis is placed on overall productivity. This includes booking activity for when it is most needed as well.

High-Versus Low-Demand Periods

Many sales departments have specific goals set for both high *and* low periods of demand. It is usually easier to book business for peak periods of demand. In other words, busy months often "book themselves," whereas slower months need more attention to get business in the door. Through goal setting, incentives are given to encourage sales activity for the need periods of the hospitality establishment.

Current Accounts Versus New Accounts

Mentioned several times thus far throughout the text is the importance of maintaining a balance between keeping good relationships with current customers and prospecting for new customers. Goals are often established to maintain this balance. A sales manager may have annual revenue goals set to book $XXX from current customer accounts and to book $YYY from new customer accounts. This scenario will vary depending on the assigned target market, the anticipated growth (or decline) of that market, and the competitive environment currently faced by that market.

Market Share and Revenue per Available Room

In addition to the goal-setting parameters presented thus far, market share and revenue per available room (RevPAR) are increasingly being used as measurements for successful selling.

Market share is viewed from two perspectives—**fair market share (FMS)** and **actual market share (AMS)**. Fair market share looks at a hotel's inventory capacity relative to the total inventory capacity of direct competition in the marketplace. All things being "fair," these properties should run similar occupancies at similar price ranges. Actual market share compares actual occupancies of each competitor to the overall occupancy of these competing facilities over a given period of time.

The FMS and AMS calculations are commonly expressed as percentages. For FMS, this would be guest room capacity for each individual hotel divided by total capacity of the competing hotels. For AMS, actual rooms sold at each hotel is divided by total rooms sold among the hotels. The AMS calculations are then compared to the FMS calculations to see "how we are doing."

Table 8.5 gives an example. Among the four hotels that compete for the same target markets, in this example, Hotel Suze is doing quite well. Its FMS is 27 percent compared to an AMS of 32 percent, five percentage points

TABLE 8.5   *Hypothetical Market Share and RevPAR Example*

Hotel	Number of Rooms	Occupancy	Average Daily Rate
Hotel Paul	350	67%	$82
Hotel John	200	72%	$95
Hotel Jane	250	55%	$102
Hotel Suze	300	81%	$91
	FMS	**AMS**	**RevPAR**
Hotel Paul	32%	31%	$55
Hotel John	18%	19%	$68
Hotel Jane	23%	18%	$56
Hotel Suze	27%	32%	$74
	100%	100%	

higher. In other words, this hotel is getting a larger share of the market relative to its size and total demand for these competing hotels. Hotel Jane has the opposite situation. Its AMS is five percentage points lower than its FMS, 18 percent compared to 23 percent. Hotel Paul and Hotel John are running about par.

This type of market share statistic can show how well (or poorly) a hotel is doing relative to its direct competitors. It is not the only measurement tool, but one of several that are frequently used for market comparisons. It is important that similar facilities in the same product class targeting similar markets be used for the FMS and AMS analysis.

Also shown in Table 8.5 are the **revenue per available room (RevPAR)** figures for these four hotels. RevPAR is calculated by taking the total room revenue (occupancy × average daily rate) and dividing by total guest room capacity for each hotel. Once again, Hotel Suze is outperforming its three main competitors from a RevPAR perspective. Although Hotel Suze has the third lowest average daily rate, it is operating at the highest occupancy. Overall, Hotel Suze has the highest AMS and highest RevPAR figures. The sales team is doing something right at this hotel.

Individual and Team Goals

Goal setting is done for team as well as for individual achievements. The AMS and RevPAR just described are the results of a team effort. A team may have the goal, of say, raising the current AMS from 32 to 35 percent. Or, raising the current RevPAR from $68 to $72. Both individual and team goals are set at many hospitality establishments.

Achieving and/or exceeding both individual and team goals are often rewarded with semiannual and year-end bonuses, as well as prominent recognition. The bonus is often configured on a percentage basis. For example, meeting an individual goal might produce a 2 percent bonus, exceeding that goal might result in a 5 percent bonus. Attaining the team goal may raise the bonus to 8 percent. Exceeding both individual and team goals may get that bonus up to 10 percent. The actual percentage figures will, of course, vary from company to company. Regardless, the spirit of winning is fostered and top performers are acknowledged. It always feels good to win and to be recognized and rewarded for hard-fought accomplishments.

PERFORMANCE APPRAISALS

It is in the best interest of the sales team and the entire hospitality establishment that sales managers continue to develop skills to ensure that sales objectives are met. As already discussed, there are many skills that lead to successful selling. It is through **performance appraisals** that strengths and areas of skill development needs are identified.

Performance appraisals are conducted with each member of the sales department by his or her immediate supervisor. This is typically done on an annual basis. For entry-level sales positions, appraisals are conducted more frequently.

Shown in Figure 8.4 is a sample management development assessment used by Marriott as part of its sales managers' performance appraisals. The assessment covers the different areas of expertise required for successful selling. These areas include sales effectiveness in gaining new business, keeping abreast of competitor activity and local-area special events, implementing various aspects of the sales process, proactively addressing need times of the hospitality establishment, contributing to the marketing plan, reaching set goals, and so forth.

In each area, the sales manager is rated as strong, proficient or improvement needed. General comments on overall progress are often included at the conclusion of the report. Both the sales manager and his or her immediate supervisor—which, in most cases, is the director of sales and marketing—sign and date the document. As a result of the assessment, a plan is put together to address how improvement will be achieved. This sales development plan will include specific goals, action steps to achieve set goals, and a timeline for each step of the plan.

The performance appraisal is an effective tool for sales manager development in hospitality sales and marketing. Sales managers receive direct feedback on areas in which they excel and areas that need improvement.

MANAGEMENT DEVELOPMENT ASSESSMENT

Discipline: Sales and Marketing   Name:

Position: Sales Manager   Date:

Rating Key:

Strength (S)	= Manager has completely mastered this skill; proactively demonstrates it and is a role model for others
Proficient (P)	= Manager has not completely mastered this skill but often able to demonstrate it
Improvement Area (I)	= Manager has not mastered this skill and needs further development to bring him or her up to the ''proficient'' level
Not Applicable (NA)	= This skill is not applicable to this manager's level or position

Sales:

_____ 1. Conducts effective sales programs in established and new group room markets.
_____ 2. Achieves sales and catering goals.
_____ 3. Conducts competitive market research.
_____ 4. Performs an effective telemarketing or outside sales program: ____ a. Prospecting
      ____ b. Qualifying
_____ 5. Uses the four-step Marriott Sales Process:
    ____ a. Determines/meets customers needs
    ____ b. Negotiates effectively
    ____ c. Uses key solicitation skills effectively
    ____ d. Lateral selling/account penetration
_____ 6. Develops and implements new market programs:
    ____ a. Knows and reacts to relevant current business trends and local area special events
    ____ b. Is aware and reacts to individual property's (area's) ''stress times''
_____ 7. Adapts to individual property's group market needs.
_____ 8. Creates and implements and follows through on sales promotions.

Communication/Account Servicing/Managing Resources:

_____ 9. Directs internal servicing of groups by:
    ____ a. Obtaining and communicating accurate and total information on a timely basis
    ____ b. Communicating and delegating interdepartmental responsibilities
    ____ c. Maintaining daily group contact
    ____ d. Reacting to and solving in-house group problems

FIGURE 8.4 *Sample sales manager performance appraisal. (Adapted from Marriott Hotels International.)*

_____ e. Reviewing and following-up to ensure customer
        satisfaction
_____ 10. Communicates effectively using verbal and written
      methods.

Marketing Plan:

_____ 11. Contributes to the group portion of the marketing plan:
      _____ a. Positioning statement for each market
      _____ b. Sets specific booking goals for each market
      _____ c. Sets plans and actions for achieving goals
_____ 12. Adapts to changes in the marketing plan.
_____ 13. Monitors the implementation of plans and actions
      according to an effective time schedule.

Comments [Use additional sheet(s) if necessary]

Reviewed Manager's Signature and Date	Reviewer's Signature and Date

FIGURE 8.4 *(continued)*

Professional development is a continuous process that enhances sales and self-esteem for each individual of the entire team.

SUMMARY

Sales management is directing the personal selling efforts of a hospitality establishment. It involves effectively managing the sales process from both an individual and a team perspective. Sales managers need to manage their day-to-day activities; sales teams need to coordinate their efforts. Various aspects of sales management include sales organization, sales account management, recruitment, training and development, goal setting, and performance appraisals.

    Sales organization addresses departmental and individual organizational issues and inventory management. Departmental organizational structure includes a director of sales and marketing with sales managers reporting to the director. Sales managers are typically organized by target market and geographic territory. Sales managers need to plan their individual daily, weekly, and monthly sales activities. In hospitality, a sales manager handles anywhere from 50 to 150 accounts. They often use trace systems to help stay organized.

Inventory management is managing the sale of inventory in a hospitality establishment. Table service restaurants, hotels, cruise lines, and the like, all "manage" their inventory. Most hospitality organizations target multiple markets. Various markets, however, do not necessarily book their reservations on the same planning horizon. Thus, portions of inventory need to be set aside to protect space for selected target audiences. Inventory management reports are produced and reviewed on a regular basis by the director of sales and marketing.

Sales account management involves developing, maintaining, and enhancing customer relationships. Sales managers develop expertise for specific market segments, industry segments, and/or customer accounts. In the 1990s, numerous hotel chains began restructuring their sales teams to account management–based systems.

Recruitment of the sales force deals with the hiring of sales personnel. Good interview skills are an important aspect of the hiring process to uncover the best candidates. Common traits among successful sales account executives include self-confidence, high energy, empathy, enthusiasm, and a strong sense of self-worth. There are several ways to find potential candidates. These include internal job postings within the organization, advertising in the print media and on the Internet offering sales position opportunities, and monitoring the competition for qualified sales personnel.

Training and development is ongoing in hospitality sales and marketing. Inexperienced sales managers need introductory training in the sales process and in sales management. Experienced sales managers require training and development in identified need areas. Strengths need to be honed; weaknesses need to be strengthened. Need areas typically include sales process skills development, sales management skills development, time management skills development, and computer literacy skills development. It is the job of the director of sales and marketing to identify, evaluate, and act on the specific needs of each individual member of the sales team. Both internal and external sources are used for sales training and development.

Goal setting is an important aspect of sales. Expectations and goals need to be stated clearly. Most sales departments have individual and team goals that can be set in several ways. These include revenue goals, high-versus-low-demand-period booking goals, current account versus new account booking goals, and market share and RevPAR goals. Often more than one of these are part of the goal-setting structure. Individuals and teams are recognized and rewarded for goal attainment. Both monetary and nonmonetary forms of recognition are awarded for meeting and/or exceeding set goals.

Performance appraisals are conducted with each member of a sales team, typically on an annual basis. It is through performance appraisals that strengths and areas of skill development needs are identified. Sales managers are rated as strong, proficient, or improvement needed on various aspects important to successful selling. As a result of the performance appraisal, a development plan is put in place. The plan will include specific goals, action steps, and a timeline for each step of the plan. Professional development is a continuous process in hospitality sales and marketing.

DISCUSSION QUESTIONS

1. Weekly sales meetings are very much a part of a sales department's organizational structure and are important for effective communication within the department. Discuss.
2. Every account should have a trace date. Why?
3. Describe the essence of inventory management. Why is it particularly important for hospitality establishments?
4. What is sales account management? Is it a new concept in hospitality sales and marketing? Discuss.
5. How can one go about finding good potential candidates for a sales position opening?
6. Several sources are available for the training and development of sales managers in hospitality. Discuss.
7. Describe what is meant by fair market share (FMS), actual market share (AMS), and RevPAR.
8. Do the calculations for FMS, AMS, and RevPAR for the occupancy statistics presented in Table 8.5. Do your calculations match those presented in the table?
9. What are performance appraisals, what do they include, and why are they done?

NOTES

1. Dina Long, "Hyatt to Realign Reps," *Business Travel News*, July 25, 1994, p. 8.
2. Harley A. Mayerson, "Better Interviews Net Better Salespeople," *Hotel & Resort Industry*, May 1994, p. 14.
3. Ibid.

Chapter 9

Sales and Technology: Part A
Management and Operations

> **LEARNING OBJECTIVES**
>
> 1. *To better understand how computer technology is used in hospitality management and operations from a sales and marketing perspective*
> 2. *To become familiar with sales office automation in a hospitality setting*
> 3. *To better understand yield management technology*
> 4. *To become familiar with point-of-sale systems and guest service technology*
> 5. *To better understand property management systems and their relationship to hospitality sales and marketing*

Cyberspace, search engines, Internet, e-mail, seamless, PMS, World Wide Web, multimedia, POS, Web site, browser, network, GDS—all are common terminology in today's vernacular of the computer tech world. Each of us in hospitality is at various points on the learning curve to understand much less comprehend what it is all about. And once we cross a major hurdle—boom—new technology comes out and we start anew. Confusion and frustration abounds. Is it worth it? Yes. In the end, it is the hospitality customer who benefits. Better systems means better sales and service. If today's computer technology is an answer to improving our systems, then let's get on with it.

In this chapter, Part A of Sales and Technology, various aspects of management and operations as they relate to technology are addressed (see Table 9.1). These include sales office automation, yield management, point-of-sale systems, guest services, and property management systems.

The next chapter, Part B, looks at reaching out to the hospitality customer through sales and technology. These areas include central reservation systems, global distribution systems, database marketing, sales support tools, the Internet, and the World Wide Web.

These various facets of sales and technology are growing in use and sophistication in the hospitality industry. Following is a more detailed discussion of the management and operations side of sales and technology.

SALES OFFICE AUTOMATION

Sales office automation is essentially automating various aspects of the hospitality sales process and sales management that were formerly done manually. For example, sales call reports were typically written by hand or typed. Inventory management for guest rooms and function space was done manually. Sophisticated calculators were used to produce monthly reports tracking market segment revenues and occupancies, sales manager booking activity, and so forth. Today, in many hospitality organizations, this is now done by computer. It is important to note that the basic tenet of sales has not changed. What has changed is the process and tools used to get the job done more efficiently and effectively.

The advent of computer technology allows the sales force to spend more time with customers, which is where they should be. Less time is spent filling out, submitting, and filing reports manually. It is done automatically with a keystroke or two. The new central location for guest room and function room inventory is on the sales manager's desk, readily accessible through his or her computer terminal, and not physically located around the corner in the

---

TABLE 9.1   *Overview of Hospitality Sales and Technology*

Part A: Management and Operations

Sales office automation
Yield management technology
Point-of-sale systems
Guest service technology
Property management systems

Part B: The Hospitality Customer

Central reservation systems
Global distribution systems
Database marketing
Sales support tools
Internet and World Wide Web

---

main office in a large, bulky, cumbersome logbook. Through the use of modems, it travels, too, in the salesperson's computer laptop or notebook. When meeting with a client on the road, the once-common phrase, "I will check space availability when I get back to the office," is no longer necessary for those on line.

The accuracy of tentative booking entries is improved as well. With a manual system, **double bookings** are all too common. A double booking is when two salespeople simultaneously book the same space for two different clients. With computer technology, it just can't happen; good software does not allow it.

There are a number of companies that market software for hospitality sales office automation. These include Newmarket Software Systems, Fidelio, CLS, and others. Miracle III (developed by National Guest Systems Corporation), for example, is a system designed specifically for function room inventory management. Sales managers "can tell at a glance which rooms are available, which bookings have been confirmed or are tentative, make changes to banqueting requirements and dates, create floor plans and immediately access information about their various accounts."[1]

Newmarket has a software product called Delphi designed for sales, marketing, and catering operations. Shown in Figure 9.1 is a graphical representation of some of the component parts of this software package. It can be purchased modularly to fit the specific needs and requirements of a particular hospitality establishment. Delphi is a good example of software available in the marketplace, and following is a brief description of each of its programs.

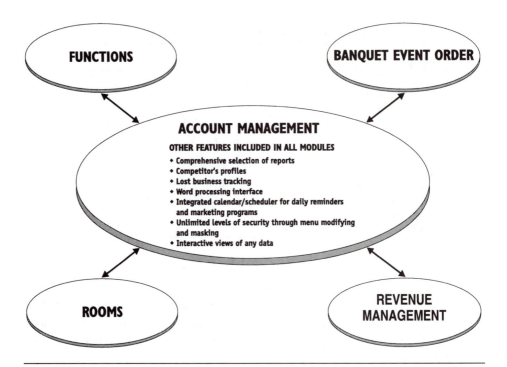

FIGURE 9.1 *Delphi sales and catering automation software system. (Courtesy of Newmarket Software Systems, Inc. © 1995–1998 Newmarket Software Systems, Inc. Reprinted with permission.)*

Account Management Programs

The account management program includes several features such as contact management, activity log, folders, traces, and competitor profiles. The contact management section gives instant access to address and phone information for all contacts entered into the program. The activity log is for entering sales call reports, site inspection correspondence, and any other activity input by the sales account executive. The folders section sorts accounts based on specific criteria set by the user such as target market, geographic territory, sales volume, and so forth. With a single keystroke one can print, edit, or export data from the folders section to another database on the system. The traces section replaces manual reminders for follow-up action on traced accounts. "To do" lists can also be created as they relate to specific accounts and/or bookings.

Competitor profiles, once input, can be called up at any time for a quick look at their major strengths and weaknesses. Tracking lost business to competitors can be compiled as well. This helps identify patterns that may develop over time, such as one competitor, in particular, that appears to attract a certain type of account.

Rooms Program

The Delphi rooms program tracks information such as tentative and definite group bookings, transient business contract accounts, average rates, and the sales manager responsible for each account. This program can shift an existing booking to a new date. It can also duplicate a booking for future dates such as a three-day corporate training seminar to be repeated every three weeks over the next four months. This feature, in particular, eliminates the time spent making repetitive entries when the process is done manually. Inventory reports of all kinds are easily produced with software such as this.

Functions Program

Similar to the rooms program, the functions program helps control function room inventory, and is referred to as the function diary. The diary is set up such that both sales and catering managers can reserve various function rooms for meetings, receptions, banquets, and so forth.

The program also includes turn-time buffers and capacity checks. A turn-time buffer is the time set aside to allow for a function room to be changed from one style of setup to another. For example, if a function room is scheduled for a meeting to be held from 9:00 A.M. to 12:00 P.M. and to be set in a classroom-style, that same room cannot be booked for a 12:00 P.M. luncheon. Time needs to be given to reset the room in a banquet-style setup. In this case, a luncheon scheduled for 12:15 P.M. would be doable, a 12:30 P.M. start time would be best, especially if the menu calls for a preset appetizer.

Capacity checks are warning signals that appear on the screen if the number of attendees scheduled to attend an event exceeds the capacity of the function room assigned for the event. These types of errors, sadly to say, are frequent in manual systems.

Banquet Event Orders Program

Banquet event orders (BEOs) are specific to the catering side of hospitality. BEOs are prepared for every function that includes food or beverage such as receptions, banquets, refreshment breaks, and so on. Typical items that need to be specified include menu details, room setup, linen, china, glassware, flatware, centerpeices, and so forth. There is space in the program to input any special arrangements or unusual requests.

The Delphi software has the capability to produce custom menu options for clients who make such requests. The program can also maintain a food and/or beverage inventory tracking system that notifies a catering manager if a selected menu item is unavailable or out of season.

Revenue Management Program

The Delphi yield management program essentially helps the sales or catering manager "sell smarter." In other words, this program helps to analyze a potential piece of business from several perspectives including total revenue generation, overall profitability, best date to book (depending on what is already on the books), and so forth. As suggested by the management at Newmarket:

> The module enables a property to analyze a piece of business from many different angles to assure you are getting the best possible rate based on time of year, amount of business already booked, number in party and type of function. It also empowers you with the tools you need to document that profitability to management.[2]

Figure 9.2 provides an overview of some of the information that Delphi reports can generate.

National Sales Automation

Thus far, we have addressed sales automation from a single-property, unit-level perspective. Technology is now available for interproperty communication for chain operations. National sales account executives at companies using this technology can access inventory status reports at all unit-level properties without having to contact the hotel directly via telephone, fax, or e-mail. Software companies such as Newmarket Software Systems and National Guest Systems have created software to do this very task. Newmarket has developed Global Delphi, which is a multiproperty sales coordination system designed specifically for off-property, regional, and corporate headquarters sales offices. National Guest Systems has introduced Visual Miracle, "a windows-based sales-and-catering system [that includes] an Internet connection, tracking of multiproperty hotels and tracking of transient business."[3]

Partnerships among buyers and sellers in hospitality sales are emerging as well. As reported in *Hotel & Motel Management:*

REPORTS

Reports let you print information stored in, and created by, Delphi. Just select the type of report you want, choose the dates or information you want in the report, and let Delphi do the rest.

Here are a few of the benefits of Delphi's reports:

- Detailed reports provide senior management with a snapshot of revenue forecasting, staff performance, sales, and profitability.

- Activity reports keep staff abreast of what's going on at your property.

- Account and contact recap reports help sales staff plan sales trips, sales blitzes, and mass mailings.

- Cover count and event summary reports provide useful information for tracking and forecasting catering revenue.

- All Delphi reports give you the choice of viewing them on screen or printing them.

FIGURE 9.2 *Overview of Delphi software program. (Courtesy of Newmarket Software Systems, Inc. Reprinted with permission.)*

Shared global account information. That's what today's sales-and-catering taskmasters are looking for. But how do regional sales offices, corporate headquarters and individual properties share information on group rooms business and catering events when disparate systems (or perhaps no systems) are being used?

One solution may be the Ajenis Project—a partnership of Starwood Hotels & Resorts Starwood, Hyatt Hotels Corp., Marriott International, the American Society of Association Executives, Meeting Professionals International and PlanSoft Holdings—which is designed to facilitate communication via the Internet between meeting planners and properties. . . .

Pat Welch, divisional director of national sales for Sheraton, is a member of the Ajenis planning committee. According to Welch, this project enables Sheraton to work with its peers to find solutions to universal sales force automation concerns.

"We want to do all we can to improve customer intimacy and speed the communication process between our customers and our sales force, our customers and the hotel, and the sales force and the hotel," Welch said.[4]

The goal is to improve and speed communication of buyers' needs and wants to a multitude of suppliers simultaneously. As stated by PlanSoft president, Ed Tromczynski, "[m]eeting planners will soon be able to send out requests for proposal to all hotels using this system, regardless of the hotel's sales-and-catering software solution."[5] Once again, the objective is to benefit the customer, including the preliminary planning stage for event planners.

The Virtual Office

Current technology allows today's sales account executives to spend less time in the office and more time on the road traveling to their *customer's* office. The notebook computer helps make this happen. The on-line sales executive can tap into most information databases at the property level and/or at corporate headquarters to clarify issues and/or book new business on the spot. In the consulting industry, for example, companies such as Ernst & Young have done away with permanent offices for their sales force and consultants altogether. Not surprisingly, this practice is called **hoteling**. When a sales manager checks in to his or her home base at headquarters, he or she is assigned a cubicle or temporary office for the duration of the stay. A senior manager in the information technology consulting division of Ernst & Young describes it this way:

> I'm usually with my clients four or five days a week. When I need to go into Ernst & Young to attend meetings or concentrate on getting new business, I call our "concierge," the hoteling administrator, and let him know when I'm coming and how long I'll be there. He checks his computer to see which offices are free, assigns me a space, puts my name on the door, and programs the phone for my extension. When I arrive I get any papers I need from my locker and plug in my notebook computer into the network, and I'm ready to start working.[6]

The hospitality industry is starting to move in this direction. Many national sales account executives at Holiday Inn, Marriott, and Hyatt, for example, use their homes as their "permanent office."

Is our industry getting connected? Yes, it is.

YIELD MANAGEMENT TECHNOLOGY

Yield management is essentially revenue management. Originating in the airline industry, yield (or revenue) management is also widely practiced in other high-fixed-cost, fixed-capacity industries such as lodging, car rental agencies, and cruise lines. The basic tenet is that generating revenue that exceeds the marginal cost of providing a service is better than no revenue at all—such as letting a guest room at a lodging establishment go empty, letting an automobile at a car rental agency sit idle, or letting a cabin on a cruise ship go unsold on departure. In other words, selling your perishable product at a discounted price is, in most instances, better than not selling it at all. As stated by Sheryl Kimes in the *Cornell Quarterly*, yield management "is a method that can help a firm sell the right inventory unit to the right customer at the right time and for the right price."[7]

Yield management entails identifying low-, medium-, and high-demand periods (or peak and off-peak periods) and adjusting rate structures accordingly. Such forecasts are initially based on an analysis of historical data. For the theme park industry in Orlando, Florida, for example, there are two peak seasons—winter and summer. Winter is attractive for the leisure market based in northern climates, especially during winter school breaks and the Easter holiday period. Summer is attractive to vacationing families when school systems are no longer in session. The availability of discounted rates during peak seasons is limited, or nonexistent. Discounted rates start to become available as the peak season begins to drop off. A good yield management system determines the parameters of peak and off-peak periods, allowing discounted rate availability to emerge as the hospitality establishment moves from peak to off-peak periods.

The concept of yield management has been around for quite some time, that is, the practice of offering discounted rates during off-peak periods to boost occupancies and increase revenues. For over a decade, many in hospitality have recognized that focusing on revenue management in the short run can be a key to bottom-line profitability in the long run. The advent of computer technology has enhanced the sophistication of yield management and its use in the industry is growing.

Several software companies market PC-based yield management systems. Highlights of such software include the ability to deal with both transient and group market segments, sales incentive and management, and volume accounts. Examples of modules included in typical software are

- Transient revenue maximization
- Group revenue maximization
- Hotel availability
- Electronic sales diary
- Forecasting
- Sales incentive program
- Configuration and utilities
- Reporting capabilities

Software systems are able to track reservations and will "open" or "close" discounted rates for various market segments depending on the volume of sales booked to date and the rates confirmed for these reservations. It is a fluid interactive system, continuously monitoring daily sales booking activity. Prior to computer technology, this task was monumental and a bit overwhelming. Much of the opening and closing of rate categories were largely done by educated guesswork. Today, much of that guesswork or "intuitive hunch" is eliminated.

Yield results are typically measured in terms of revenue per available unit of inventory (or RevPAR as discussed in Chapter 8). If a 100-room hotel sells 80 rooms for a given night at an average rate of $75, the yield for that night would be $60. If 90 rooms are sold at an average rate of $70, the yield is $63. If 95 rooms are sold at an average rate of $60, the yield is $57. (See Table 9.2 for the calculations.) The message here is that a higher average rate per room does not necessarily imply a larger yield. Overall occupancy is a major variable, too. Selling some rooms at a discounted rate when predicted occupancies are lower than expected can often mean *higher* revenues, not lower profits. Salespeople's goals are often set in terms of yield. For example, a goal might be set to increase yield from $60 to $63 per room over a given period of demand.

Yield management can be practiced in hospitality because of the varying price sensitivities of differing segments of demand both within and among business and leisure travelers. Some (but not all) business travelers, for example, are more sensitive to the timing of a trip than to the cost of making that trip. Some vacationers, on the other hand, are more sensitive to the price than to the timing of the planned vacation. Thus, many hospitality establishments vary their rate structure depending on anticipated levels of demand from various market segments for the period in question.

Some vacationers headed for Disney World very much *want* to take that trip in February when there is five feet of snow in the backyard. This segment is ready and willing to pay peak season price to escape the frigid north, and is affectionately known as the "snow bird" segment in the south. Others may

---

TABLE 9.2   *Sample Yield Calculations*

Number of Rooms Sold	Average Rate	Guest Room Capactiy	Yield
80	$75	100	$60
90	$70	100	$63
95	$60	100	$57

Yield Calculations

80 × $75/100 = $60 yield
90 × $70/100 = $63 yield
95 × $60/100 = $57 yield

opt to wait until April or May, still wanting to visit the renowned theme park, but preferring to do so when the cost is somewhat lower. Based in part on historical data, hospitality organizations can estimate or predict these travel patterns and set their yield management systems accordingly. Once in place, the system can adjust rate structures based on actual demand, which may vary somewhat from the forecasted estimate.

Yield management is not a crystal ball. Yet it can help smooth out demand. When implemented properly, it can enhance revenue as well as customer satisfaction. Loyal patrons will return when they feel they have received fair value for the right product at the right time at the right place at the right price.

POINT-OF-SALE SYSTEMS

Food and beverage **point-of-sale (POS) systems** are abundant in hotels, restaurants, and institutions across the hospitality foodservice industry. Not only are they easy to install and use, they improve the accuracy of menu orders and billing and systematically keep track of items sold for reporting purposes. These reports, analyzed by management, identify daily revenues, customer counts, contribution margins, average checks, popular items, and not-so-popular items.

There are a number of software programs designed specifically for foodservice management. These include MenuSoft by MenuSoft Systems, Prohost by Micros, NOVA-GRATUIT by NOVA Information Systems, and Advantage Series by Remanco International. Advantage Series offers two types of programs. The Spectrum Advantage system is designed for medium-sized hotels and restaurants. The Vision Advantage system is intended for larger hotels and restaurants and is capable of supporting 90+ terminals throughout the establishment.

Developed by Digital Dining of Australia, MenuSoft was the first PC-based system to be marketed in the United States. It is interesting to note the history of this pioneering venture in North America:

> Digital Dining was originally developed and installed in Australia in 1978. The product was introduced in the United States in 1984, and the Virginia corporation, MenuSoft, was formed. In 1984, the first U.S. Digital Dining system was installed at a small Washington, D.C. tavern with three workstations. At that time, PC-based systems were virtually unknown. The hospitality industry was using proprietary cash registers.
>
> Today, Digital Dining has emerged as an industry leader and is installed in independent restaurants, chain restaurants, country clubs, racetracks, institutions, hotels, casinos, fast-food outlets and virtually every type of foodservice concept.[8]

Various POS software programs offer many features in addition to those outlined previously. These include labor scheduling, the paging of patrons when their table is ready, credit card verification, economical monochrome keyboards or color-graphic touch screens, and the monitoring of server tips and gratuities. Also, "NOVA is working on a product known as SmartCards [for restaurants], which can be used like cash for purchases. Frequent-diner or frequent-stay point accumulations, for example, can be stored on a magnetic-stripe card for redemption by the customer at the point-of-sale."[9] POS systems, similar to sales office automation, help managers and servers—the sales account executives of the foodservice business—work smarter. The real bottom line, of course, is better service and enhanced customer satisfaction.

GUEST SERVICE TECHNOLOGY

Guest service technology has proliferated in hospitality, especially in the lodging industry. Recall that step 5 of the sales process is service delivery. Service delivery in lodging involves many facets including check-in, check-out, and in-room services. Each of these lends itself quite well to computer technology and is discussed next.

Automated Check-In

Automated check-in for hotels was first introduced in the early 1990s. As reported in *Hotels* at that time:

> Hotel check-in procedures entered a new stage in March [1994] as both Marriott and Hyatt announced tests of new technology, which they have been trying out since the beginning of the year. Marriott is using hand-held terminals. Hyatt is using self-service machines, much like automated-teller machines at banks.[10]

This service is available to guests who have made reservations and have preregistration privileges such as members of Marriott's or Hyatt's frequent-guest programs. Guest room keys are obtained from a hotel staff member stationed in the lobby or at the airport where check-in can also take place. Keys can also be dispensed by kiosk machines in the lobby at hotels that use this type of service.

Fast-food restaurants are experimenting with similar "check-in" procedures as well. At the time of this writing, Taco Bell and Burger King are testing touch-screen systems to be used by a patron to place an order. At Taco Bell, "a customer first selects the category of food she wishes to order (e.g., categories include burritos, tacos, drinks) and then she selects specific items in that category (e.g., chicken soft taco, regular beef taco). This process is repeated until the order is complete."[11] The machine prints out a ticket with the items selected and includes the familiar order number as well. The customer then proceeds to the counter to pick up the order and pay for the meal. Simple.

Automated check-in, however, is not for everybody. Some guests are very comfortable with this technology; others are not. Some guests want fast, efficient, high-tech, nonpersonal service, while others prefer human interaction. The following excerpt from the *Wall Street Journal* helps illustrate this point:

> After a busy day of shopping and sightseeing, Karen Showman was grateful to come across an automated check-in machine at an Embassy Suites hotel in Alexandria, VA. A long line of people was waiting to check in, but no one was using the kiosk. "I remember thinking when I was done, 'Why are these people still in line?' " says Mrs. Showman, a homemaker from Smithsburg, Md. "People would walk right past it to go to the front desk."
>
> It could be that these people didn't realize what the kiosk was for, but it's also possible that they were travelers who choose interaction over automation. "I prefer to go to the front desk," says Jimmy Lake, a petroleum advisor with Carpoven Inc. in Caracas, Venezuela, who was staying recently at the Dallas/Fort Worth Airport Hyatt hotel. "I like to know the people I'm dealing with because you can tell what kind of service you're going to get."[12]

Automated Check-Out

Check-out lines at hotels have trimmed down dramatically with the introduction of in-room guest check-out. The guest simply turns on the television, clicks to the hotel's check-out channel, reviews his or her bill for accuracy, and checks-out. No lines, no hassles, and off to the airport to catch a flight. Receipts for credit card billings can be mailed on request. At many hotels, a copy of the billing charges to date is also slipped under the guest room door in the early morning of the scheduled departure date. Although not an official receipt, this gives the guest a printout of the various charges.

In-Room Services

Today, hotel guest services have gone well beyond express check-in and check-out services. At many hotels, guests can now readily access TV-based interactive guest information services. Providers of in-room entertainment and information services are numerous. Players such as InfoTravel, City Key,

LodgeNet Entertainment, On Command Video, CNN Text, and WebTV Networks offer various technology-driven in-room guest services to hotels. Following are some highlights of these service delivery product offerings.

InfoTravel and City Key are in-room programs giving guests access to information for the local area. City Key offers information on local dining, shopping, attractions, sports, recreation, and entertainment. InfoTravel provides four categories of multimedia interactive options including (1) places to eat, (2) things to see and do, (3) services, and (4) getting around.

On Command Video lets in-room guests view various movie options when it is convenient for the guest. Instead of arranging his or her schedule around a preset time for a particular movie, the *guest* chooses when to watch a film or documentary.

CNN Text is "essentially a newspaper that can be read on the guest-room television. News and other information are available 24 hours a day, and updated constantly. To access the text, guests turn on the terminal, tune to CNN International, then press the teletext button on the remote control."[13] It is widely used in Europe where teletext television sets are the standard. English is the primary language for CNN Text. However, headlines and news summaries can be obtained in the European language of selected major national newspapers.

Many guests can access the Internet through their in-room television sets. This access includes sending and receiving e-mail, checking stock quotes, making future hotel reservations, and surfing the World Wide Web. The Radisson Encore in Sioux Falls, South Dakota, was the "first hotel to have every guestroom equipped with in-room Internet service via the hotel television and the LodgeNet Entertainment system."[14] Shown in Figure 9.3, the LodgeNet system also provides movies, games, languages, and so forth. On Command Video and WebTV have hooked up and offer similar in-room Internet access services. Tut Systems is another player offering high-speed Internet connections to guest rooms and to hotel convention facilities (see Figure 9.4). These types of services are attractive to both business and leisure travelers, and are increasingly sought by hoteliers to offer to their guests across the United States and Canada. Regulations on Internet access vary from country to country, presenting challenges to international hotels wanting to provide this service. As noted in *Hotels*, "[w]hile Germany tries to restrict Internet access, some countries in the Middle East and Asia may outright forbid it."[15]

Emerging technology for in-room guest services is, needless to say, a common topic at hospitality conferences and conventions. Shown in Figure 9.5 is an excerpt from a well-written article reporting on guest service technology discussions at recently held American Hotel & Motel Association

FIGURE 9.3 *LodgeNet Entertainment in-room guest services. (Courtesy of LodgeNet Entertainment Corporation. Reprinted with permission.)*

(AH&MA) conferences.[16] In short, predictions are made that thumbprints will replace electronic door keys and robots will carry luggage to the guest room. Additionally, should a guest prefer a different guest room decor, just push the button, and—voila!—the Western-style motif is now a Japanese-style design. Will virtual reality become "real" reality in the not too distant future?

PROPERTY MANAGEMENT SYSTEMS

Property management systems (PMSs) first entered the hospitality industry in the early 1970s. Their purpose is to facilitate and expedite interdepartmental communications in lodging establishments Originally, the computer-based PMS connected back-office accounting to front-office registration and billing procedures. Today, it is a highly integrated system connecting sales, reservations, front office, accounting, housekeeping, purchasing, POS, and other facets of hotel operations. For example, when the sales department

Internet Access for Your Guests

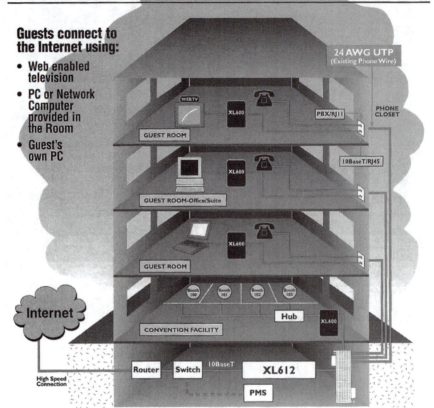

Guests connect to the Internet using:

- Web enabled television
- PC or Network Computer provided in the Room
- Guest's own PC

Offer a high speed Internet connection to every room in your hotel with the Tut Systems plug-n-play network extenders. Tut Systems shows you how to increase your occupancy rate and increase your revenue/room/night by 10% to 30%. Visit our web site at http://www.tutsys.com/hotels to learn more about Tut's XL600 family of 10Mbps Ethernet network extenders.

See us at

HITEC
97

 TUT SYSTEMS

2495 Estand Way | Pleasant Hill, CA 94523
510.682.6510 | 510.682.4125 fax
www.tutsys.com

For more information, contact Jason Johnson, ext 150

For FREE information circle **47**

FIGURE 9.4 *Tut Systems Internet access for hotel guests. (Courtesy of Tut Systems. Reprinted with permission.)*

Two years ago at the AH&MA conference in Denver, 20 PCs were set up for people to list technological ideas they want to see implemented in a hotel in year 2020. About 330 people from all segments of the industry participated. They were asked to comment in four areas: check-in, check-out process; guestrooms; guest services; and their wildest fantasies. The most telling result of this survey was that many of the ideas exist and are already in place at hotels, such as express check-in, in-room faxes, doors that lock with credit cards, and electronic key entries.

At the AH&MA conference this past spring, about 800 delegates stopped by the virtual reality booth, Hotel 2020, to experience the future. By donning VR helmets, delegates experienced being a guest who checks in using his or her thumbprint. A robot carries the luggage to the room and the guest uses his or her thumbprint to gain electronic entry. The guest exclaims he or she had the same Western-style room the previous week and then changes the decor with a voice command that activates holograms of a Japanese decor on the walls. While this vision may appear to be a quantum leap ahead of what is possible, the technology exists. . . .

While hotels are not expected to reach a Star Trek holodeck experience anytime soon, the future is sure to be dynamic, reflective of changing technologies, lifestyles, and workstyles.

FIGURE 9.5 *Excerpt from "Just Around the Corner."* (*Source:* Kathleen Cassedy, "Just Around the Corner," *Lodging,* January 1996, pp. 44 and 46.)

confirms a group booking, the reservation department automatically gets the room block details. Or, when the reservation department makes a guest room reservation, the front office will automatically get the detailed requirements for this reservation on the day of arrival.

In the U.S. market alone, there are over 80 suppliers of property management systems. CLS SOFTWARE is one such player and key features of its PMS are shown in Figure 9.6. As can be seen, this system automates and integrates such areas as front office, guest history, housekeeping, yield management, and back-office accounting. Encore Systems is another supplier and its PMS is installed in over 1400 Holiday Inns across North America.

Some hotel companies develop their own customized systems using a commercial PMS as their base. For example, Radisson has developed "Harmony," its own PMS, which is "based on the front-office PMS from Fidelio [of Munich, Germany], modified to meet Radisson requirements."[17] Other

No Property Management System Supports Your Staff Like CLS

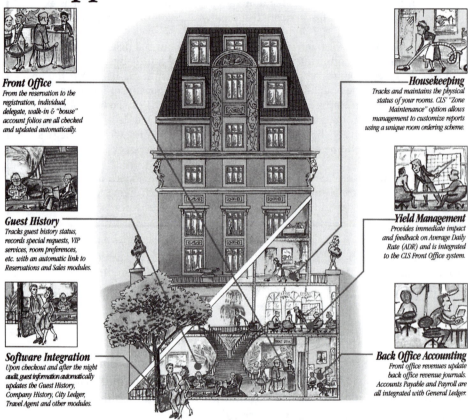

Front Office
From the reservation to the registration, individual, delegate, walk-in & "house" account folios are all checked and updated automatically.

Guest History
Tracks guest history status, records special requests, VIP services, room preferences, etc. with an automatic link to Reservations and Sales modules.

Software Integration
Upon checkout and after the night audit, guest information automatically updates the Guest History, Company History, City Ledger, Travel Agent and other modules.

Housekeeping
Tracks and maintains the physical status of your rooms. CLS' "Zone Maintenance" option allows management to customize reports using a unique room ordering scheme.

Yield Management
Provides immediate impact and feedback on Average Daily Rate (ADR) and is integrated to the CLS Front Office system.

Back Office Accounting
Front office revenues update back office revenue journals. Accounts Payable and Payroll are all integrated with General Ledger.

Your guests may not be able to see your **CLS Property Management System** at work, but they will certainly feel the results!

CLS Software can direct your staff in their day-to-day duties throughout your property making them more efficient in their delivery of services to your guests.

From the registration desk to the cashier window, your guests will feel pampered by your pleasantly efficient staff and improved guest services.

CLS' Property Management System is a result of over 20 years of on-going software development within the hospitality industry. Experience with over 2,000 installations has contributed to the sophistication and ease of use for which **CLS** Software has become known.

CLS' seamlessly integrated modules provide your staff with the most feature rich PMS package available. Improve productivity and increase occupancy – automate your property with **CLS Software** today.

CLS SOFTWARE
DIVISION OF MAI®

CLS SOFTWARE
9600 JERONIMO RD.
IRVINE, CA 92718
800 -711- 4CLS
(714) 580-6821 FAX
*Software, Hardware, Networking,
Support Services for the Hospitality Industry*

FIGURE 9.6 *CLS SOFTWARE property management system. (Courtesy of CLS SOFTWARE, a division of MAI. Reprinted with permission.)*

hotel companies custom design their entire property management system such as Marriott Hotels, Resorts, and Suites.

Sales office automation systems, such as Delphi and Miracle III described earlier in this chapter, are usually linked to the property PMS. The same holds true for point-of-sales and yield management systems, too. For example, Encore Systems, as part of its PMS package, offers to interface the Fisher Restaurant System point-of-sales program to hotels that want this feature. Indeed, Encore Systems "has acquired exclusive distribution rights within the hotel industry of the point-of-sale system from Fisher Restaurant Systems [of Atlanta, Georgia]. Encore plans to market the POS system under the Encore name to hotels worldwide."[18]

The reservation portion (and increasingly the yield management portion) of a property PMS in chain operations is linked with the hotel company's central reservation system (CRS). Central reservation systems are an important aspect of sales and technology and are addressed in the next chapter.

SUMMARY

This chapter looked at the management and operations side of how technology is impacting hospitality sales and marketing. Areas discussed included sales office automation, yield management, point-of-sale systems, guest services, and property management systems.

Sales office automation has grown tremendously since the early 1990s. It essentially deals with automating various aspects of the sales process and sales management that were formerly done manually. These areas include sales call reports, trace dates, tentative and definite booking entries, inventory management, and monthly reports. The advent of technology allows sales managers more time to spend with their customers. Less time is now spent on the administrative tasks of filling out, submitting, and filing reports. Although these tasks are important and need to be done, they should be done quickly and efficiently. Good technology lets this happen.

Yield management is essentially revenue management. The objective is to maximize revenues during both peak and off-peak periods of demand. Technology has made it possible to monitor more closely the sale of guest room inventory. In low periods of demand, yield management systems allow rooms to be sold at discounted rates, when necessary, as opposed to not being sold at all. Conversely, in high periods of demand, fewer rooms, if any, are sold at a discounted rate. With yield management, revenues are enhanced by responding to the ups and downs of supply and demand in the marketplace.

Point-of-sale (POS) systems are used by many in the hospitality food-service industry. They systematically record and analyze daily sales of menu items. POS systems automatically prepare bills, calculate average checks, and monitor popular and not-so-popular items. In hotels, many POS systems automatically post foodservice charges to the guest's room bill. Point-of-sale technology is timely and accurate, enhancing customer satisfaction and management efficiency.

Guest service technology continues to evolve in hospitality. Service delivery is a key aspect of the sales process and technology lends itself well to customers' on-premise experience. Automated check-in and check-out at hotels is commonplace today for guests desiring this service. Technology-based in-room services are also available at many lodging establishments. Guests can now readily access TV-based interactive guest information services, view on-command movie and video entertainment, and access the Internet and World Wide Web. It is predicted that thumbprints may soon replace electronic door locks. Who knows what is next.

Property management systems are integrated computer systems connecting sales, reservations, front office, accounting, housekeeping, POS, and other facets of hotel operations. Hotels can purchase these systems from outside vendors or create their own in-house systems, which has been done by some of the larger hotel companies such as Radisson and Marriott. For chain hotels such as these, the reservation portion of the PMS is linked with its central reservation system, which has come to be known as the CRS. The CRS and other aspects of sales and technology that reach out to the customer are the subject of the next chapter.

DISCUSSION QUESTIONS

1. Discuss the impact of sales office automation on the hospitality sales process and sales management.
2. What is "hoteling"?
3. The advent of computer technology has enhanced the sophistication and effectiveness of yield management and its use in the hospitality industry is growing. Discuss.
4. What advantages do POS systems offer the hospitality foodservice side of the business?
5. Discuss how guest service technology has improved service delivery in hospitality including check-in, check-out, and in-room services.

6. Property management systems facilitate and expedite interdepartmental communications. Discuss.

NOTES

1. "Westin Stamford Modernizes Room-Booking Process," *Hotel & Motel Management*, November 6, 1995, p. 119.
2. Delphi Brochure, Newmarket Software Systems, Inc., Portsmouth, NH, 1996.
3. "Tech Talk: National Guest Unveils Visual Miracle," *Hotel & Motel Management*, April 7, 1997, p. 53.
4. Barbara A. Worcester, "Sales Automation Across the Nation," *Hotel & Motel Management*, April 7, 1997, p. 53.
5. Ibid., p. 56
6. Alison L. Sprout, "Moving into the Virtual Office," *Fortune*, May 2, 1994, p. 103.
7. Sheryl E. Kimes, "Perceived Fairness of Yield Management," *Cornell Quarterly*, February 1994, p. 23.
8. "MenuSoft," *Hotel & Motel Management*, August 12, 1996, p. 34.
9. Susan Bard Hall, "Tableside Technology," *Hotel & Motel Management*, June 17, 1996, p. 62.
10. "Marriott, Hyatt Test New Check-In Procedures," *Hotels*, May 1994, p. 76.
11. Stowe Shoemaker, "Scripts: Precursor of Consumer Expectations," *The Cornell Quarterly*, February 1996, p. 46.
12. Jon Bigness, "Impersonal Touch: More Hotels Automate Front Desk," *Wall Street Journal*, June 18, 1996, pp. B1 and B12.
13. James Carper, "News Service Keeps Travelers Informed," *Hotels*, February 1994, p. 64.
14. "LodgeNet Expands Its Services," *Hotel & Motel Management*, March 17, 1997, p. 40.
15. Steven Shundich, "Guestroom Internet Experiments Abound," *Hotels*, February 1997, p. 62.
16. Kathleen Cassedy, "Just Around the Corner," *Lodging*, January 1996, pp. 41–42, 44, and 46.
17. "Harmony: A Model PMS," *CKC Report*, October 1994, p. 4.
18. Ibid., p. 6.

Chapter 10

Sales and Technology: Part B
The Hospitality Customer

LEARNING OBJECTIVES

1. *To better understand how computer technology is used to reach out to the hospitality customer*
2. *To become familiar with the technological aspects of hospitality sales and marketing, which include:*
   - *Central reservation systems*
   - *Global distribution systems*
   - *Database marketing*
   - *Sales support tools*
   - *The Internet and the World Wide Web*

The previous chapter, Part A, looked at the managerial and operational aspects of sales and technology. In this chapter, Part B, we move on to the various ways in which we reach out to the hospitality customer. These include central reservation systems, global distribution systems, database marketing, sales support tools, and the Internet and World Wide Web. Following is a more detailed discussion of each.

CENTRAL RESERVATION SYSTEMS

The **central reservation system (CRS)** has become a mainstay for booking reservations at chain hotels, car rental companies, airlines, cruise lines, and now even restaurants. In the lodging industry, for example, total rooms sold through CRS sales has grown from less than 10% in the early 1980s to over 50 percent in the 1990s.[1] In other words, growth in sales activity through the use of central reservation systems has risen dramatically over the past decade.

The CRS is essentially a data bank that keeps track of inventory for the entire chain. The familiar toll-free 800 telephone number is the principal vehicle that individuals and travel agents use to connect to a central reservation system. (Computer electronic access is also common and will be discussed shortly.)

The reservation component of a property management system at a unit-level operation is, in most cases, connected directly to the CRS. Thus, for instance, one can make a reservation directly with a hotel or through the hotel chain's 800 number. In theory, the same rate should be quoted depending on space availability, forecasted occupancies, yield management systems in place, and so forth. However, studies have shown this is not always the case, and hotels, in particular, are working on this issue.

Many chain hotel companies have several product lines and/or multiple brands under their umbrella (see Table 4.5). Some offer one 800 number for access to their central reservation system such as Howard Johnson and Holiday Inn. Others have separate 800 numbers for each of their product offerings such as Marriott and Choice Hotels International. Table 10.1 shows a more detailed picture of the preceding examples. The phone numbers shown in Table 10.1 are for calls originating in the United States or Canada. Every country has its own toll-free numbering system. Thus, hotel chains with properties located around the world typically have a separate toll-free number in each country. Figure 10.1 shows the various numbers in the Middle East to be used by customers of Radisson SAS. When a customer is in Kuwait, for example, and wants to make a Radisson SAS reservation in, say, Austria,

TABLE 10.1 *Examples of 800 Number Access to Central Reservation Systems*

Choice Hotels International

Sleep Inns	(800) 753-3746
Comfort Inns and Suites	(800) 228-5150
Quality Inns, Hotels, and Suites	(800) 228-5151
Clarion Hotels, Suites, and Resorts	(800) 252-7466

Bass Hotels and Resorts

Holiday Inn	
Holiday Inn Select	
Holiday Inn Express	
Holiday Inn SunSpree Resorts	(800) 465-4329
Crowne Plaza Hotels and Resorts	
StayBridge Suites	

Howard Johnson

Howard Johnson Plaza	
Howard Johnson Lodges	
HoJo Inn by Howard Johnson	(800) 446-4656
Howard Johnson Park Square Inns	
Howard Johnson Hotels	

Marriott

Marriott Hotels, Resorts, and Suites	(800) 228-9290
Fairfield Inn by Marriott	(800) 228-2800
Courtyard by Marriott	(800) 321-2211
Residence Inn by Marriott	(800) 331-3131
TownePlace Suites by Marriott	(800) 257-3000
Marriott Vacation Club International	(800) 845-5279
Marriott Executive Apartments	(800) 800-5744

that customer would call toll free 800 288 and be connected to the Radisson SAS reservation center in Dublin.

Even when there are different 800 numbers for one hotel chain, the reservation sales agents are still basically working through one central reservation system. At Marriott, for example, the CRS is affectionately known as MARSHA. Over 400 reservation sales agents work at Marriott's CRS headquarters based in Omaha, Nebraska. Any one of these agents can respond to separate reservation inquiries for Fairfield by Marriott, Courtyard by Marriott, Residence Inn by Marriott, and Marriott Hotels, Resorts, and Suites. By offering separate 800 numbers, chain hotel companies can more strongly differentiate each of their brands and make life a little bit easier for the loyal customers of each. It is felt by management at these companies that more

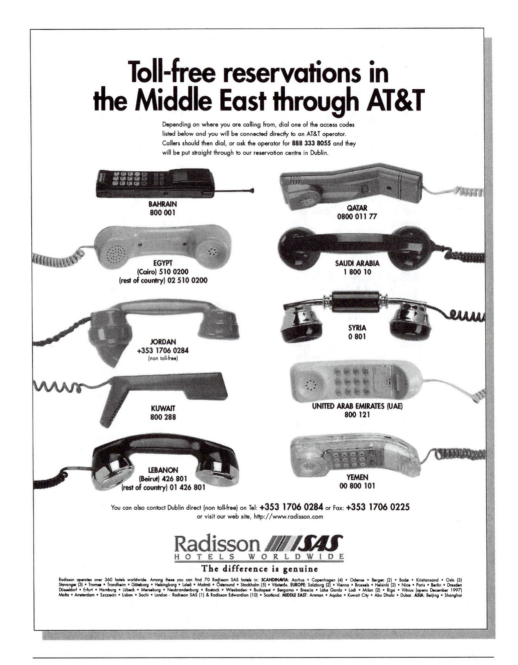

FIGURE 10.1 *Toll-free CRS telephone numbers for Radisson SAS. (Courtesy of Radisson SAS Hotels Worldwide. Reprinted with permission.)*

distinctive positioning results from the use of separate 800 numbers for each individual brand.

Thus far, we have been addressing individual reservation inquiries either directly from the customer or the customer's travel agent. At some hotel chains, there are specific 800 numbers for group sales requests (which is typically 10+ rooms) including Marriott's (800) 831-4004 or Hyatt's (800) 882-1234. Radisson has group sales reservation agents at its CRS headquarters, who are available through Radisson's regular toll-free numbers. Group sales (as discussed in Chapters 6 and 8) can be quite complex. Group sales reservation agents at CRSs are specially trained to handle these types of requests. Often times, the potential account may be routed directly to a national sales account executive.

Yield Management and the Central Reservation System

Yield management (see Chapter 9) is increasingly being practiced at the CRS level. Today's technology allows hotel chains to implement this strategy. When central reservation systems were first introduced, the CRS "fed" the unit-level properties on a limited basis only. In other words, hotels allotted some but not all of their available inventory to the CRS for sales. Some inventory was held back to retain control of this inventory at the unit level. This scenario, however, is changing. At several chains, such as Westin Hotels and Resorts and Powder Resort Properties (of Whistler, British Columbia), *all* guest room inventory is "plugged" into the CRS. This is necessary for yield management to work most effectively. As noted by Cherie Hensdill, technology editor for *Hotels:*

> Most hotel companies practice some form of yield management, but generally only at the property level. Now, with the trend of moving inventory to a central repository for single imaging across all distribution channels, centralized yield management is becoming an obvious necessity.
>
> "For yield management to become truly effective," says Roger S. Cline, a partner at Andersen Consulting, New York, "much more will need to be accomplished in terms of technology support and interface between the market reality at the property level and the centralized reservation systems that have become such an important part of the industry's distribution system."[2]

Powder Resorts has installed Spring Miller System's SMS/Host. SMS/Host is actually a multiproperty management system that includes a CRS and a yield management program encompassing all 10 of the Powder Resorts lodging establishments. "A top priority . . . was a sophisticated yield management system to manage rates for the company's 700 rooms, consisting of 76 available room types at 10 different properties, all located in Whistler."[3] Three of these properties are Radissons and one is a Sheraton. SMS/Host was specifically designed to interface with the Radisson CRS and the Sheraton CRS for these particular properties, respectively. We realize this may seem confusing, and it is. But it works. The sales technology is there to make this all happen.

Several technology companies aligned to develop a centralized yield management system for the Westin Hotels and Resorts central reservation system. "Bookings made at the property level are instantly reflected in the CRS, and rates are adjusted accordingly. [The system] also allows direct connection to the global distribution systems so yield management goes all the way back to the travel agent."[4] Most central reservation systems are now interfaced with what has come to be known as the global distribution system, which is discussed next.

GLOBAL DISTRIBUTION SYSTEMS

A **global distribution system (GDS)** is a network of worldwide computer reservation systems for booking hotel, airline, car rental, and other travel-related reservations. GDS bookings are made electronically, and not via the traditional toll-free 800 number discussed previously. As stated in the *Cornell Quarterly*, following is a brief history of the global distribution system:

> In the late 1950s, airlines developed computer systems to manage their reservations. The early '70s saw airline computer-reservation terminals installed in travel agencies to enable agents to book airline seats without using the telephone. Airlines expanded their reservation systems in the late '70s to encompass hotel bookings and other travel-related services. . . .
> Today, GDSs have evolved from narrowly focused airline-distribution channels to generic broad-based travel-reservation systems.[5]

In the lodging industry, by 1996, an estimated 30 million hotel reservations and 60 million room-nights were booked through a GDS.[6]

At the core of global distribution systems are major airline reservation systems including (but by all means not limited to) SABRE, Gemini, Apollo/Galileo, System One/Amadeus, and Fantasia. The CRSs of most hotel chains, other airlines, car rental companies, and cruise lines are interfaced with these systems. Thus, one can electronically book a hotel room, an airline seat, or a rental car using the GDS.

Travel agents across North America are increasingly doing business through a global distribution system. The option of booking electronically is appealing, especially when arranging international travel itineraries. European travel agents, too, are making expanded use of electronic computer reservations. As noted by Kurt Ritter, president and CEO of Radisson SAS:

> Travel agents are changing the way they make hotel reservations. They are shifting from a reliance on toll-free numbers to booking hotel rooms directly through their computer systems. For years these were referrred to as [Airline] Computer Reservation Systems . . . , now they have been renamed Global Distribution Systems.[7]

Many travel agencies, especially large agencies, have a GDS installed and pay a monthly fee for its use. The GDS supplier, such as Apollo/Galileo, sets up computer reservation terminals at the agency enabling the travel agents to access their system. Once in place, the travel agent is now hooked up to do business, literally, worldwide. Frederick Travel of Guelph, Ontario, for example, uses the Gemini GDS. Five terminals are installed and virtually 100 percent of its business is booked through this system.

Global distribution systems offer access to a multitude of hospitality product offerings. "[They] are packed with a huge roster of global travel products. Everything from cars to hotels and ferry schedules to ecotours is available in real time and organized.";[8] SABRE (officially known as SABRE Travel Information Network), for example, has what management refers to as "associates" comprising over 300+ international hospitality businesses. These associates include airlines (in addition to the parent company, American Airlines), car rental companies, ticket, agencies, firms that provide foreign currency and exchange rate information, sightseeing and tour operators, railways, insurance companies, limousine services—you name it, it's all there in this rather large GDS.

Travel agents are sales agents for all of these products. Many of our customers rely on travel agents for current, up-to-date information and access to hospitality products for sale. In turn, we rely on the travel agent to help us sell hospitality services. Global distribution systems help make this happen.

Recent Developments in Global Distribution Systems

Before closing this discussion on GDSs, two additional issues need to be addressed. These include (1) recent developments in inventory access for independent operators and (2) what has come to be known as "seamless" reservation systems.

Independent Operators

In the mid-1990s, the American Hotel & Motel Association (AH&MA) and SABRE together brought to market a way for noncomputerized independent operators to get connected to the GDS. This service is called "Direct Request for Hotels" and is available (for a fee) to all members of AH&MA. No hardware or software is required by the lodging establishment; a fax machine with a dedicated touch-tone phone line is all that is needed. The hotel hooks up with a travel agency that is connected to the SABRE GDS. The independent operator is now able to sell its product through a global distribution system without having to be part of a chain operation CRS.

Brian Kinsella, vice president of corporate/industry affairs for AH&MA, comments that "[t]his agreement [with SABRE] will prove to be invaluable worldwide exposure for independent properties. Utilizing this global distribution system will produce extra bookings from untapped markets."[9] Feedback thus far from properties that have signed on to Direct Request for Hotels has been quite positive.

Seamless Connectivity

The term "seamless" was the new buzzword in the business world by the mid-1990s. Seamless refers to how business entities are connected. In hospitality sales technology, this refers to how unit-level inventory is connected to central reservation systems, and how central reservation systems, in turn, are connected to global distribution systems. Seamless implies having no seams, having no lines of demarcation. It means a continuous and complete flow of inventory information from one system to another without interruption.

Prior to this technological innovation, the availability of inventory for sale was forwarded from the hotel's property management system to the hotel chain's CRS. The information received from the hotel was then added to the CRS inventory. This was done in somewhat of a block formation, often several times a day. Once received by the CRS, this inventory information would then be forwarded on to the global distribution system with which the hotel chain was affiliated. As noted earlier, not all inventory is necessarily released to the CRS from the property management system. The same holds true for rooms inventory transmitted from the CRS to the global systems. John Burns, a well-known hospitality technology consultant, explains the GDS database transition as follows:

> When the booking capability for non-air travel products was first added in the GDSs, the listing and descriptive opportunities were limited. As an example, hotels could list a maximum of eight to twelve room types, depending on the GDS, with usually six or fewer rate types (rack, corporate, government, military, weekend, etc.). Description opportunities,

both for individual hotels and for the chain-wide policies and programs, were similarly restricted.

In this limited display environment room types were described with three letter codes—A1K, for example. The A indicated that the room was the best category in the house; the 1 that it had one bed; K that the bed was king size. The best king size bed equipped room in every hotel—whether Rodeways, Ramadas, or Ritz-Carltons—were described simply as A1Ks.

By 1993, with implementation of enhanced non-air product listings and sales capabilities in all GDSs the situation improved considerably. Two fundamental limitations on the volume of bookings—caps on the number of product types and lack of adequate descriptions—were considerably lessened.[10]

The seamless technology arrived next. Instead of forwarding information from the CRS to the GDS, technology is now available such that global systems can draw directly from the central reservation system. "In the seamless connectivity mode, room type information and descriptions (including availability and specific rates) are not taken from the GDSs data base, but are instantly extracted from the hotel company's computer [reservation system]."[11] It is now seamless. This same technology is being applied to CRS/PMS connections, too. Unit level properties no longer have to forward their room inventory and corresponding rates to the CRS periodically, it can be done automatically.

What does all this really mean? It means hotels, car rental agencies, cruise lines, and others now have the capability to offer the full array of their product offerings through the PMS, the CRS, and/or the GDS. The customer no longer has to hunt and peck for specific queries, special promotions, and so forth. The seamless connectivity evolving in today's hospitality sales technology helps make this happen.

DATABASE MARKETING

"A Potent New Tool for Selling: Database Marketing,"[12] "Database Marketing: The New Frontier in Revenue Enhancement,"[13] and "The Future for Database Marketing Is Present"[14] read typical headlines by the mid-1990s. The use of database marketing is growing across many industries including hospitality.

Database marketing is a technology-driven tool used to reach out to identified customers in the marketplace. It is precision marketing, a one-on-one sales approach to individual customers and clients. Database marketing applies the concept of market segmentation. Yet, instead of targeting a particular group of customers, database marketing reaches out to customers individually. The names, addresses, and buying habits of individual customers are culled from databases. "Now, new generations of faster, more powerful computers are enabling marketers to zero in on ever-smaller niches of the population, ultimately aiming for the smallest consumer segment of all: the individual."[15]

Building a Database

Database marketing in the hospitality industry began with building a guest history database for regular clientele. This database entailed basic information such as name, address, purpose of travel, preferred method of payment, room type preference, nickname, and so forth. Thus, when Mr. Jones checked in, information such as this was on file and readily accessible for the guest service agent to register Mr. Jones in an efficient and personalized manner. Prior to this type of database, regular guests such as Mr. Jones were repeatedly asked the same questions over and over again each time they checked in to the hotel.

Four Seasons and Ritz-Carlton hotels are renowned for their extensive guest history databases. They include such details as a preference for feathered or nonfeathered pillows, breakfast menu item preferences, and preferred times for wake-up calls. For many frequent travelers, having someone know and care about your personal preferences, your likes and dislikes, is an asset. This type of service enhances guest satisfaction and encourages repeat customer patronage.

Frequent-flyer programs, frequent-traveler programs, and frequent-diner clubs are also major sources for database development. Marriott, for example, has over five million members in its Marriott Rewards frequent-traveler program. This program "requires the efforts and attentions of around 200 full-time staff—ranging from system designers to customer service personnel—to maintain it. Marriott's vice president–database marketing Lynne Roach has no doubts the money is well spent. 'We regard our program as an asset which enables superior customer understanding.' "[16]

Members of these programs are building points to get "deals" such as a free airline ticket, a free restaurant meal, or a free weekend stay at a hotel or resort. The hospitality organization is attempting to build loyalty through a points-earned award distribution system. A member of a program accumulates points with each purchase of that particular product. Awards are then distributed based on the number of points earned. Figure 10.2 shows the innovative ways to earn miles on American Airlines "AAdvantage Program."

You can also earn Bonus Miles for flying on a purchased Business Class or First Class ticket on American Airlines and all participating airlines, adding to your total even faster:

- 25% of flight mileage flown in Business Class
- 50% of flight mileage flown in First Class

More Ways to Earn Miles

We've teamed up with a variety of travel, hospitality and service companies to provide even more opportunities to earn AAdvantage mileage credit. Participating companies include:

- World-class airlines
- Leading hotel chains
- Car rental agencies
- Financial services (credit cards) and investment companies
- Long distance providers

and many more. (See the back cover of this guide for a complete list of participants and their phone numbers.)

Imagine, you can earn AAdvantage miles by eating out at a participating restaurant or by sending flowers to someone special through our participating floral service. You'll be amazed at how quickly and easily your AAdvantage miles add up. Here are a few typical examples:

YOU'LL BE AMAZED AT HOW QUICKLY AND EASILY YOUR MILES ADD UP!

A Possible Day in the Life of an AAdvantage Member

7:00 a.m. Pick up dry cleaning and grab breakfast.
Earn 58 AAdvantage miles by using the Citibank® AAdvantage card.

7:45 a.m. Renew gym membership.
Earn 650 AAdvantage miles, again by using the Citibank AAdvantage card.

10:55 a.m. Fly American Airlines from Dallas/Fort Worth to Miami.*
1,121 AAdvantage miles.

3:00 p.m. Pick up a rental car in Miami at a participating rental car company.*
500 AAdvantage miles.

4:00 p.m. Check into a participating hotel.*
500 AAdvantage miles.

7:30 p.m. Dinner with clients.*
AAdvantage Dining earns you 1,000 miles.

8:45 p.m. Call home with MCI. Coach kids through tough geography homework.
50 AAdvantage miles.

10:15 p.m. Check next day's schedule, discover it's your anniversary; wire flowers via 1-800-SEND-FTD.*
300 AAdvantage miles.

Total for the day: 4,679 miles!

* *By using the Citibank AAdvantage card as payment for these other transactions, you can further increase the number of miles you earn in a day.*

5

FIGURE 10.2 *American Airlines frequent-traveler awards program. (Courtesy of American Airlines. Reprinted with permission. American Airlines reserves the right to change AAdvantage program rules, regulations, travel awards and special offers at any time without notice, and to end the AAdvantage program with six months notice. American Airlines is not responsible for products or services offered by other participating companies.)*

In return for awarding points for purchases, the hospitality organization is garnering a tremendous amount of information about your purchase habits, travel patterns, and so on. Management can learn more about you than perhaps you yourself are aware. Following are some examples of what management is looking for:

- How frequently is the customer purchasing this product?
- For what dates and/or times of year are purchases most frequently being made?
- What specific products are being (or not being) purchased? (Room service? Spa facilities?)
- What is the size of the purchase?
- Is the purchase amount consistent or does it vary from purchase to purchase?
- How far in advance are reservations typically made?
- What is the duration (or length of stay) of the purchase?
- Is the duration (or length of stay) consistent or does it vary from purchase to purchase?
- Where does this customer live?
- How many customers do we have from a particular area or region?

These are just a sampling of the kinds of questions for which management is looking for answers. The more management knows and understands the buying habits and preferences of its customers, the better management can respond to the needs and wants of its customer base.

Using the Database

Product and service improvement is just one result of tapping into a database. Developing special promotions and employing direct mail to promote these campaigns is another major use of database marketing.

For example, a sales team may have just completed a review of the upcoming summer months. This review may have revealed that bookings to date are somewhat below forecast and that a special promotion may be in order to spur business. The sales team would then develop a special promotion package to encourage bookings for this period of demand. They would search the database to identify customers who tend to (1) book in the summer months, (2) book on a short-term basis, and (3) respond to promotional campaigns. A direct mailing could then be used as the principal means to reach out to these customers and say, "We have been thinking about you and have put together a special package designed just for you. . . ." Activities such as this are today referred to as database marketing. It is aggressive selling to potential customers who have particular needs and wants that match or "fit" the needs of the hospitality establishment.

Cindy Green, a specialist in this field, offers the following advice for a successful direct mail campaign using the database marketing approach:

> Most successful campaigns require multiple efforts on several levels, and database marketing supports these efforts. If you are interested in attracting more weekend package guests, it is not enough only to do a mailing to all the people who have purchased a package from you in the past. An effective strategy using database marketing calls for mailing to all travel agents who have booked packages in the past, all guests who have booked packages in the past, all guests who have indicated through market research that they are interested in weekend package offerings, and outside lists of prospects who match the demographic and lifestyle profiles of your past package purchasers.[17]

Outside lists are external databases that can be purchased by a hospitality establishment. This is often done to enhance and augment internal databases already developed. Suppliers of outside lists are numerous. American Express, for example, sells lists that are frequently purchased by hospitality organizations. These lists can be organized in a number of ways, including the buyer behavior patterns and geographic locations of hospitality customers.

Database Mining

Database mining is "the process by which you distill your target customer groups out of the massive data files typically found in hospitality operations."[18] In other words, there are systematic ways to sift through a database or a multitude of databases to get the information for which you are searching.

Hyatt Hotels, for example, extracts information from several databases including its Gold Passport frequent-guest program, the guest history database of its leisure travel customers, the database of its travel agent customers, and "joint data from travel partners like airlines, car rental companies, and credit card companies."[19]

Some hospitality organizations outsource this task to companies that specialize in this field. For example, Driving Revenue (a Rockville, Maryland–based firm) developed Kaleidoscope, a database marketing system that

> [E]nables users to integrate data from internal and external sources, such as guest history, reservation files, travel agent files, business prospects and demographic overlays. The data can then be used to generate customer profiles, purchasing profiles, and reports on geographic/demo-

graphic penetration, travel agent performance and the use of frequent stay programs, all on a property- or chain-wide basis.[20]

Data Designs is another database marketing system developed by Group 1 Software (also a Maryland-based firm). This system captures data from various sources within the hospitality establishment. As noted by Group 1 Software's public relations specialist:

> It easily integrates with property management, reservations, and point-of-sale systems, automatically extracting operating data from legacy databases for use in the marketing database. . . . The system's analysis tools allow users to profile their most profitable customers, analyze their buying habits, and develop and assess the performance of targeted marketing campaigns.[21]

The bottom line is that a new profession is emerging in hospitality to get and keep a customer. It is technology-based, it is sophisticated, and it is called database marketing. Companies in hospitality that are adopting the database marketing approach to enhance sales are seeing increased customer satisfaction as well as increased revenues.

SALES SUPPORT TOOLS

In hospitality, the best approach for sales presentations is the on-site property visit (see Chapter 6). This site inspection allows potential customers to visually see, touch, and, to some degree, experience the product offering they are considering for purchase. Support tools for on-site visitations are minimal as they are not really necessary. The prospective client is physically on premise to see for his- or herself what it is that you have to offer. The sales manager is present to probe, respond to questions, highlight features and benefits, and so forth.

However, when personal visits are not possible, various tools are used to assist in helping to make a presentation for you. **Sales support tools** are used when a customer cannot make a site inspection, has to delay a site inspection, or wants to review material prior to making a decision of whether or not to do a site inspection.

The most common support tool for sales is the printed brochure. It typically consists of text describing the hospitality establishment including photos and exhibits. Brochures are given to prospective clients prior to or during a site visitation.

Today, a new breed of technology-driven "brochures" is increasingly being used as part of the sales process. These include videos and CD-ROMs. They are similar to the printed brochure in that they describe the property for the prospective customer. They are different, and more advanced, in that more than one medium is used.

Table 10.2 highlights the similarities and differences among these sales support tools. As can be seen, brochures use only one medium, which is the printed page including text, photos, charts, and diagrams. Videos use two media, which are sight and sound. CD-ROMs use multimedia or several formats of media including text, sight, sound, and graphics. Brochures and videos have previously been discussed in Chapters 2 and 6. Following is a more detailed discussion of CD-ROMs. They are the support tools that make use of multimedia and are largely driven by computer technology.

CD-ROMs

CD-ROMs are similar to the CDs that you put into your disc player sound system at home. What differs is that a CD-ROM is inserted into a computer and offers more than sound. For hospitality sales, it is a first-class technology-driven brochure that customers can view on their office or home computer.

There are a number of advantages for using CD-ROMs as a support tool for sales. First, it makes effective use of multimedia. Clients can read the text, view the "video," hear the commentary, and study accompanying charts and graphs that may be part of the CD-ROM package. This use of multimedia offers several ways for a prospective customer to get a better "picture" of what your hospitality establishment is all about. It delivers so much more than the traditional printed brochure.

Second, most CD-ROMs are interactive. This means that the customer can guide the "tour." If a travel agent, for example, is interested in the

TABLE 10.2 *Sales Support Tools*

Support Tool	Number of Media Used	Options for Media Format	Interactive
Printed brochure	1	Text	No
Video	2	Sight Sound	No
CD-ROM	Multi	Text Sight Sound Graphics	Yes
Web site	Multi	Text Sight Sound Graphics	Yes

number and types of suite accommodations available at a hotel, he or she can "click" specifically to that section of the CD-ROM. Should meeting planners want details on function room sizes and setup configurations, they can easily guide themselves to where this information is located (and skip the suite accommodations section altogether should they so desire). Each of the preceding "tour" examples typically includes several media including sight, sound, and text—multimedia. Interactive means that customers can choose what they want to see and how they want to see it. Again, multimedia.

CD-ROMs are durable, long lasting, environmentally friendly, lightweight, and economical, too. As a contributor to the *HSMAI Marketing Review* commented:

> From the standpoint of cost, a CD-ROM-based presentation can be a very economical choice. Compact (4–3/4 inches in diameter and one millimeter thick) and very lightweight (half an ounce), CD-ROMs can be mass produced and mailed very economically. Magellan Interactive Multimedia of Calgary, Alberta, Canada, notes that one firm has determined that its costs to produce and distribute 30,000 CD-ROM discs amount to $8,000—a figure that translates to a unit cost of less than 27 cents. This is less than the price of a single First-class postage stamp![22]

Use of CD-ROMs as a sales and marketing tool is growing rapidly in hospitality. Hotels use it, cruise lines use it, airlines use it. Even the American Automobile Association (AAA) is "making all of the information contained in its well known AAA tourbooks available in an interactive multimedia format on CD-ROM."[23] The CD-ROM will not totally replace the printed brochure or video. It will, however, become more and more the medium of choice as customers and hospitality organizations alike become more savvy with computer technology and the opportunities it offers to help make a sale happen.

THE INTERNET AND WORLD WIDE WEB

The Internet

The Internet is a communication tool used by a variety of people for a variety of reasons. Kids play games on the Net. Kids and adults send e-mail messages back and forth on the Net. Faculty at educational institutions conduct research on the Net. Parents do their family grocery shopping on the Net. Companies conduct business on the Net. The Internet is a new electronic medium, a new source for information, "a new mode of communication."[24]

It is an avenue to reach out to customers. As stated by Ron Evans, past president and CEO of Best Western International; ''[our] strategic goal is to provide cyberspace travelers with a new way to access inventory and rates while providing Best Western with a new method of attracting room-night business.''[25]

Of interest to business is that the Internet is a source for customers to learn about their products. It also provides a means for consumers to purchase their products. ''Companies in all industries are rushing to set up computer sites to tell their story and to conduct business.''[26]

The hospitality industry launched full steam ahead on the Internet in the 1990s. Much commerce, the exchange of goods and services between buyers and sellers, in hospitality already takes place on the Internet. Bob Coyne, a technology expert and frequent consultant to hospitality, offers the following brief history of the Internet and future predictions for hospitality business conducted on the Internet:

> Around since the late 1960s, its original use was restricted to the military. In the early 1980s, it was opened up to the university, research and government communities. In the late 1980s, the Internet was opened up to the world—hence the growth in number of users, fueled mainly by the on-line service providers (America On Line, Compuserve, Microsoft Network, Prodigy) that have easy to use tools and relatively inexpensive access.
>
> The Internet is not a single network—and it isn't censored. It is a global network of networks.
>
> By some estimates, there may be 5,000 different networks, connecting possibly 15 million users at any one time out of 100 million (200 million by 2000, some say 300 million) with access. There are about 1 million Web sites now. That number is expected to double in a year.
>
> One estimate states that 90 percent of commerce will take place on the Internet by 2000. I have doubts about the accuracy of this 90 percent estimate. However, I don't think many experts would disagree that the percentage might be approaching 50 percent by 2000 and 90 percent by 2005.
>
> In terms of one Internet aspect for hotels, some predict that the mix of global hotel rooms inventory access will be 40 percent global-distribution system, 20 percent voice and 40 percent Internet within five years. I concur.[27]

Table 10.3 illustrates a broader view of projected revenues for on-line shopping including purchases of travel and entertainment. As can be seen, Forrester Research predicts that over $7 billion in sales of travel-related products will be conducted on line by the year 2001.

In hospitality, much of the on-line commerce is being done on the World Wide Web. The remainder of this chapter focuses on this aspect of hospitality sales and technology.

TABLE 10.3   *Projected On-Line Shopping Revenue (in millions of dollars)*

	1997	1998	1999	2000	2001
PC hardware and software	$863	$1,616	$2,234	$2,901	$3,766
Travel	654	1,523	2,810	4,741	7,443
Entertainment	298	591	1,143	1,921	2,678
Books and music	156	288	504	761	1,084
Gifts, flowers, and greetings	149	264	413	591	802
Apparel and footwear	92	157	245	361	514
Food and beverages	90	168	250	354	463
Jewelry	38	56	78	107	140
Consumer electronics	19	34	60	93	143
Sporting goods	20	29	43	63	84
Toys and hobbies	13	21	32	47	71
Health, beauty, and drugs	11	16	25	36	50
Tools and gardening	10	22	31	44	59
Home furnishings	9	15	21	28	38
Other (pets, photo, etc.)	22	28	35	42	52
Total	$2,444	$4,828	$7,924	$12,090	$17,387

Source: Forrester Research, Inc. Reprinted with permission.

The World Wide Web

The World Wide Web (also referred to as WWW or the Web) is part of the Internet. It is a computerized, interactive, multimedia system to impart and/or access information worldwide. It is used for both personal and business purposes. Our focus here will be on the business side of using the Web.

Web sites are the major vehicle of the WWW. They are the "homes" or "addresses" for business enterprises (called URLs—uniform resource locators—in WWW language.) In hospitality, there are several avenues that one can take to set up a Web site to share information and conduct business with a potential customer. These include company Web sites, and travel Web sites, and destination and directory Web sites. Following is a discussion of each. (For the interested reader, Table 10.4 offers a refresher on Web terminology.)

Company Web Sites

Most hospitality organizations, especially large and/or multiunit chain operations, set up their own sites on the Web. Examples here are many including Hertz Car Rental (www.hertz.com), Sheraton Hotels & Resorts (www.sheraton.com), Delta Air Lines (www.delta-air.com), and Windsor Vineyards (www.windsorvineyard.com). Holiday Inn Worldwide

TABLE 10.4	*World Wide Web Terminology*
World Wide Web	A computerized, interactive, multimedia system to impart and/or access information worldwide electronically. It is often referred to as the WWW or the Web.
Web site	The "home" or "address" of a business enterprise. It consists of a home page and subsequent pages created by the organization for potential viewers. (Referred to as URLs in WWW technology.)
Home page	The first page of a Web site.
Search engine	A Web site that helps a viewer search for Web sites on specific topics when addresses (or URLs) are not known.
Link	Software that provides the ability to move from one Web site to another or to move from one page to another within a Web site.

(www.holiday-inn.com) has its own Web site, and its home page is shown in Figure 10.3. As can be seen, the customer has a number of choices from which to choose including viewing the worldwide directory, taking a hotel tour, making a reservation, and so on. Note that potential customers are prompted on the home page to ask questions that they may not have thought to ask, such as "I want to find out about current promotions." In the past, hotels used to hide special rates. Today, they actively promote discounts in an attempt to reach out to the price-sensitive market, especially on the Web.

Choice Hotels International launched its Web site in 1995. As stated by Donald Landry, former president of Choice Hotels:

> Internet users spend $38 billion in domestic leisure travel per year. Though not all make travel arrangements on-line, travel ranks as the sixth most popular item that "Internauts" buy on-line today. In the coming years, Internet experts expect travel to rank third.
>
> Numbers like these are the reason Choice created its own Web site last year (http://www.hotelchoice.com) that links directly to our CHOICE 2001 reservation system. We carefully created a useful, easy-to-navigate site with real-time availability and booking capabilities that enable Internet users to find and book the room that suits them best. Relying on publicity and word-of-mouth alone, the site has been a tremendous success, leading to hundreds of thousands of dollars in extra revenue for our licensees.[28]

Setting up one's own Web site is one way for a hospitality establishment to get on the WWW. Another alternative is to be part of a travel Web site, which is discussed next.

HOLIDEALS from Holiday Inn — **Click Here to Save at Least 40% on Last Minute Weekend Rooms!**

Holiday Inn Garden Court — Holiday Inn — Holiday Inn EXPRESS — Holiday Inn SELECT

Holiday Inn SunSpree Resorts — Holiday Inn HOTEL & SUITES — Holiday Inn EXPRESS HOTEL & SUITES

"Hello? Holiday Inn? I need a room."

"I need to make a reservation."
"I need to cancel a reservation."
"I want a great deal on last-minute weekend travel."
"I want to plan my next meeting."
"Boston or Chicago is my final destination."
"I want to find out about current promotions from Holiday Inn®."
"Tell me about the different kinds of Holiday Inn® hotels."
"I travel a lot...Tell me about the Priority Club® Worldwide program?"
"What's new at Holiday Inn®?"
"I want to know more about your programs, especially rates."
"I want to see individual hotel web pages!"

1-800-HOLIDAY

▼ CLICK ON ANY ITEM

CONTACT

Holiday Inn

[Contact Us] [Directory/Reservations] [Family of Hotels] [FAQ] [Meetings]
[Hotel Tours] [Leisure Time] [More Info] [What's New] [Priority Club] [HOLIDEALS]

Rev: 02/08/99

FIGURE 10.3 *Holiday Inn Worldwide Web site home page. (Courtesy of Bass Hotels & Resorts. Reprinted with permission.)*

Travel Web Sites

Travel Web sites are gaining in popularity as destinations on the Web. Many hospitality establishments, both small and large, are placing their Web site as an integral part of a broader travel Web site. Major players in the travel Web site business include:

- Internet Travel Network
  (www.itn.net/itn)
- PC Travel
  (www.pctravel.com)
- TravelWeb
  (www.travelweb.com)
- Travelocity
  (www.travelocity.com)
- TravelQuest
  (www.travelquest.com)

Hyatt Hotels, for example, chose to hook up with TravelWeb. Its Web site address is www.travelweb.com/hyatt.html. A customer can find the Hyatt Web site directly by using the preceding address or by going to the TravelWeb site and then linking to the Hyatt site from there. Best Western, another large international hotel chain, also chose TravelWeb as its home base.

TravelWeb is owned by a consortium of 15 major lodging firms (including Hyatt and Best Western) representing over 8000 hotels worldwide. Another 50 or so lodging chains link to this travel Web site as well.

Travelocity's home page is shown in Figure 10.4. Customers visiting this travel Web site have several options to explore, including reservation inquiries and direct booking capability for airlines, car rentals, cruises, hotels, and bed-and-breakfasts.

Some Web sites target the business traveler such as TravelWeb. The 15-member consortium represents largely business hotels targeting individuals, groups, and conventions traveling for business purposes. Travelocity, on the other hand, also targets the vacation traveler. Items displayed on this Web site are geared to the leisure market including cyberspace tours that have "vivid graphics and animation, such as an airplane that takes you on a simulated tour of a destination."[29] A simulated tour of a destination is of more interest to the leisure-minded traveler than to the business-minded traveler. Any individual can use any of these sites. Nonetheless, travel Web site setups and layouts are designed with specific target markets in mind.

We have described thus far company Web sites and travel Web sites. A

FIGURE 10.4 *Travelocity Web site home page. (Courtesy of the SABRE Group, Inc. Reprinted with permission.)*

third alternative for consumers to explore travel options on the Web is destination and directory Web sites.

Destination and Directory Web Sites

Numerous destination and directory Web sites are readily accessible on the Internet. Similar to company and travel Web sites, they offer "electronic brochures" for potential customers to view the product offerings. Many destination and directory sites provide reservation capabilities, too.

Destination Web sites are dedicated to a particular region, city, or geographic area of a country. Beyond the French Riviera is one such site located at www.beyond.fr/. This site shows viewers that the French Riviera is more than just a famous ritzy resort area along the Mediterranean Sea in the southeast corner of France. The site explores the back country and the perch-top villages that wind in and about this pristine region of southern France. According to the developer of the site, Russel Collins, "I now get e-mail from people who tell me they are coming to visit the Riviera's back country because of what they discovered on my site."[30]

A directory site is a grouping of similar type hospitality establishments. Guild's Guide to Independent Hotels (www.hotelreservation.com), for example, is a listing of independent hotels where a customer can make on-line reservations should he or she wish to do so. The Guild was developed specifically for independent, nonchain-affiliated operators that desired access and visibility on the Web. It is an organization where members can develop a home page in the directory or a link for properties that already have a home page.

Several restaurant directories are easily accessible on the Web. The Great Canadian Restaurant Survey (www.restaurant.ca) and the A la Carte Guide to North America (www.westweb.com/alacarte/) are two such examples. The A la Carte Guide to North America covers both the United States and Canada. The listing includes over 300,000 restaurants categorized by city, state, or province and cuisine. As stated in the *Cornell Quarterly*, "the text only [restaurant home] page is the equivalent of a Yellow Pages advertisement except that it is available electronically to anyone in the world."[31] The A la Carte Guide is maintained by Westcoast Web Works based in Brier, Washington.

Search Engines

Search engines are programs on the Internet that help users search for a particular product, destination, and the like. They are used when potential customers do not know the Web site address of a particular hospitality organization or travel destination in which they are interested in searching.

There are many search engines available. These include Alta Vista (www.altavista.com), Infoseek (www.infoseek.com), Lycos (www.lycos.com), and many others. Yahoo! (www.yahoo.com), for example, has an entertainment subdirectory. In this subdirectory is a food and eating section offering numerous Web site options in this category. Yahoo Canada is a regional directory that has over 250 related sites for those searching the Canadian marketplace.

Places and ways to explore the Web just in searching hospitality are monumental and daunting. Each day, however, more and more customers are using the Web to search and seek travel possibilities worldwide.

SUMMARY

This chapter looked at several ways in which the hospitality industry reaches out to hospitality customers through sales and technology. These include central reservation systems, global distribution systems, database marketing, sales support tools, and the Internet and World Wide Web.

Central reservation systems (CRSs) are data banks of inventory for hospitality chain operations. Guest rooms at hotels, autos at car rental companies, and cabins on cruise lines are made available for sale on central reservation systems. This is usually done through a toll-free 800 telephone number. Sometimes separate telephone lines are dedicated specifically for group inquiries. Each unit-level operation feeds its inventory status to the CRS on a regular basis.

A global distribution system (GDS) is a network of computer reservation systems for booking airline, hotel, car rental, and other travel-related reservations. These bookings are made electronically and not through the traditional toll-free telephone number. Global distribution systems have evolved from airline reservation systems to broad-based travel reservation systems. They are, for the most part, still owned and operated by major airlines worldwide. Hospitality companies pay a fee to have their inventory available for sale on a global distribution system. Travel agents, in particular, are frequent users of the systems. The option of booking electronically is appealing, especially when arranging international travel itineraries. Travel agencies pay a monthly fee for access to the GDS of their choice.

Database marketing is a technology-driven tool used to reach out to identified customers in the marketplace. It is precision marketing, a one-on-one approach to individual customers. It is not necessarily direct personal selling. The names, addresses, and buying habits of individual customers are culled from databases often for direct-mail and special promotion purposes.

The databases are either developed internally by a hospitality establishment or produced externally by a major source of hospitality purchases such as credit cards companies, airlines, and so forth.

Sales support tools assist in the sale of hospitality products. They are used as support material for a personal sales call or when personal selling is not possible. Brochures, videos, and CD-ROMs are the most common sales support tools in hospitality. Printed brochures use one medium, which is the printed page of text, charts, and diagrams. Videos use two media, which are sight and sound. CD-ROMs use multimedia or several formats to present the message. These include text, sight, sound, and graphics. CD-ROMs are interactive. This means that customers can choose what they want to view and how they want to view it. Because of their multimedia format and durability, use of CD-ROMs as a sales support tool is growing in popularity by buyers and suppliers alike.

The Internet is a technological communication tool used by a variety of people for a variety of reasons. It is an avenue for hospitality businesses to reach out to their customers and for customers to learn more about hospitality product offerings in the marketplace. Much commerce, the exchange of goods and services between buyers and sellers, in hospitality already takes place on the Internet. It is predicted that over $7 billion in sales of travel-related products will take place on the Internet by the year 2001.

The World Wide Web (WWW) is part of the Internet. It is a computerized, interactive, multimedia system to impart and/or access information worldwide. Web sites are the major vehicle of the WWW and are the "homes" or "addresses" for business enterprises. Most hospitality businesses have a Web site. Customers can access these Web sites to learn more about a hospitality product or service and, in most instances, make a purchase. Travel, destination, and directory Web sites are locations on the Web with multiple travel options to explore.

Central reservation systems, global distribution systems, database marketing, sales support tools, and the Internet and World Wide Web are very much a part of sales and technology. They are ways in which we can reach out and let buyers know we have the product they are looking for. Electronic media will continue to grow and expand as a means of communication with hospitality customers worldwide.

DISCUSSION QUESTIONS

1. Growth in sales activity through the use of central reservation systems has risen dramatically over the past decade in hospitality. Discuss.

2. Discuss the relationship between yield management and the CRS.
3. What are global distribution systems? Have they had a major impact on the hospitality industry?
4. Discuss the significance of the PMS/CRS/GDS connection in the hospitality industry.
5. What is database marketing? What types of information are helpful to management in a customer database?
6. Compare and contrast database marketing and database mining.
7. Four sales support tools include printed brochures, videos, CD-ROMs, and Web sites. How are they similar? How are they different?

NOTES

1. "Technology to the Rescue Balancing Rates, Occupancies," *Hotels*, August 1993, pp. 37–38.
2. Cherie Hensdill, "Centralized Yield Becoming a Necessity," *Hotels*, January 1997, p. 73.
3. Ibid.
4. Ibid.
5. Rita Marie Emmer, Chuck Tauck, Scott Wilkinson, and Richard G. Moore, "Marketing Hotels Using Global Distribution Systems," *Cornell Quarterly*, December 1993, pp. 81, 83.
6. "GDS Bookings Up in 1996," *Hotel & Motel Management*, March 17, 1997, p. 19.
7. Kurt Ritter, "The GDS Revolution," *Leaders*, January–March, Vol. 18, No. 1, 1995.
8. "Travel Technology," [SABRE advertising supplement], *Business Travel News*, August 10, 1995, p. 33.
9. "AH&MA Inks Deal with SABRE," *Hotel & Motel Management*, August 12, 1996, p. 8.
10. John Burns, "Hospitality Marketing Through Global Distribution Systems," *HSMAI Marketing Review*, Winter 1996, p. 14.
11. Ibid., p. 16.
12. Jonathon Berry, "A Potent New Tool for Selling: Database Marketing," *Business Week*, September 5, 1994, pp. 56–62.
13. Cindy Estis Green, "Database Marketing: The New Frontier in Revenue Enhancement," *HSMAI Marketing Review*, Fall 1994, pp. 22–25.
14. Laura Koss-Feder, "Future for Database Marketing Is Present," *Hotel & Motel Management*, June 17, 1996, p. 66.

15. Berry, "A Potent New Tool for Selling," pp. 56–57.
16. Clive B. Jones, "Applications of Database Marketing in the Tourism Industry," Occasional Paper Series, Pacific Asia Travel Association (PATA), 1993, p. 4.
17. Green, "Database Marketing," p. 23.
18. Cindy Estis Green, "Data Mining," *Hotel & Motel Management*, July 7, 1997, p. 24.
19. Koss-Feder, "Future for Database Marketing Is Present," p. 66.
20. Cherie Hensdill, "What's New in Technology," *Hotels*, June 1997, p. 76.
21. Ibid., pp. 76 and 78.
22. Donald E. Bender, "CD-ROM: The New Technology of Choice for Marketing Your Organization," *HSMAI Marketing Review*, Fall 1994, p. 13.
23. Ibid., pp. 14–15.
24. Jamie Murphy, Edward J. Forrest, and Edward Wotring, "Restaurant Marketing on the World Wide Web," *Cornell Quarterly*, February 1996, p. 63.
25. Ron Evans, *Hotel & Motel Management*, June 17, 1996, p. 27.
26. Murphy et al., "Restaurant Marketing on the World Wide Web," p. 61.
27. Bob Coyne, "Internet: A Global Network of Networks," *Hotel & Motel Management*, June 16, 1997, p. 46.
28. Donald J. Landry, *Hotel & Motel Management*, June 17, 1996, p. 30.
29. Scott McCartney, "Poised for Takeoff," *Wall Street Journal*, June 17, 1996, p. R6.
30. Joel Stratte-McClure, "Cybertravel Now Widely Available," *International Herald Tribune*, March 9–10, 1996, p. 19.
31. Murphy et al., "Restaurant Marketing on the World Wide Web," p. 67.

PART FOUR

Intermediaries and Partnerships

Chapter 11

Intermediaries

LEARNING OBJECTIVES

1. To understand how intermediaries are very much a part of the sales effort in hospitality
2. To become familiar with the various kinds of intermediaries and the role they play in hospitality sales. These intermediaries include:
   - Travel agents
   - Wholesale tour operators
   - Incentive travel houses
   - Independent meeting planners
   - Convention and visitors bureaus

Intermediaries can be found throughout the travel industry. They are organizations that assist in the sale of hospitality product offerings. They are in the business of providing travel services to hospitality customers. Travel agents, wholesale tour operators, incentive travel houses, independent meeting planners, and convention and visitors bureaus are all intermediaries. They essentially package and/or sell hospitality. They are all customers. Hospitality organizations "sell" to intermediaries. In turn, intermediaries then "sell" to consumers.

Table 11.1 gives an overview of each of the travel intermediaries listed previously. This chapter gives a detailed discussion of their role in the hospitality sales process.

TRAVEL AGENTS

Travel agents are in the retail business, much like department stores and supermarkets. Retail agents sell goods and services that are produced and/ or developed by a third party. Travel agents sell travel services developed

---

TABLE 11.1 *Overview of Travel Intermediaries*

Travel Agent

Person, firm, or corporation qualified to sell tours, cruises, transportation, lodging accommodations, sightseeing, and other elements of travel to the public.

Wholesale Tour Operators

Organizations that contract with transportation, lodging, foodservice, and other hospitality companies to develop and manage tour packages. Tour packages are typically sold through the retail division of wholesale tour operators and/or travel agents.

Incentive Travel Houses

Incentive travel is a reward given to employees, especially sales personnel, for reaching and/or exceeding company-set goals. Incentive travel houses (sometimes referred to simply as incentive houses) are in business to develop, package, and sell incentive travel programs to companies that offer such reward systems.

Independent Meeting Planners

Entrepreneurs who specialize in meeting planning. They are hired by organizations (on a contractual basis) to plan meetings for them.

Convention and Visitors Bureaus

Municipal, state, or provincial nonprofit organizations responsible for promoting tourism for a specific area.

Source: Adapted, in part, from Charles J. Metelka, *The Dictionary of Hospitality, Travel and Tourism,* 3rd ed., Delmar Publishers, 1990.

by lodging, transportation, cruise lines, wholesale tour operators, and other hospitality services. Travel agents sell their own services, too. These services largely involve customer knowledge and product knowledge. Who is the customer? What are they looking for? What products are available to meet their customers needs and wants? In other words, travel agents are sales agents, and follow the same sales process as a hospitality sales account executive. Travel agents are travel professionals whose numbers are strong and growing.

Industry Statistics

There are an estimated 400,000+ travel agents worldwide selling daily to hospitality customers.[1] Specific to the United States, "America's travel agents represent a sales force 200,000 strong."[2] A travel agency survey conducted by *Travel Weekly*, a travel industry news publication, reported that, in 1995, "[t]he total dollar volume of all U.S. travel agencies has passed the $100 billion mark for the first time in the industry's history."[3] There are approximately 35,000 travel agency locations in the United States with an average of six travel agents per agency. Some of these agencies are chain operations such as Carlson Wagonlit with over 4000 agencies worldwide.

The survey mentioned previously reported that the bulk of agency revenues resulted from airline reservation sales, followed by cruise lines, car rentals, and hotels. The survey also showed that individual travelers—those who travel for both leisure and business purposes—are the vast majority who use travel agents when making travel arrangements. (See Table 11.2.)

A Day in the Life of a Travel Agent

Lori Nicoll is one of five full-time travel agents at Frederick Travel in Guelph, Ontario. Frederick Travel has three locations in southern Ontario, including the Guelph location. Lori's typical day is varied and hectic, similar to a sales manager's day at a hotel, resort, or conference center.

Throughout the day, she is working with a multitude of customers—both in person and on the phone—on various aspects of upcoming travel plans. For example, a regular client from the nearby university calls to have her start working on travel arrangements for a scheduled conference in San Antonio, Texas, next month. A couple walks in to the agency seeking assistance for travel to Australia. The couple has never flown before, has two small children, wants an eight-day stopover in Honolulu, has never traveled in a foreign country, and will be living in Australia for one year. Another client, just returning from a trip, stops by to question a car

TABLE 11.2 *U.S. Travel Agency Survey Results*

Travel Agency Revenues by Type of Product Sold

Product	Revenue (in billions)	Percentage
Airlines	$61.2	61%
Car rental	7.5	7
Cruises	14.4	14
Hotels	10.1	10
Miscellaneous	7.8	8
Total	$101.0	100%

Market Segment Usage of Travel Agency Services

Segment	Revenue (in billions)	Percentage
Individual leisure travel	$44.5	44%
Individual business travel	46.5	46
Group travel	10.1	10
Total	$101.1	100%

Source: U.S. Travel Agency Survey, *Travel Weekly*, August 1996. Reprinted with permission of *Travel Weekly*.

rental bill. The bill seemed outrageously high but he had no time to "dicker" with the car rental company as he had been in a hurry to catch a return flight home.

Each of these examples represents various stages of the sales process. Lori is at the beginning stage of "opening the relationship" with the couple traveling to Australia. Much "probing" will follow to learn of particular needs, wants, and preferences, especially for a young couple with little travel experience. Lori will also need to do a lot of coaching and advising regarding international travel such as the need for passports, visas, vaccination shots, medical insurance coverage, and so forth.

The university client represents the "presenting the message" stage of the sales process. This customer is a regular client. Lori's records will show that this customer, for example, prefers flying Air Canada (to build frequent-flyer mileage points), wants early-morning flight departures, needs transportation to/from the airport, and uses the American Express card for payment. Lori mainly needs to know specific dates of travel and preferred lodging accommodations for this particular trip. "Closing the sale" should move quickly for this regular account.

The client stopping by regarding the questionable rental car billing represents a "service delivery" aspect of the sales process for travel agents. Although this customer has essentially completed the hospitality purchase, the client is still seeking service from the travel agent to help resolve a customer complaint issue. As Lori commented:

> It is part of my job to help clients in these situations to do what I can to ensure customer satisfaction. In the above case, I may or may not get a rate reduction from the car rental company for my client. Nonetheless, I will try. Most clients get a sense of satisfaction from a travel agent if we do our best to do whatever we can to resolve legitimate complaints from our customers. It is all part of the commission we earn as travel professionals in the travel industry.

In other words, from a travel agent perspective, the sale is not complete until the traveling customer returns home, and returns home satisfied with the travel agent services provided.

Travel Agent Commissions

Travel agents are generally paid on a commission basis. A commission is a percentage of the price charged to the customer for a hospitality purchase. The commission is paid by the hospitality establishment (and not the customer) and is typically 10 percent. Thus, when a travel agent books a $450 airline flight for an individual client, he or she earns $45 from the airline for making the sale. Commissions are common practice when travel agents book individual airline, car rental, lodging accommodation, and cruise line reservations. (Foodservice reservations are not normally commissionable.) The travel agent does not receive the full 10 percent, however. Part of that commission is paid to the travel agency for whom the agent works.

In 1995, major U.S. airline carriers put a cap on the commissions they will pay to travel agents. The cap, or the most they will pay per reservation booked, is $50 for round-trip U.S. air travel. The cap was introduced to help contain operating expenses in the airline business.

Needless to say, travel agents were not pleased with this action. (We, too, question the long-term implications for airline/travel agent relationships.) However, according to a U.S. travel agency survey, conducted by *Travel Weekly*, revenues at many travel agencies have not declined as a result. Revenues are actually up. This is in large part due to more efficient travel agency management and an increase in foreign travel sales. As suggested by a spokesperson from the Rosenbluth International travel agency, "[a] lot of our growth is driven by multinational corporations."[4] These multinational corporations have much international travel and this travel does not necessarily originate in the United States. Agencies targeting the U.S. domestic business and leisure travel markets are more challenged by the commission caps.

Promoting to Travel Agents

There are several ways in which hospitality establishments reach out and promote to travel agents. The more traditional approach is sending printed brochures to identified agents. CD-ROMs are growing in popularity as a promotional sales tool for travel agencies, too. A mailing list can easily be developed from a history of travel agents who have previously booked reservations at the establishment. Membership listings of travel agency associations, such as the American Society of Travel Agents (ASTA), can also be obtained.

Sales managers from large hospitality organizations make personal calls on travel agencies, especially those organizations that receive a fair amount of business from this segment. Radisson SAS, for example, has identified more than 80 travel agency key accounts. Sales managers from Radisson SAS regularly call on the travel agents at these agencies. Reservations are not necessarily directly booked as a result of the sales call. Rather, the sales manager is building a relationship, discovering of trends about his or her clients, and learning of changing needs within the agency.

Radisson Hotels Worldwide (of which Radisson SAS is a partner) offers an aggressive loyalty/recognition program directed specifically at travel agents. It is called "Look To Book" (see Figure 11.1). Similar to frequent-flyer and frequent-guest programs, the Look to Book program awards points to travel agents who book reservations at the 400+ Radisson Hotels Worldwide and on Radisson's Diamond Cruise Line. "Agents earn 10 points for every dollar booked and consumed. . . . Prizes can range from a free, one-day Avis car rental after earning 12,500 points all the way up to free cruises on the Radisson Diamond which require at least two million points."[5]

Radisson purposely does not offer commission above the standard 10 percent to spur sales.

> Like other chains, Radisson does not pay commission overrides to travel agents. . . . [A]ward programs such as Look to Book are the commission overrides of the future. They are actually more appreciated, says Maureen O'Hanlon, senior director for distribution channel marketing at Radisson. She points out that many times travel agents must split their commissions with their agency owner and/or manager. But a Radisson television set or CD player directly rewards the frontline agent.[6]

Majesty Cruise Line has a different approach. Instead of an award points incentive program, Majesty promotes a "Double Your Commission"

LOOK TO BOOK® FACT SHEET

WHAT:	Look To Book, the travel industry's premier on-line travel agent loyalty program, was awarded a patent in 1995.
WHO:	Over 360 Radisson Hotels Worldwide and over 170,000 travel agents in 95 countries (120,000 with activity in any given year).
WHEN:	Since 1992
HOW:	Participating agents earn ten points per $1 U.S.D. each time they book a client through the GDS/CRS at a Radisson hotel or Country Inn & Suite by Carlson. Once the agent has completed the reservation, a message appears on the terminal stating the number of points the agent earned with that transaction and their total number of accumulated points.
FEATURES:	Participating agents can attain "ELITE" status by earning 80,000 points in the program between a qualification period of Jan. 1 and Dec. 31. The 80,000-point threshold is needed to maintain "ELITE" status each year. "ELITE" members receive additional mailings, the ELITE Focus newsletter and invitations to special events. There are currently 12,500 "ELITE" agents.
PROGRAM TO DATE:	Since its inception in 1992, the program has awarded more than $14 Million in awards to 26,000 agents.

FIGURE 11.1 *Radisson Hotels Worldwide "Look to Book" travel agent incentive program. (Courtesy of Radisson. Reprinted with permission.)*

incentive to travel agents. In its 1996 booking season promotion, when a travel agent booked double the number of cabins from the previous year, agents earned up to 20 percent commission from the cruise line. This promotion was also offered to travel agents who had not booked with Majesty the previous year. Sales promotions such as these are typically advertised in trade publications targeted at the travel agency business. For example, the

Majesty Cruise Line sales promotion was advertised in *Travel Weekly*, a major publication of this type.

Travel Agents and Technology

By the mid-1990s, most travel agents continued to use central reservation systems and/or global distribution systems as their primary tool for booking business. The 1995 U.S. Travel Agency Survey reported that GDS usage was 39 percent SABRE, 26 percent Apollo, 20 percent Worldspan, and 19 percent System One.[7]

Few travel agents responding to the survey booked reservations on the Internet. "A fifth (21%) of the agents surveyed said they could access the Internet at their agency location compared with 77% who could not." For those who had access, primary use of the Internet was for e-mail and destination research purposes.[8] With today's technology expanding at such a rapid rate, we predict this scenario will change.

WHOLESALE TOUR OPERATORS

Wholesale tour operators are intermediaries that are major players in the hospitality industry. The following discussion looks at what they do and how they do it.

Developing Tour Packages

Wholesale tour operators develop tour packages to be purchased by consumers. They contract with lodging, transportation, foodservice, and other hospitality companies to develop the packages. Tour package bookings are usually done in bulk with hospitality suppliers in exchange for deeply discounted rates. In other words, the wholesale tour operator often books a series of tour packages, or "back-to-back" tour bookings as they are sometimes called. A series may consist of 2-to-20-day packages covering a 10-to-12-week period or season.

For example, a wholesale tour operator may reserve a block of 20 double-occupancy rooms at a hotel for a series of seven-day periods and a block of 40 round-trip airline seats for the first and seventh day of each period. The operator will then package the hotel room and airline seats together at a single price to be marketed as a one-week tour package for individual consumers. This week-long tour package might be offered throughout a summer season from July 1 to August 31. Figures 11.3 and 11.5 show additional samples of tour package offerings. Packages such as these are typically priced at per person rates.

The tour package is sold to customers at the retail level through travel agents and/or the retail division of the wholesale tour operator. The "retail price" paid by the consumer is slightly higher than the "wholesale price" paid by the operator to the hospitality organizations that are part of the tour package. For the consumer, however, the price paid is normally lower than if the consumer had put the package together on his or her own.

Following is an example of a French Alps package put together by New Frontiers, a New York–based wholesale tour operator:

> New this year is a tour of the French Alps based in Lyon that starts at $1,199 (U.S.) and features round-trip scheduled flights from New York, first and last night's accommodations at a quality hotel in Lyon, four nights at a succession of country inns, most meals (wine, too), and a rental car with unlimited mileage. Prices are effective from June 29 to Sept. 7.[9]

New Frontiers arranged for all the transportation, lodging, and foodservice aspects of the tour package. All the customer has to do is arrive on time in New York for the scheduled departure (with appropriate passport, etc.).

Trafalgar Tours is a wholesale tour operator. It specializes in tour packages exploring northern Europe. One such tour is its 20-day "Best of Scandinavia." The tour

> [B]egins and ends in London and visits Denmark, Sweden and Norway, as well as Belgium, Holland and Germany. Highlights include: the medieval Swedish city of Orebro; the Olympic sites in Lillehammer, Norway; and a cruise across the Geirangerfjord. The price per person, double occupancy, is $2,370 land only, $2,870 air and land.[10]

This example demonstrates the flexibility that can be achieved when developing tour packages. Note that the package can be purchased with or without air service to/from London to get to the Scandinavian start and finish points of the tour. The price with round-trip air service from London is $2870, without $2370, or a difference of $500. Thus, if one is already or planning to be in the Scandinavia area, one does not have to pay the extra $500 to get to London to start the tour. This flexibility broadens the reach and affordability for various market segments that may be interested in the "Best of Scandinavia."

Delta Air Lines promotes tour packages through its private label brand, Delta Vacations℠. Shown in Figure 11.2 is an advertisement promoting five such Delta Vacations packages. Consumers can book their reservations directly through a toll-free 800 number or on the Web, or contact their travel

▲ Delta Vacations™

Don't let this moment pass you by

Day and night, you're always on the run.
So, isn't it time for a breather?

Time to finally use your passport again
(it's been collecting dust in your nightstand
for ages). To wiggle your toes in the sand
(and leave those heels behind). Or to do
the hula (don't forget the grass skirt). Time to
discover a place where your only decisions are
whether to sleep late or catch an early show.
Whew...

The Bahamas
from $389

Rates Begin From:	4 DAYS/3NTS
Simply	
BRITISH COLONIAL BEACH RESORT Includes **FREE** unlimited non-motorized watersports	$389
Preferred	
RADISSON CABLE BEACH RESORT *All-Inclusive* - Includes all meals, beverages, plus more	$799
Ultimate	
ATLANTIS - PARADISE ISLAND Includes **FREE** use of 14-acre waterscape	$629

Rates also include transfers.
TRAVEL DATES: 7/5/98 - 8/28/98.

Sparkling shores, glittering casinos...
Discover vacation fun at its very best!

Grand Cayman
from $699

Rates Begin From:	4 DAYS/3NTS
Simply	
TREASURE ISLAND RESORT	$699
Preferred	
MARRIOTT GRAND CAYMAN BEACH RESORT●	$939
Ultimate	
HYATT REGENCY GRAND CAYMAN RESORT●	$969

Rates also include transfers.
● Includes Chillin 'n Cayman Bonus
Features, such as discounts on
watersports, dining, shopping,
sightseeing, and more. Ask for details.
TRAVEL DATES: 7/6/98 - 8/27/98.

Endless beaches, cobalt seas...
So this is what paradise looks like!

Waikiki
from $829

Rates Begin From:	7 DAYS/6NTS
Simply	
OUTRIGGER MAILE SKY COURT	$829
Preferred	
OUTRIGGER EAST Includes 6th Night FREE and $25 in Big Kahuna Bucks & Fun Pack	$999
Ultimate	
OUTRIGGER WAIKIKI Includes 6th Night FREE and $50 in Big Kahuna Bucks & Fun Pack	$1199

Rates also include transfers, a fresh flower
lei greeting upon arrival, a welcome "Aloha"
breakfast the morning after arrival and
24-hour customer service representation.
TRAVEL DATES: 9/2/98 - 10/27/98.

Standing on the shore, surrounded by lovely
vistas of mountains and sea... Lucky you.

Puerto Rico
from $769

Rates Begin From:	4 DAYS/3NTS
Simply	
RADISSON NORMANDIE	$769
Preferred	
EL SAN JUAN HOTEL & CASINO	$979
Ultimate	
HYATT DORADO BEACH RESORT & CASINO	$939

All rates include transfers and are part of
the *Endless Summer Sounds Promotion*
which features **FREE** deluxe continental
breakfast daily.

TRAVEL DATES: 7/27/98 - 9/3/98.

Ask about Kids Stay & Eat FREE and
FREE Night promotion.

Sapphire waters splash to the sound of the
saucy Latin beat... Now you're on vacation!

France
from $1089

Rates Begin From:	8 DAYS/6NTS
Simply	
PARIS HOTEL FRANTOUR PARIS BERTHIER Includes 6th Night FREE	$1089
Preferred	
NICE RADISSON SAS HOTEL NICE	$1429
Escorted Tour	
ESSENTIAL FRANCE - 12 DAYS/10 NTS 7 Cities – Plus sightseeing, transfers, & select meals Paris arrivals/departures	$1849†

Rates also include breakfast daily and are
based on NONSTOP service.
TRAVEL DATES: 8/4/98 - 8/31/98,
†9/16/98 & 9/23/98 departures only.

A quaint bistro along the Champ-Elysees.
So this is what escargot tastes like.

▲Delta Air Lines
SkyMiles®

Air, hotel, room taxes, and more!
Call **1-800-872-7786** or contact your travel agent for details
Or make reservations online at **www.deltavacations.com**

Simply - COMFORTABLE HOTELS & ALL THE ESSENTIALS   **Preferred** - ATTRACTIVE HOTELS & QUALITY FACILITIES   **Ultimate** - SUPERIOR ACCOMMODATIONS & SERVICES

FIGURE 11.2 *Delta Vacations™ package promotion. (Courtesy of Delta Air Lines, Inc.*
© 1998 Delta Air Lines, Inc. Reprinted with permission.)

agent to make the reservation. In the latter case, a commission would be paid to the travel agent. The advertisement is aimed directly at consumers. A similar advertisement promoting the same packages could be directed to travel agents as well.

Escorted Tours

Many tour packages are marketed as **escorted group tour** packages. This means that a representative of the wholesale tour operator meets at the departing gate and travels with the group throughout the tour. The group is met and assisted by local guides once they arrive at their destination. The escort manages on-site activity throughout the duration of the tour package (see Figure 11.3). The escort (sometimes referred to as a tour director) may also be the guide to specific planned activities and/or work closely with a local guide hired for these purposes (see Figure 11.4). In other words, tour escorts are responsible for the service delivery aspects of personal selling in the tour package business.

There are essentially two types of escorted group tours. One type is a grouping of people who purchased the package independently. Members of this type of tour group do not know each other and may have varied backgrounds and/or reasons to be on the tour such as a common interest in the destination. The second type is a group of people who travel together and have a special interest such as belonging to a travel club, a university alumni association, a senior citizens group, or a special topics organization such as photography, archeology, and so on. Individuals in this type of group may or may not know each other personally, but they do have a common thread linking them together as a group. Customized tour packages are often put together by wholesale tour operators on request from organizations of this type.

Personal Selling to Travel Agents

Like hotels, cruise lines, and other hospitality establishments, wholesale tour operators actively sell to travel agents. Many wholesalers do not have their own retail division and, thus, rely heavily on travel agents to sell their product offerings. Tauck Tours of the United States and Regent Holidays of Canada are two well known wholesale tour operators of this type. As remarked by Jan Jennings, a sales representative for Regent Holidays, "Regent Holidays has no retail division. Our strategy is to not compete with our primary source of business which is the travel agent."

Jan Jennings' job is to call on travel agents throughout her region keeping them updated on Regent Holidays tour packages (see Figure 11.5) and

PERFECTING THE ART OF TRAVEL

Understanding a country and its cultural nuances is a multi-sensory adventure which invites the explorer to delight in the unfamiliar and exotic. One must experience all that a land has to offer – its people, customs, and cuisine – to fully appreciate its beauty and uniqueness. Herein lies the secret to perfecting the art of travel and the promise of Cultural Tours.

During our many years exploring the lands of the great Asian continent, we have embraced a changing tapestry of extraordinary images.

Cultural Tours members have traced the steps of Marco Polo over the sand dunes of the legendary Chinese Silk Road, witnessed the mysterious dances of the Balinese, and sipped rice wine with Dyak tribesmen in the rainforests of Borneo. They have also known the bright lights of Hong Kong's Fragrant Harbour and haggled over silks and rubies with Thai shopkeepers in Bangkok.

Always with our eyes to the future, Cultural Tours has expanded into new frontiers. Travellers may now journey with

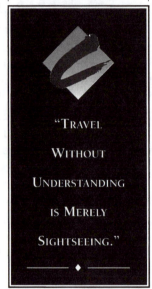

"TRAVEL WITHOUT UNDERSTANDING IS MERELY SIGHTSEEING."

us to destinations in the South Pacific. We have broadened our horizons, venturing into lands newly open to the western world and exploring a myriad of diverse cultures and landscapes.

While we believe in the importance of cultural pursuits, we have not forgotten the recreational side of travel. Cultural Tours members are accommodated in uncompromised luxury. Hotels used in our tour itineraries exemplify the very best in service and amenities. In places where there are no deluxe properties, we take care to use the best accommodation available.

Naturally, we have also set aside leisure time for those treasured moments of quiet relaxation. Our vision is to present to the discerning traveller a complete tour experience.

Cultural Tours' philosophy remains fundamentally the same. We look to new destinations, and the tides of the world shift and change, but our commitment to excellence is resolute. We strive, as always, to perfect the art of travel.

DAVID SIU
MANAGING DIRECTOR

2

FIGURE 11.3 *Escorted tour package advertisement: Cultural Tours wholesale operator. (Courtesy of Cultural Tours. Reprinted with permission.)*

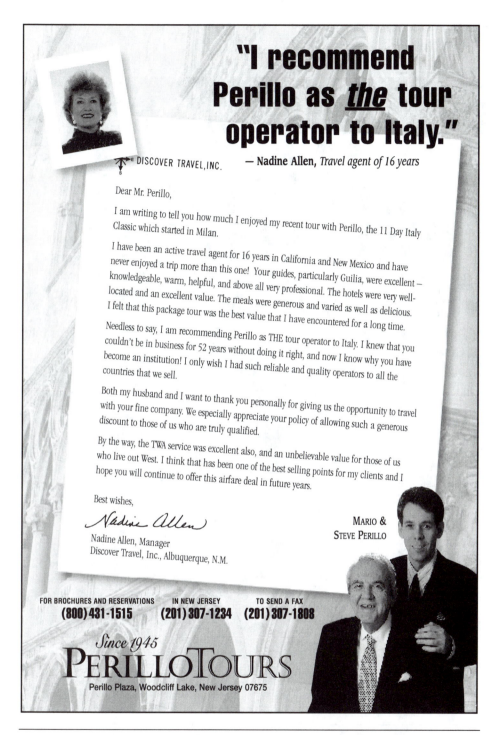

FIGURE 11.4 *Escorted tour package advertisement. PerilloTours wholesale operator. (Courtesy of PerilloTours and Discover Travel, Inc. Reprinted with permission.)*

℞EGENT HOLIDAYS

NEW FOR SUMMER 1998

MORE SUMMER FUN!
INTRODUCING COSTA REAL HOTEL AND SUITES CANCUN

ALL INCLUSIVE!

The courtyard of this beachfront Mediterranean style resort features a beautiful pool surrounded by lawns and colourful gardens. Although Costa Real is all-inclusive featuring both buffet and à la carte dining at two restaurants, our studio accommodation also includes a kitchenette with a small dining area.

LOCATION: On the beach near shops, restaurants, nightlife, 30 minutes from the airport.

FACILITIES: 316 rooms in five buildings, two restaurants, beach and lobby bars, pool, exercise facilities, beauty salon, sundry shop. Watersports rentals for jet-skis, water-skis, parasailing, banana boat rides.

CHOICE OF ACCOMMODATION:
Hotel room: Air conditioned with two double beds or one king-size, satellite TV, phone, half-fridge, bathroom with shower only.
Studio: Same as hotel room but with a kitchenette which has a two burner hot plate, half fridge, small dining area and balcony or terrace.

INCLUDED BONUS FEATURES:
▶ Buffet breakfast, lunch and dinner daily including three theme dinners. A la carte also available for all meals
▶ Unlimited domestic drinks including house wine 10 am to midnight
▶ Daily activities programme
▶ Kayaks, pedal boats, snorkeling (one hour daily–reservations required)
▶ Pool scuba clinic (once per stay)

STUDIO

New Bookings Only. Prices are in Canadian dollars based on double occupancy. For full terms and conditions of booking see Regent's Glorious Greece™ Summer 1998 brochure. Printed in Canada July 17, 1998. Ontario Registration #1742827.

YOUR TRAVEL AGENT

COSTA REAL HOTEL AND SUITES	HOTEL ROOM ADULT		STUDIO ADULT		HOTEL/STUDIO CHILD	
	1 WK	2 WKS	1 WK	2 WKS	1 WK	2 WKS
JUL 26 TO AUG 9	1199	1869	1269	1989	659	849
AUG 16	1199	1869	1269	1989	659	849
AUG 23	1199	1779	1269	1849	659	849
AUG 30	1089	1699	1149	1839	659	849
SEPT 6 TO 27	1049	1609	1099	1769	619	799
OCT 4 TO 25	1099	1669	1159	1779	659	849
SGL SUP	370	740	420	840	–	–
EACH OF 3/4	30/40	60/80	30/40	60/80	–	–

NOT INCLUDED: CANADIAN DEPARTURE TAX ($30), MEXICO DEPARTURE TAX ($26), AND TRANSPORTATION RELATED FEES ($20) ARE EXTRA AND WILL BE ADDED TO YOUR ACCOUNT.

FIGURE 11.5 *Sample Regent Holidays tour package. (Courtesy of Regent Holidays Ltd. Reprinted with permission.)*

keeping herself updated on trends emerging in the marketplace. She has 462 travel agency accounts in her southern Ontario region of Canada. These accounts are categorized as follows:

A	Regular/good high-producing accounts
B	Building business from strong-potential accounts
C	Building business from moderate-potential accounts
D	Weak/low-producing accounts

Jan routinely makes personal sales calls with all her travel agency accounts, giving priority to the A and B accounts.

Sales representatives from Regent Holidays give semiannual formal presentations to travel agents in various locations throughout their respective regions. In the tour package business, there are generally two seasons—winter and summer. Thus, the semiannual presentation is given to personally sell and promote upcoming packages for the season about to begin. News releases (see Figure 11.6) and subsequent sales calls support these efforts.

The one-to-two-hour sales presentation is typically held at area hotels or restaurants. Travel agents in the area are invited to attend. For large agencies that have more than 10 travel agents, the presentation is usually done on premise. The presentations are often early-morning breakfast meetings sponsored entirely by Regent Holidays. Most agents prefer the early-morning sessions so as not to take away from regular daytime sales activities. The presentation includes slide presentations and videos of destinations of the various tour packages being offered and a discussion and question/answer period at the end of the session. New brochures highlighting details for the upcoming season are distributed at these events as well.

For wholesale tour operators, personal selling is very much a part of the sales representatives' daily activity. They do not actually "book" business as a hotel or conference center sales representative does. Rather, their job takes a more indirect approach to help make "bookings" happen. Their productivity is measured in terms of how many bookings are made from the various travel agencies in the region for which they are assigned.

INCENTIVE TRAVEL HOUSES

Incentive travel houses are in business to develop, package, and sell incentive travel programs to companies that offer such rewards to their employees. **Incentive travel** is a reward given to employees, especially sales personnel, for reaching and/or exceeding company-set goals. The incentive travel market is truly a subset of the corporate market. The employees themselves do not purchase the product. It is the corporation that buys incentive travel for

REGENT HOLIDAYS

REGENT BONUS POINTS!
OUR POPULAR INCENTIVE PROGRAM FOR TRAVEL COUNSELLORS

For Winter 1998/99, Regent continues our popular Bonus Points programme, now entering its seventh year. You earn one Regent Bonus Point for every passenger (adult or child) whom you book on any Regent package holiday, cruise, or air only ticket; even children and third and fourth persons sharing count as one full point.

BLOCKBUSTER VIDEO JOINS REGENT BONUS POINTS! **NEW!**
Regent is pleased to welcome Blockbuster Video to our supplier group for Regent Bonus Points. Effective immediately, your Bonus Points may be exchanged for movie rental coupons valid at all Blockbuster Video locations. See our Regent Bonus Points flyer for all the details. And watch for new Bonus Point suppliers coming soon!

REDEEM YOUR REGENT BONUS POINTS FOR VALUABLE MERCHANDISE!
Your Regent Bonus Point coupons, issued with your invoice, can be redeemed for valuable merchandise with Regent's Bonus Points programme suppliers. You can shop for items at Zellers stores, take in a movie with Cineplex Odeon theatre passes, or enjoy a home video rental. The choice is yours.

REDEEM YOUR BONUS POINTS FOR TRAVEL WITH REGENT!
Best of all our Bonus Points offers, Regent allows you to redeem Bonus Points for travel with Regent, for you and one travelling companion. Every booking brings you closer to your own holiday!

BONUS POINTS SPECIALS!
Periodically you can earn extra Bonus Points on our Bonus Points Special—watch for our announcements.

Don't forget…
Bonus Points can be pooled!

BOOK 70 PASSENGERS WITH REGENT THIS WINTER, AND YOUR AGENCY WILL EARN 15% COMMISSION FOR WINTER 1998/99!

Your agency's starting commission rate for Winter 1998/99 (defined as passengers departing November 1, 1998 through April 30, 1999) will be determined by the number of passengers your agency has booked with Regent on our current published override plan. If your commission rate is changing for Winter 1998/99, you will be advised by your Sales Representative by November 15, 1998.

Your agency's commission rate at source will increase automatically as you pass each threshold as listed to

the right. Commission increases are not retroactive to the previous level.

Agency passenger targets apply to all Regent product.

Groups Bonus! Group passengers are included in your total winter sales figures!

PASSENGERS BOOKED DEPARTING BETWEEN NOVEMBER 1, 1998 THROUGH APRIL 30, 1999	COMMISSION LEVEL YOUR AGENCY WILL EARN FOR SUMMER 1998 AND WINTER 1998/99
1 TO 20 PASSENGERS	10%
21 TO 29 PASSENGERS	11%
30 TO 45 PASSENGERS	12%
46 TO 55 PASSENGERS	13%
56 TO 69 PASSENGERS	14%
70+ PASSENGERS	15%

SELL REGENT WITH CONFIDENCE!
REGENT'S CANADIAN DOLLAR GUARANTEE!
BOOK NOW…NO CURRENCY SURCHARGE THIS WINTER!
Beat the battered buck! Regent is offering the first 20,000 clients who book their 1998/99 fall or winter holiday this exceptional guarantee… no currency surcharges even if our loonie slips even further against the American dollar!

You can assure your valued clients that when they book early with Regent, they have no further concern about our slipping dollar. The price of their previous holiday is protected against any future currency surcharge!

OUR TORONTO WINTER LAUNCH IS A Latin Fiesta

To introduce our exciting new video on our exclusive Latin American destinations, we're throwing a big "Latin Fiesta" night for you in October, in Toronto. You can anticipate food, drinks, exciting entertainment, dancing and door prizes!

Watch for details.

FALL 1998 FAM TRIPS!
Here's a fabulous opportunity to see several of our exclusive Latin American destinations! We're planning the following fams:

PANAMA CONTADORA ISLAND SAN ANDRES ISLAND
OCTOBER 15 TO 18
ONE NIGHT PANAMA CITY, ONE NIGHT CONTADORA ISLAND, ONE NIGHT SAN ANDRES ISLAND (GREAT FAM!)

Dates also pending for **MARGARITA ISLAND**

Watch for flyers with details.

FIGURE 11.6 *Regent Holidays news release. (Courtesy of Regent Holidays. Ltd. Reprinted with permission.)*

WEDDINGS!

"Weddings in Paradise" are more and more popular as when compared to what you pay here for very little, the price is next to nothing and many hotels offer memorable services and locations. Great opportunity for you to develop your group business too, as friends and family frequently join the bride and groom for the ceremony.

Watch for this "flash" on our hotels. It alerts you to see page 7 where you'll find information related to wedding services or packages available at the following hotels.

WEDDINGS! SEE PAGE 7 FOR DETAILS

CANCUN
Calinda
Club Las Velas
Omni
Costa Real
PUERTO PLATA
AMHSA Paradise
Club Bahia San Juan
El Portillo
PUNTA CANA
Fiesta Palace
SANTO DOMINGO
Coral Costa Caribe
Coral Hamaca

NEW WEDDING SYMBOL
Wherever you see this symbol, wedding services in some form are available at the hotel.

GOLF SYMBOL

As a quick reference for you, on page 7 of our brochure we have listed those hotels where we offer *golf specials, golf packages* or *free golf.* There are many other hotels throughout the brochure which are near golf, so keep an eye out for our golf symbol.

BEAT THE CANADIAN DOLLAR BLUES!

SELL REGENT'S ALL INCLUSIVES ...AND CRUISE
Regent offers a product lineup that allows your clients to purchase their holidays in Canadian dollars prior to departure.
See our flyer for more thoughts on this issue...

EARLY BOOKING SAVINGS UP TO $360 PER COUPLE!

Cash savings from $50 per couple right up to $360 per couple are available on all winter sunshine ITC holidays. Each hotel has a bright blue box reflecting that hotel's special savings offer including any specific date references.

AN EXCEPTIONAL OFFER...
Exceptional for two reasons: Savings apply to every ITC holiday in the brochure departing between January 1 and April 30, 1999 without restriction.

Secondly, these Early Booking Savings may be combined with our "Kids Free" offers, providing substantial savings for families who want to book now and save big! Full details may be found on page 3 of the brochure.

NEW OFFER!
SAVINGS NOW APPLY TO THIRD & FOURTH IN ROOM!
Third and fourth passengers in a room will now save 50% of the applicable per couple savings for each hotel.

KIDS STAY FREE!

When your client asks if anyone has a "terrific deal" for kids—Reach for Regent as we like to say! You'll not find better savings opportunities for families with children anywhere. Throughout our brochure, green "kids boxes" appear on our hotel and price pages highlighting a variety of offers for children: **Kids Free; Kids Eat and Stay Free; and Kids Stay Free.**

Although we encourage all passengers to book early with our money saving Early Booking Bonus, our kids offers are in effect for bookings *made at anytime.* Full details may be found on page 5 of the brochure.

Remember!
Kids 5 – 16 cruise free on beautiful Bolero

EXCLUSIVE! JANUARY 1 TO 29
CHIN WINTER PICNICS
AT DECAMERON LOS COCOS IN PUERTO VALLARTA
PORTUGUESE: JANUARY 1 TO 15
GERMAN, GREEK, CROATIAN, POLISH: JANUARY 15 TO 29

The picnics are open to the general public and can be booked through any retail travel agency.

For the second consecutive year, Regent is hosting the Portuguese, Greek, Polish, Croatian and German CHIN Winter Picnics at the all-inclusive Decameron Los Cocos Resort in Puerto Vallarta.

In addition to the full host of activities and entertainment for which Decameron Resorts are so well-known, additional Portuguese, Greek, Polish, Croatian and German entertainers are scheduled to perform. All participants are provided with a CHIN/Regent passport which enables them to participate in the schedule of activities and qualifies them for great prizes.

HERES HOW TO BOOK YOUR CLIENTS...
VIA RESERVATIONS AGENT
Advise our Res Agent that your client is a CHIN Picnic passenger and request the free CHIN/Regent passport.

DIRECT ACCESS
(LEISURELINK/DIRECTOURS)
Please ensure you select the package that specifies **CHIN Picnic**

The CHIN/Regent passport will accompany the travel documents sent to your agency.

See our flyer for full details on pricing.

For more information contact: Jens Grodt, Manager, Regent Holidays Groups Department at (905) 673-0777 or 1-800-263-8776 Ext. 340.

AIR ONLY PRICES!

Back by popular demand, you'll find a complete list of Air Only prices for all sunshine destinations on brochure pages 8 to 11. Air only prices are also found in our hotel price panels.

"ODD DURATIONS" OFFER GREAT SAVINGS
In the destinations below, along with one and two week holidays, we offer other durations. Watch our price panels for our specialy priced "odd durations" in the following destinations:

SANTO DOMINGO:
8, 9, 10, 15, 16, 17 nights
MARGARITA ISLAND, PUERTO LA CRUZ, SAN ANDRÉS ISLAND:
21 nights
CARTAGENA: 10, 17 nights
VARADERO: 6, 13 nights

COMING SOON!
FALL/WINTER FLIGHTS
LONDON GATWICK,
MANCHESTER,
GLASGOW, BELFAST
NOVEMBER TO MAY
VIA AIR TRANSAT B757/L1011

GLORIOUS GREECE™ & MED CRUISES!

Due to your unprecedented support, this summer over 15,000 of your clients will have enjoyed a Regent holiday in Glorious Greece or aboard our Mediterranean cruises.

GLORIOUS GREECE
GROUP QUOTES READY FOR 1999
We're ready now with Glorious Greece group quotes for 1999. Give us a call!

MED CRUISE UPDATE!
Cruise sold out: August and September 2, 16, 23, October 14

Cruise limited availability: September 9, 30, October 7, 21

Air only and hotel: Limited availability

GLORIOUS GREECE 98/99
LONG STAY AIRFARE (VIA AIR TRANSAT)
$738 net plus tax
Depart between August 15 to September 27, 1998
Return May 17, 22, 24, 29, 31 or June 5, 1999

FIGURE 11.6 *(continued)*

its award-winning employees. The Society of Incentive Travel Executives (SITE) officially defines incentive travel as "a modern management tool that motivates salespeople, dealers, distributors, customers, and internal employees by offering rewards in the form of travel for participation in the achievement of goals and objectives."[11]

Incentive Awards

Travel is awarded in one of two ways. Award winners are sometimes offered individual travel to popular destinations such as Hawaii, the Caribbean, Mexico, Europe, and North Africa. The trip is taken at an agreed-upon time between management and the recipient of the award. The trip normally includes being accompanied by a spouse or companion and is typically a 3- to 4-day or 7-day excursion. The individual trip type of award is a growing trend in incentive travel.

More commonly, a group of award winners travel together (with spouse or companion) and are often joined by various members of the management team of the sponsoring organization. Similar to individual travel awards, locations chosen for the group trips are popular destinations including cruise ship adventures as well.

For example, Aetna Life Insurance may offer an incentive trip award to its top 50 sales account executives over a given period of time, say, one year. The award program is announced at the beginning of the year as a motivation for sales personnel for the coming year. The award may be a 10-day cruise in the Caribbean with ports of call at various islands throughout the region. Round-trip airfare to reach the cruise ship departure point is included as part of the award. This group of 100+ sit back, relax, explore port-of-call excursions, and enjoy the "rewards" of their professional accomplishments. Specific group activities are usually planned as part of the itinerary for incentive trips such as this.

Incentive House Contracts

Incentive houses contract with a corporation to develop its incentive travel program. It is the incentive house planner (and not the corporate travel manager or meeting planner) who makes all arrangements for the program including details and logistics of the trip being awarded. As stated in *Meetings & Conventions*, "[t]hey have the staff and capabilities to help determine objectives, design the program, handle promotions and mailings and provide the awards."[12]

There are several ways in which incentive houses bill their clients. Some simply charge a straight flat fee. Sometimes the charge is a flat fee per participant. For instance, an incentive house might charge a per person fee for 300 qualified sales personnel in an organization, for which only 30 may in the end be recipients of the award.

Another billing method uses a specified percentage of the total corporate budget for the incentive travel program. If the budget is $750,000 and a 10 percent billing fee is charged, the incentive house will earn $75,000 for developing and managing the program.

Another method is the cost-plus approach. It is growing in popularity as a way for incentive houses to bill their clients. "[I]ncreasingly, firms are using cost-plus pricing, with the supplier itemizing the cost of each element of the program for the planner, then [the planner] adding 10 percent on top of each charge, says Bob Vitagliano, executive vice president of the Society of Incentive & Travel Executives."[13] Suppliers are the hotels, the airlines, the cruise lines, or whomever that is "supplying" various aspects of the incentive travel program.

Personal Selling to Incentive Houses

Hospitality organizations that are based in and/or have routes to prime destinations actively seek incentive travel business. Upscale establishments, in particular, target this market. Sales account executives from hotels, resorts, airlines, and cruise lines of this type regularly make personal sales calls on incentive house planners to garner their business. These planners are very influential on the choice of location and facility selection when developing incentive travel programs for their corporate clients.

Chain hotels and resorts often have national sales account executives who specialize in incentive travel. Their sole job may be to exclusively call on incentive houses to solicit business.

Incentive travel is lucrative. The corporation sponsoring the program wants top-of-the-line facilities and services and is willing to pay for quality. For airlines, this means business-class or first-class seating, perhaps even private chartered jet service. For hotels, resorts, and cruise lines, this means double occupancy at premium rates and lavish food, beverage, and entertainment for the award winners.

Winning incentive house accounts is highly competitive. Upscale chains such as Hyatt, Marriott, and Four Seasons compete aggressively to secure this business. Price and service negotiations can be quite complex. Part of the complexity is the issue that there are two key players buying. The incentive house (the intermediary) is purchasing the product for a corporation that is paying the bill. In other words, it is the corporation that is "picking up the tab," so to speak. This is why sales account executives who are assigned the incentive house market are highly trained experienced professionals. They have to understand and apppreciate the needs and wants of both parties. In addition, the incentive house planners and their clients are very much aware of the desirability of their business to the hospitality industry.

INDEPENDENT MEETING PLANNERS

Independent meeting planners are entrepreneurs who specialize in meeting planning as their business enterprise. They contract out with various organizations to plan off-premise meetings for them. In some organizations, this is referred to as outsourcing. As noted elsewhere in this text, outsourcing is the hiring of an outside firm or agency to conduct business for the organization that was previously done in house.

Independent meeting planners work on a project basis. They may have several clients at the same time in various stages of the meeting planning process. Their fee structure varies in the same way that it does for incentive houses (see the discussion in the previous section).

Small-to-medium-sized firms are frequent users of independent meeting planners to manage their meeting activity. These organizations either choose to outsource or are not large enough to warrant the expense of a full-time in-house meeting planning department. Many large organizations have their own meeting planning department and only occasionally hire independents for the task. However, for some large organizations, this is not always the case.

Corporate downsizing that began in the late 1980s and early 1990s saw the job of full-time meeting planning as one avenue for corporate restructuring. In a number of large organizations, such as IBM and Sprint International, meeting planner positions were reduced substantially or eliminated altogether. Thus, many professional meeting planners on corporate payrolls saw their jobs literally disappear. It was not the meeting activity that was curtailed. Rather, it was who actually did the planning that got "restructured." The job was outsourced to independent planners.

A number of today's independent meeting planners are former full-time planners of large organizations. Indeed, many went into business for themselves and are now planning meetings for their former employers. "Karen Durkee, CMP [Certified Meeting Professional], first planned meetings for Sprint International as an employee and later as an independent."[14] She has her own meeting planning company, based in Atlanta, Georgia:

> At present, she has two employees, one of whom is her husband, a former
> pharmaceutical marketer who now prospects pharmaceutical meetings for

the company. Durkee expects to have about a dozen people working for her within four years. She herself is doing less planning and more selling and marketing.

"I did not have a difficult time making the transition from corporate to independent whatsoever," she says. "In the meeting planning industry, you need to be disciplined, and to make the transition from corporate to independent you need to have still more discipline. I didn't have a problem."

Still, she recognizes the challenges others may face. "It's scary because corporate planners are dinosaurs," she says. "And there are a lot of independent planners out there who are not going to succeed. They are good planners, but they don't have sales and marketing skills."[15]

Entrepreneurship is a challenging vocation. It takes courage to set out on your own and build a business. As Karen Durkee realizes, you may have a great product—and hers is meeting planning expertise—but sales and marketing are also essential to the long-run success of any business endeavor.

It is not easy for hospitality sales account executives to find independent meeting planners to solicit business. One source, however, is Meeting Professionals International (see Chapter 3). Over a third of its membership are independent meeting planners. Many salespeople regularly attend MPI conferences and conventions at the local, regional, and national levels. Here they meet and network with independents as well as with association and corporate meeting planners who attend these events.

CONVENTION AND VISITORS BUREAUS

Intermediaries discussed thus far include travel agents, wholesale tour operators, incentive travel houses, and independent meeting planners. They are similar in that each acts as an agent for a buyer to contract business with a seller, that is, a hospitality establishment. **Convention and visitors bureaus (CVBs),** however, are somewhat different.

As described in Table 11.1, CVBs are municipal, state, or provincial organizations responsible for promoting tourism for a specific area. Examples include the Atlanta Convention and Visitors Bureau in Atlanta, Georgia; the Greater Raleigh Convention and Visitors Bureau in Raleigh, North Carolina; and the Irving Convention and Visitors Bureau in Irving, Texas (see Figure 11.7). CVBs are nonprofit service organizations that act on behalf of the constituencies they represent. These constituencies include hotels, restaurants, conference centers, convention centers, local attractions, and so forth.

Convention and Visitors Bureau Sales Managers

CVBs have sales managers whose job is to sell and market the destination. Melissa Pappas, for example, was a convention sales manager for the Greater

FIGURE 11.7 *Irving Convention and Visitors Bureau advertisement. (Courtesy of Irving (Texas) Convention and Visitors Bureau. Reprinted with permission.)*

Boston Convention and Visitors Bureau. Her various assignments included selling Boston to associations based in the Chicago and Midwest area. The primary job responsibility of CVB sales managers is prospecting and generating leads for hotels, convention centers, and other constituencies in the area that they represent.

Corporate and association meeting planners, in particular, are frequent users of CVB services. Reported in a study conducted by *Meetings & Conventions* magazine, approximately 50 percent of association planners and 25 percent of corporate planners use CVBs.[16] The sales manager at a convention and visitors bureau is often the first contact planners have when exploring meeting and convention opportunities at a selected destination.

For example, an association planner may have selected the Northeast as the region to hold an upcoming convention. The planner (and sometimes jointly with a site selection committee) may have identified three metropolitan areas they are considering for the event—say, Philadelphia, New York, and Boston. This planner may contact the CVB in each of these cities to learn more about the facilities, accommodations, and services each offers. The planner's first contact would be with a sales manager at the CVB, such as Melissa Pappas. Following the initial meeting, leads are distributed by Melissa to hotels (and other hospitality establishments) that are members of the CVB and that meet the criteria specified by the planner.

A CVB sales manager may also help arrange site inspections for the planner and the site selection committee. The site inspection entails visitations to the various hospitality establishments selected by the prospective buyer. A general tour of the area is often done as well. This type of site inspection of a major destination can take two to three days, especially for large, complex convention requirements.

Convention and visitors bureau sales managers do not initiate or sign contracts for hotels and convention centers. Rather, the CVB sales manager puts the planner in contact with hospitality establishments that meet their specific needs and requirements. CVB sales managers assist in the opening, probing, qualifying, and presenting stages of the sales process. They are not involved with the "closing" of the sale.

Convention and Visitors Bureau Services

CVBs are often involved with service delivery aspects of the sales process. On request, many provide services such as assistance with housing reservations, convention registration, welcome programs, and so on. The Atlanta (Georgia) CVB, for example,

> [O]ffers a variety of services ranging from the personalized invitations of the mayor and governor to providing skilled personnel to assist with

meetings. The Atlanta bureau also provides publicity materials, dining and entertainment information, facility arrangements and housing needs.[17]

Similarly, the Birmingham (Alabama) CVB

[W]ill assist with pre-convention planning, registration, housing, publicity, guest activities and tours, and will provide promotional materials and brochures. Publications available include the Visitors Guide, newsletters, tourist maps and Publicity Guide.[18]

The preceding examples represent the various kinds of services typically offered by convention and visitors bureaus across the United States and Canada. Most bureaus are members of the International Association of Convention and Visitors Bureaus (IACVB). Membership is currently at 400+ CVBs representing 30 countries worldwide. Most, however, are located in the United States.

Convention and Visitors Bureau Cost Structure

The cost of supporting CVB activity is determined in several ways. Most are primarily funded by membership dues paid annually by hospitality establishments in the local area or region. Some of these areas or regions have hotel/motel occupancy taxes (usually 5 to 10 percent of the room rate paid by the guest of a lodging facility). A portion of this tax is typically distributed to the CVB.

State or provincial grants or awards are sometimes awarded, too. In Massachusetts, for example, the Greater Boston CVB periodically receives grants from the Boston-based Hynes Convention Center and from the Massachusetts Office of Travel and Tourism. In summary, CVBs are nonprofit organizations largely supported by the constituencies they serve.

SUMMARY

Intermediaries are organizations that assist in the sale of hospitality product offerings. They are in the business of providing travel-related services to hospitality customers. Travel agents, wholesale tour operators, incentive travel houses, independent meeting planners, and convention and visitors bureaus are all intermediaries.

Travel agents are in the retail business. They sell goods and services that are produced and/or developed by a third party such as lodging, transportation, cruise lines, and other hospitality organizations. Travel agents are sales agents and use the same sales process as hospitality sales account executives. Most travel agents are paid on a commission basis. The commission is paid by the hospitality establishment (and not the customer) and is typically 10 percent of the sales price.

Wholesale tour operators develop tour packages to be purchased by consumers. They contract with hospitality companies such as hotels and airlines to develop packages. Tour package bookings are usually done in bulk in exchange for deeply discounted rates. The tour packages are then sold to customers at the retail level through travel agents and/or the retail division of the wholesale tour operator. The "retail price" paid by the consumer is slightly higher than the "wholesale price" paid by the operator to the hospitality suppliers that are part of the tour package. Wholesale tour operators also engage in the sales process. They promote their tour packages to travel agents as well as to consumers directly. They compete for business with other operators offering similar packages.

Incentive travel houses are in the business of developing, packaging, and selling incentive travel programs to companies that offer such reward systems. Incentive travel is a reward given to employees who meet and/or exceed company-set goals. The employee does not pay the travel expenses. It is the company offering the incentive travel program that purchases the product, which typically includes air transportation, lodging, foodservice, and entertainment. Incentive houses have their own planners who develop and implement all aspects of the incentive program. Hospitality organizations that are based in and/or have routes to prime destinations actively seek incentive travel business. Upscale establishments, in particular, target this market. Sales account executives from hotels, resorts, airlines, and cruise lines of this type regularly make personal sales calls on incentive house planners to garner their business.

Independent meeting planners are entrepreneurs who specialize in meeting planning as their business enterprise. Organizations hire these entrepreneurs to develop, plan, and implement their off-premise meeting activity. Independent meeting planners work on a project basis. They may have several clients at the same time in various stages of the meeting planning process. Small-to-medium-sized firms are frequent users of independent meeting planners. These organizations either choose to outsource meeting activity or are not large enough to warrant the expense of a full-time in-house meeting planning department. Larger organizations, however, are increasingly using the expertise and "simplicity" of hiring an outside firm to perform the task.

Convention and Visitors Bureaus (CVBs) are municipal, state, or provincial organizations responsible for promoting tourism for a specific area. They are nonprofit service organizations that act on behalf of the hospitality organizations they represent. CVBs have sales managers whose job is to market and sell the destination. These sales managers do not initiate or sign contracts. Rather, the CVB sales manager puts interested meeting planners and association executives in contact with the hospitality establishments that they serve. Most CVBs are funded, in part, by membership dues paid annually by hospitality establishments in the local area or region.

Travel agents, wholesale tour operators, incentive travel houses, independent meeting planners, and CVBs help sell hospitality. They are customers, too. Hospitality organizations "sell" to intermediaries, which, in turn, "sell" to consumers. Intermediaries are very much a part of the sales process for hospitality sales and marketing.

DISCUSSION QUESTIONS

1. Travel agents are in the retail business. Discuss. What do they sell?
2. What are wholesale tour operators? Are they, too, in the retail business?
3. What is incentive travel? Who are the customers of incentive travel houses?
4. Independent meeting planners are entrepreneurs who own and manage their own businesses. What do they do? Who are their customers?
5. Convention and visitors bureaus (or CVBs) are nonprofit service organizations that act on behalf of the constituencies they serve. Discuss.
6. Why are each of the preceding organizations considered intermediaries? What are intermediaries?

NOTES

1. Christopher Schulz, "Expand Your Sales Potential by Marketing to Travel Agencies," *HSMAI Marketing Review*, Summer 1993, pp. 10–13.
2. Christopher Schulz, "Hotels and Travel Agents: The New Partnership," *Cornell Quarterly*, April 1994, p. 45.
3. "U.S. Travel Agency Survey," *Travel Weekly*, August 29, 1996, p. 24.
4. Ibid., p. 53.
5. M. L. Pina, "The Travel Agent's Best Friend," *Lodging*, November 1994, p. 68.

6. Ibid.
7. Jim Glab, "U.S. Travel Agency Survey," *Travel Weekly*, August 29, 1996, p. 129.
8. Scott Bittle, "U.S. Travel Agency Survey," *Travel Weekly*, August 29, 1996, p. 122.
9. "Yes, Tourists, There Is a Virginia," *Globe and Mail*, May 31, 1997, p. F6.
10. "Trafalgar Tours Offering Scandinavian Tours This Summer," *Travel Trade*, June 16, 1997, p. 16.
11. Margaret Shaw, *The Group Market: What It Is and How to Sell It*, HSMAI Foundation, 1985, p. 45.
12. Susan J. F. Braley and Lisa Grimaldi, "The Complete Guide to Outsourcing Meetings and Incentives," *Meetings & Conventions*, March 1997, p. 85.
13. Ibid.
14. David Ghitelman, "Return Engagement," *Meetings & Conventions*, May 1997, p. 70.
15. Ibid., p. 69.
16. Lisa Grimaldi, "Both Sides Now," *Meetings & Conventions*, February 1997, p. 65.
17. "Atlanta" [advertising supplement], *Meetings & Conventions*, June 1996, p. 182.
18. "Birmingham" [advertising supplement], *Meetings & Conventions*, June 1996, p. 174.

Chapter 12

Hospitality Partnerships

LEARNING OBJECTIVES

1. *To appreciate the growth of partnerships in the hospitality industry and its impact on hospitality sales and marketing*
2. *To become familiar with the two major types of partnerships, which include supplier partnerships and customer partnerships*
3. *To better understand the various kinds of supplier partnerships*
4. *To better understand customer partnerships, which has come to be known as relationship marketing*

A phenomenon of the 1990s in the hospitality industry has been the increasing occurrence of partnering. Variously called strategic alliances, affinity relationships, joint ventures, and other names, these terms actually apply to specific situations. The umbrella concept that covers them all, and the one we will use here, is **partnerships**. These are just what they sound like—two or more firms getting together to benefit mutually from better selling and marketing and enhanced customer satisfaction.

There are essentially two major kinds of partnerships, supplier partnerships and customer partnerships. As shown in Table 12.1, hospitality partnerships with suppliers include reservation networks, consortia and affiliations; frequent-traveler programs; hotel and restaurant partnerships; and like-kind and related-business partnerships. The concept of partnering with customers has come to be known as relationship marketing. This chapter takes a closer look at hospitality partnering activity occurring in the marketplace.

RESERVATION NETWORKS, CONSORTIA, AND AFFILIATIONS

Reservation Networks

Reservation networks are organizations that offer central reservation systems and services to independent and chain-affiliated hospitality organizations including hotels, car rental companies, and cruise lines. Although many larger organizations have their own central reservation systems, this is often not enough. They, too, join reservation networks to gain more exposure, especially in the international arena.

REZsolutions, (Figure 12.1) became the world's largest reservation network system with the merger of Utell International and Anasazi. It represents more than 7000 hotels worldwide in over 140 countries. These include such

---

TABLE 12.1 *Partnerships in Hospitality Sales and Marketing*

Supplier Partnerships

Reservation networks, consortia, and affiliations
Frequent-traveler programs
Hotel and restaurant partnerships
Like-kind business partnerships
Related-business partnerships

Buyer Partnerships

Relationship marketing

well-known names as Ciga, Delta, Embassy Suites, Euro Disney, Four Seasons, Fairmont, Golden Tulip, Hilton International, Holiday Inn, Hyatt, Choice, Omni, Marriott, Nikko, and many others. REZsolutions major customer base is the travel agent. Agents worldwide can find the CRS on every major global distribution system. Another example is Steigenberger Reservation Systems (SRS) of Germany.

Reservation network companies started primarily as reservation systems. However, many now exceed that scope. Some have grown to sophisticated marketing support services working closely with their supplier clients to identify and tap new business, improve rate delivery, and boost occupancies. Thus, they offer marketing and sales support services as well as reservation systems.

A hotel or hotel company can, in effect, partner with a range of network choices. These choices include (1) a basic reservation answering service, (2) a hotel chain reservation system, (3) an independent full-service reservation marketing system such as REZsolutions described previously, and (4) the airline-based global distribution systems.

A basic reservation answering system simply answers the phone with the name of the client's hotel or hotel company. The REZsolutions and SRS full-service reservation marketing systems are well known and carry the clout of their brand name, especially among travel agents. And, not surprisingly, these types of systems are more expensive to join than a basic reservation service.

Consortia

Consortia are niche-based reservation marketing systems, such as Leading Hotels of the World, Preferred Hotels, and Relais et Chateaux of France. These reservation networks partner only with upscale/luxury properties and have stringent standards and tight membership requirements. Consortia are considered brand names and have strong marketing pull. Consortia charge annual membership fees and per booking fees for each reservation made at a member hotel. Memberships are typically limited in consortia. For example, Preferred Hotels has about 100 members strategically located across the globe. Each member hotel actively promotes other members of the consortia to which it belongs.

Affiliations

Affiliations are partnerships that are less stringent than consortia and reservation network systems. Inter-Continental Hotels, for example, has a division called "Global Partners." The partners are independent hotels or small

REZsolutions, Inc. is a powerful new force in the global hospitality industry, formed by the merger between Utell International, the world's leading hotel reservations and marketing company, and Anasazi Inc., the leading supplier of IT-based solutions to hotel businesses worldwide.

By combining the strengths of these two highly successful companies, REZsolutions, Inc. is the industry's first 'one-stop shop' for integrated technology, reservations and marketing solutions.

Here's how you will benefit:

What does REZsolutions mean to me?

Increased visibility …extended distribution …higher margins …lower costs …and endless possibilities. The creation of REZsolutions has opened up a whole new world of opportunities for existing Utell and Anasazi customers as well as for new prospects, through an unparalleled portfolio of products and services. Now you can profit from both companies' proven track records in terms of innovative research and development, access to leading edge technology, comprehensive reservations and data management solutions, worldwide business development and marketing planning, distributed globally through a network of offices worldwide. No other company has this unique ability to offer complete end-to-end integrated solutions to its customers. What's more, you can benefit from the high value of these products and services with total confidence, knowing that REZsolutions is committed to helping you achieve a real competitive advantage.

How will REZsolutions help me reach my target markets?

REZsolutions puts the hotel industry's most extensive distribution network at your disposal, with 56 sales and reservations offices in 38 countries and automated connections to over half a million travel agent terminals. We do business in more than 180 countries, from Bombay to Buenos Aires and from Vladivostok to Venice. In fact, wherever you need us, we have local experts ready to help. Our services encompass the international and domestic markets, covering the travel agency, corporate, leisure, meetings and group business sectors.

FIGURE 12.1 *Utell International reservation network. (Courtesy of Utell International, on REZSolutions Company. Reprinted with permission.)*

How will REZsolutions help develop my business?

REZsolutions not only offers you the benefit of international marketing expertise, but also has the appropriate products and services to generate business effectively from specific target markets. Using our extensive knowledge of local cultures and business customs, we can help you establish an effective presence in your chosen areas. We provide extensive consultancy services for marketing planning and global business development, working closely with you on a partnership basis.

How will I benefit from REZsolutions' integrated solutions?

Unique to the hotel industry, REZsolutions offers you a complete yet highly flexible 'end-to-end' technology solution. Our broad information technology platform can be used to deliver business efficiently to each of your

The data generated by our IT systems can be channeled back into planning and development, thus optimizing business from the worldwide market through REZsolutions' extensive worldwide network and marketing solutions.

properties, maximize the yield from that business and process data into meaningful market information and reports. An example of this is ALESA (Anasazi Lodging Enterprise System Architecture), REZsolutions' integrated suite of complementary products which can provide a central reservation system, property management system, revenue management, guest history and recognition, data warehousing and decision support technology – all in one.

What changes can I expect to the products and services I currently use?

You will not notice any change at all. All existing products will continue to be offered and enhanced. In addition to the current portfolio of products and services, you will have access to property management, yield management and data warehousing systems within the next six months. Further information will be published in regular newsletter updates, and you will also be kept fully informed by your Account Manager.

What level of support and customer service can I expect?

Our global presence means that we are in a unique position to meet your systems, marketing and distribution needs wherever you are in the world. REZsolutions has all the necessary resources and personnel to provide full business development and operational support for your objectives at the local level. All activity is coordinated by a single Account Manager for maximum convenience and efficiency. Whatever your objectives, REZsolutions will be there to guide you every step of the way.

How do I find out more?

Contact any one of the offices listed on the back of this brochure. The REZsolutions representatives at these locations will be pleased to answer your questions and provide you with any assistance you may need.

FIGURE 12.1 *(continued)*

chains that fit a similar profile of quality, reputation, and upscale location. These properties get access to Inter-Continental's worldwide sales, marketing, and reservation services, while Inter-Continental gets representation in strategic locations. Guests at these properties benefit from Inter-Continental's frequent-guest program including recognition and VIP treatment, but not points or prizes.

The Adolphus Hotel was one of the first Inter-Continental "Global Partners." It is one of several Noble House Hotels and Resorts, a small luxury chain based in Dallas, Texas. Within the first two years of this partnership, room nights and revenue at the Adolphus more than doubled. Much of this was attributed to the newly formed link with Inter-Continental.[1] Noble House now has five of its hotels in the Global Partners program.

FREQUENT-TRAVELER PROGRAMS

Frequent-traveler program partnerships are common today. Just about every hotel chain, airline, car rental, and credit card company has a partnership with one or more of the others for the purpose of awarding frequent traveler points. And the traveler can pretty much use his or her own discretion as to where, when, and how to get and use the points. The idea, of course, is to build customer loyalty by having points available from suppliers of related products. In return, hospitality organizations are building databases on frequent travelers (see Chapter 10). Companies then develop profiles of their most frequent users and can target advertising, design special promotions, and provide other benefits that appeal to the frequent user of their product.

Figure 12.2 displays Radisson SAS's partnership with 23 airlines. Note that the airlines represent various regions throughout the world, including Scandinavia (SAS), Germany (Lufthansa), Great Britain (British Airways), Australia (Qantas), Iceland, Mexico, Canada, and the United States.

It is important to comment that no airline or hotel company has exclusivity with one or the other. That is, the growth of these frequent-traveler program partnerships gives the customer a multitude of choices. Customers can build points in numerous ways without having to be loyal to just one company. Business travelers, in particular, purposely belong to a number of frequent-traveler programs to take full advantage of program benefits. Thus, building customer loyalty through these types of partnerships is getting a bit convoluted and perhaps diminishing *true* customer loyalty—which was the original intent of frequent traveler programs in the first place. Nonetheless, and perhaps more important, the customer has a choice—lots of choices from which to make a hospitality purchase decision.

Sales and marketing executives can no longer rely on frequent-traveler

FIGURE 12.2   *Radisson SAS partnership with airlines advertisement. (Courtesy of Radisson SAS Hotels Worldwide. Reprinted with permission.)*

programs to differentiate their product offering. These programs, especially when coupled with the rapid growth of partnership programs, have become routinely expected from all major players. Today's travelers expect more from the programs. There is much debate as to the true ability of the programs to increase customer loyalty.

HOTEL AND RESTAURANT PARTNERSHIPS

For a number of years, foodservice operations in many hotels have been considered "loss leaders" or necessary evils. That is, they were thought to be essential to the hotel in attracting customers but they often operated at considerable loss. Hotel foodservice has a European heritage, particularly French and Swiss, where the culinary arts subsumed the guest room side of the business. In other words, food and beverage operations took priority over the lodging side of the business from a management perspective. Although this is still true in some smaller hostelries across Europe, many hotel managers today, at least in North America, consider themselves in the business of managing hotels and not operating restaurants.

The deluxe five-star Palace Hotel in New York City, for example, operated a deluxe restaurant that lost over $2 million a year. A very successful five-star restaurant in the city, Le Cirque, was looking for a new location. The two developed a partnership with Le Cirque moving into the hotel restaurant site in 1997. The restaurant operates independently of the hotel, yet the two share a common clientele. Le Cirque provides an upscale restaurant facility that many hotel guests want, and it attracts local clientele that the previous hotel restaurant had not been able to do. Once again, a win–win situation has been created and, to date, is very successful.

Today, many hotels lease their food and beverage facilities to outside operators. This reduces the hotel's exposure to the high cost (and high risk to the hotel operator) of the food and beverage business. Some lodging establishments retain part of the food and beverage operation such as coffee kiosks, room service, banquet facilities, and cocktail lounges. In a sense, assuming they get a good foodservice operator, the hotels give up very little, probably save money, and have the same or better foodservice facilities.

Restaurant operators also gain. They get access to prime locations, a built-in customer base, instant name recognition, and joint sales and marketing services. Of course, if the restaurants are well branded, they also bring their own recognition factor. For example, Bonanza and Ponderosa steak houses are locating in many Choice Hotel properties with which they do joint marketing and sales. More upscale, Ruth's Chris Steak House, with over

40 freestanding units in the United States and Canada, is expanding further by locating in upscale hotels. Morton's of Chicago, also a posh steak house, is in the five-star Nikko Hotel in Beverly Hills, among others. Tony Roma's rib restaurants are in Hiltons, the Stardust Hotel in Las Vegas, and two Continental Plaza hotels in Mexico. A Red Lion Inn in San Jose livened up its too quiet bar off the lobby by leasing it to a local sushi bar operator. Elephant and Castle of Vancouver operates English-style restaurants in some hotels in Canada and the United States.

Off-Premise Foodservice Providers

Another variation on the theme is when outside operators provide a hotel's room service meals. This is more likely to be the case with limited-service hotels that do not have an in-house restaurant. Hawthorne Suites Hotels offers considerable choice in ordering meals from nearby restaurants for room delivery. Menus from several nearby restaurants are promoted together in an in-room flyer. The guest simply calls the restaurant of his or her choice to place a "home delivery" order.

More limited menu choices from off-premise foodservice providers, such as pizza, are also common. When hotel managers observed the number of pizzas being delivered to their hotels by local pizza establishments, some decided they might as well join the process and reap the benefits of "customer satisfaction." Pizza Hut has table tents in the rooms of numerous hotels across the United States and Canada, and delivers on demand.

In still another twist to off-premise foodservice options, the Radisson Suite hotel in Boca Raton, Florida, has teamed up with the local Pete's Restaurant to offer meeting and banquet facilities in separate yet nearby buildings connected by a lakeside promenade (see Figure 12.3). Through this joint partnership, Pete's Restaurant has expanded its customer base and the Radisson has enhanced the foodservice options for its guests without having to "get into" the foodservice business.

Freestanding Foodservice/Hotel Relationships

Limited-service and budget properties are, for the most part, not in the food and beverage business at all. But they do need and want to have foodservice accessibility for their guests. This has led to joint arrangements between lodging and foodservice operators to build independently yet side by side or nearby. A number of restaurant chains have participated in this kind of partnership including Burger King, McDonald's, Denny's, Taco Bell, Hardee's,

Boca Radisson and Pete's Restaurant team to offer superior meeting facilities

Pete's Restaurant of Boca Raton and The Radisson Suite Hotel of Boca Raton that share the wooded, waterfront environment at the Arvida Parkway Center on Glades Road, recently announced that they have officially formed a long-awaited joint venture. The two neighboring establishments have combined their marketing services to offer one of the finest full-service meeting and banquet facilities in the Southeast. For meeting banquet planners within the South Florida business community, as well as the many out of staters who utilize Florida locations for their meetings and conventions, the partnership simplifies the initial contact and coordination process. Whereas, it was previously necessary to work with separate entities to take advantage of these two superb facilities, clients may now plan every detail of an event with the help of a single, experienced coordinator. More importantly, the partnership combines the benefits and resources of a nationally reknown restaurant and caterer and a premier hotel into one convenient package. Widely recognized for their excellence, both Pete's Restaurant and Radisson Suite Hotel have received numerous awards. The Radisson has been honored as the number one Radisson within the world-wide chain two years consecutively as well as receiving the Five Star President's Award. Pete's lakefront restaurant has been hailed by the food critics and has been the recipient of several prestigious national awards for its fine cuisine and exceptional architecture, placing it in the same groupings as The Four Seasons and Spago's.

Peter Boinis, developer and owner of Pete's Restaurant, noted that the facilities are ideal for board meetings, seminars, company banquets, or entertaining corporate guests.

"Professionals who want the best for their guests will be delighted with our unique catering facilities," he stated. "Not only do we offer the finest cuisine, and serve it in the most beautiful surroundings, we also pride ourselves on our presentation, service, and attention to detail."

The ambiance, first-class style and service continue with the Radisson Suite Hotel, which features 200 luxurious spacious suites, complimentary breakfasts and cocktails, and courteous treatment by an excellent staff under the direction of General Manager Tom Perregaux. By using the two facilities, planners can efficiently host events of all types and sizes. While the Radisson's meeting rooms are perfect for mid-sized group meetings and conferences, Pete's versatile catering facilities can easily accommodate large meetings, receptions, cocktail parties, banquets and board meetings. As Boca Raton's premier restaurant and top-flight hotel, Pete's and the Radisson will transform your plans into a memorable special occasion or a smooth and successful business affair.

Out-of-town guests can take advantage of on-site recreational opportunities including a heated swimming pool, lakeside jogging trail, and exercise room. Hotel guests also have privileges at several nearby golf courses, tennis centers and health spas. The center also provides convenient access to major expressways, shopping malls and airports.

For additional information contact Alisa Farrell or Robert Tedesco, Pete's Catering Coordinators at (407) 487-1600 or Renee Bacher, Director of Sales and Marketing for the Radisson Suite Hotel, (407) 483-3600.

FIGURE 12.3 *Radisson Suite Hotel and Pete's Restaurant partnership article. (Courtesy of Boca Radisson Suite Hotel. Reprinted with permission.)*

Sizzler, and many others, with properties like EconoLodge, Days Inn, Super 8, and Holiday Express. Generally, the partnership is formed before building commences.

Marketing-oriented hotel management, whether for a one-, three-, or five-star operation, needs to consider the following issues with regard to partnering its food and beverage service[2]:

- What kind of food and beverage choices do our customers want and expect?
- What kind of concept is most consistent with the hotel's positioning?
- Would an outside operator, particularly a brand name one, enhance our sales and marketing and provide a competitive advantage?
- Which operators can provide a better product at a lower cost than we can do ourselves?

On the other hand, the foodservice operator with a particular concept needs to consider the following:

- Will the hotel deliver enough customers, and the right kind, who will provide a substantial customer base?
- Is there potential for customers from local businesses, residences, and other hotels?
- How much competition is there? Are we sufficiently differentiated?
- Are we a good match?

These, of course, are the marketing questions that need to be answered but they need to be answered first. If the answers are not positive, there would be no point in proceeding with further negotiations for a partner relationship. In the final analysis, partnerships must be mutually beneficial.

LIKE-KIND BUSINESS PARTNERSHIPS

Like-kind partnerships are those where two or more organizations in the same business form an alliance to benefit all parties. For example, and shown in Figure 12.4, the Westin and Marriott hotels in Copley Place, Boston, formed "The Copley Connection" in order to attract larger groups between them. Although these two hotels normally compete head to head for convention business, each has only so much capacity. By partnering, they can go after large conventions that neither could handle alone.

A global like-kind business partnership example is the strategic alliance between Radisson Hotels of Minneapolis and SAS International Hotels of Brussels. Following an extensive search for a global partner "fit," the Radisson SAS partnership emerged. Radisson had a large presence in North

FIGURE 12.4 *The Copley Connection (Boston, Massachusetts) advertisement. (Courtesy of Boston Marriott Copley Place, Westin Hotel Copley Place, and Copley Place Shopping Galleries. Reprinted with permission.)*

America; SAS had a large presence in northern Europe. Both companies were seeking to grow in the international marketplace. SAS was given use of the Radisson name in Europe and the Middle East and all rights for development in those areas. Its hotels now carry the name Radisson SAS, which provides recognition for North Americans and Europeans alike. Radisson also has an elaborate central reservation system. When tied into the SAS system, this permits powerful joint marketing and sales efforts around the world.

Figure 12.5 illustrates a partnership among airlines called the "Star Alliance." Although these airlines compete with each other on some routes, they can now offer "seamless" travel around the world. Each sells the others' products. Travel agents can book all of them with one reservation. And, of course, frequent travelers get their mileage points no matter which airline they are flying at any one time. As a result, customer satisfaction is enhanced.

Foodservice chains do likewise. This is quite common on major highways in both North America and Europe, although in a little different context. Not that you will see McDonald's and Burger King sharing the same site. Very unlikely. But you will see either one of them on highway stops along with, perhaps, KFC, Baskin-Robbins, TCBY, Mrs. Fields' Cookies, or any number of other combinations. The cost of space is shared, the cost of signage is shared, and the customer has options. Each member of a traveling family has a choice. In other words, these are partnerships that enhance sales, reduce costs, and, most important, elevate customer satisfaction.

Another form of like-kind partnerships is when organizations get together to share advertising and related marketing expenses. Joint advertising is done commonly in printed newspaper ads. Publications charge the same amount for an ad whether it contains the name of one establishment or the names of ten. Proportionately, however, the larger the ad the less cost for a given amount of space. In other words, a large ad costs less than the total cost of 10 small ads. This difference can be significant. Figure 12.6 shows an example. In this case, nine inns have partnered together in four ways: first, in newspaper advertising; second, in a toll-free 800 number; third, in a joint guidebook; and, finally, in a joint Web site. Yet, individually, they all compete with each other.

RELATED-BUSINESS PARTNERSHIPS

We refer to **related-business partnerships** when related, and sometimes competitive, hospitality organizations partner together for joint sales and marketing activity. Organizations such as hotels, cruise lines, foodservices, theme parks, and credit card companies often team up to enhance their presence in the marketplace.

FIGURE 12.5 *Star Alliance airline partnership. (Courtesy of Star Alliance. Reprinted with permission.)*

OVER 100 WINTER PACKAGES
AT ONTARIO'S FINEST COUNTRY INNS

Cross Country Skiing... for two!
Award Winning Four Diamond Dining
Enjoy exceptional dining from our "Modern Country House Menu" and free use of our 16 kms of cross country trails. Luxury rooms with whirlpools and fireplaces available. 3 night packages start at $252 pp including breakfast & dinner for 2, use of the Idlewood Health Club, cross country skis and trails. All just 2 hours north of Toronto!
Reservations: 1-800-461-4233
SHERWOOD INN
Lake Joseph, Port Carling, Muskoka

RELAX and RECHARGE WITH SUPERB FOOD, FINE WINE and A WARM FIRE.

Try a "Magical Midweek" Break! from: $98 p.p./ per day
SIR SAM'S INN
DOWNHILL AND CROSS-COUNTRY SKIING
1-800-361-2188 • (705) 754-2188
Eagle Lake P/O, Haliburton, Ont. K0M 1M0

THE WOODLAWN TERRACE INN, Cobourg Ontario
Elegant mansion circa 1835. Luxurious guest rooms with romantic fireplaces, king size beds, whirlpool tubs and 12' ceilings. Exquisite gourmet dining, fresh, home-made pastas, traditional family recipes for decadent sweets. Extensive wine cellar. Relaxing activities. Only 1 hour east of Toronto in historic, lakeside Cobourg.
"The King of Cobourg" - 2 day package
$74 p.p./ per day
Call 1-800-573-5003

Langdon Hall
Country House Hotel
Is that a key in your pocket ...or did you only reserve a table?
My Lovely Valentine Package available February 12-16.
Treat your valentine to a special affair that includes a bottle of champagne upon arrival, two nights accommodation, breakfast each morning, Valentine dinner one night and "something silky to take home".
Space is limited, so don't leave until the last minute.
Gift Certificates for the Spa are available for those who can't get away.
R.R.33 Cambridge, Ontario N3H 4R8
1•800•268•1898 1•519•740•2100

Domain of Killien
At the south tip of Algonquin Park, there is a small, personal inn amidst a 5000-acre private estate offering quiet comfort, French regional Cuisine and Hospitality in the tradition of the finest European Inns.
In the Winter you can enjoy our 28km of ski trails, skate under the stars, read by a crackling fire or...
MASTER THE ART OF DOING NOTHING... *BEAUTIFULLY*
...in the Haliburton Highlands
(705) 457-1100
www.domainofkillien.on.ca

Ski Magic at The Millcroft Inn
Enjoy great alpine skiing, first class accommodation and fine dining! The package includes: first class accommodation, (1) dinner for two, (2) breakfasts and 2 days of skiing and lift tickets at The Caledon Ski Club.
from $129.00* per person, per night
MILLCROFT Inn
* Based on double occupancy, and a 2 night stay. Some rooms have hot tubs, fireplaces or Jacuzzis. Tax and service charges are additional.
Ask about our NEW Spa Facilities!
55 John St., Alton, Ontario, L0N 1A0
1-800-383-3976 Fax:(519) 941-9192
...or visit our website: www.millcroft.com
CALEDON HILLS

A Perfect Valentine's Gift
Give your loved one an experience to remember... an escape to our romantic country inn. Call us now to book a gift certificate for a *couple's getaway*, or perhaps a personal spa retreat. Your sweetheart will *love* you for it!
1-800-265-1711
Benmiller Inn
R.R.#4, Goderich, Ontario (2 hrs from Toronto)
Email: benmiller@odyssey.on.ca

Call 1-800-340-INNS (4667) for your FREE, full-colour, 22 page **Guidebook and Passport to Ontario's Finest Country Inns**. Or visit our website! http://www.countryinns.org

FIGURE 12.6 *Like-kind partnership advertisement. (Courtesy of Independent Innkeepers of Ontario and the Globe and Mail. Reprinted with permission.)*

Hyatt, for example, has joined forces with Royal Caribbean Cruise Line. Travelers can combine three- or four-night stays in Puerto Rico at the Hyatt Regency Ceromar Beach or the Hyatt Dorado Beach Resort and Casino with three- or four-night sails in the Caribbean aboard the *Nordic Empress.* These are all-inclusive tour packages put together by these two hospitality organizations. "It's the lure of cruising that's the real spoiler . . . Hyatt, for one, has applied an age-old approach to competition: If you can't beat 'em, join 'em."[3] The program is called "Cruise Hyatt," a creative nomenclature to capture the attention of the Caribbean-going vacation market. Hyatt has a special toll-free number devoted to programs such as these, Hyatt Vacations at (800) 772–0011.

Looking at another area of hospitality, McDonald's has secured a 10-year marketing partnership with Disney. McDonald's has exclusive rights to promote everything from Disney movies and videos to TV shows and theme park rides in its own promotional campaigns. Disney also has McDonald's as its "presenting sponsor" at the Animal Kingdom theme park (in Walt Disney World in Florida), which opened in 1998. This agreement prevents McDonald's from working with other entertainment entities (as it previously did with the movies *Jurassic Park* and *Batman and Robin*). Likewise, this partnership breaks the arrangement that Disney had with Burger King, McDonald's arch rival. Nonetheless, Burger King is now free to pursue partnerships of a similar nature.

Still another related-business partnership is when a credit card company seeks to encourage the use of its card and teams up with a hotel company offering a benefit for using the card with that organization. For example, Hilton offered the customers benefit of a free night's stay at participating Hiltons when they used the American Express card to pay their bill. This type of promotion is usually short-term, with restrictions that apply to reap the reward. For the frequent traveler, however, the restrictions are not overbearing.

Related-business partnerships are numerous, and growth in this area of hospitality sales and marketing will continue to expand. It is spreading in popularity among suppliers (and buyers) as another avenue to the ultimate goal of customer satisfaction. The core product has to be right, yet why not enhance that product offering to introduce repeat and new customers to the many facets of hospitality.

RELATIONSHIP MARKETING

Building a lifelong customer relationship has come to be called **relationship marketing**. There is nothing more important than the ongoing relationship with a customer, which is, in effect, a partnership. As Thomas Stewart points out, a satisfied customer is not enough. He recounts an experience at a well-known hotel in Washington, DC, after which he felt satisfied but not ready to return because of minor irritations. "We're used to thinking—assuming really—that satisfaction and loyalty move in tandem," says Stewart. "In vigorously competitive markets, a graph—with satisfaction on the horizontal axis and retention on the vertical axis—doesn't rise diagonally. Instead, it dawdles along a curve: Loyalty rises a bit as satisfaction increases, swooping abruptly up only at the highest levels of satisfaction."[4]

Others have found similarly: "If satisfaction is ranked on a 1-to-5 scale, from completely dissatisfied to completely satisfied, the 4's though satisfied are six times more likely to defect than the 5's."[5] Stewart states, a "way to stop customers from playing the field is to marry them—to forge intimate, mutually beneficial partnerships based on an exchange of knowledge about each other's desires, needs, abilities, and character."[6] Again, we call this relationship marketing.

Relationship marketing is the building and maintenance of customer relations. It is based on the premise that buyers and sellers enter an exchange between them with expectations for future exchanges. It is the responsibility of sales, marketing, and the entire team of the hospitality establishment to foster this exchange relationship.

Although relationship marketing is applicable in any industry, it is especially so in the hospitality industry. As suggested by Leonard Berry of the American Marketing Association, there are several key considerations when relationship marketing is of particular significance.[7] These include the following:

- When there is an ongoing and/or periodic desire for service by the customer
- When the customer controls the selection of the service supplier
- When there are alternative supplier choices
- When customer loyalty is weak and switching suppliers is common and easy
- When word of mouth is an especially potent form of communication about a product

Each of these very much reflects the purchase of hospitality goods and services.

Theodore Levitt probably stated the case best almost 20 years ago:

The sale merely consummates the courtship. Then the marriage begins. How good the marriage is depends on how well the relationship is managed by the seller. That determines whether there will be continued or expanded business or troubles and divorce, and whether costs and profits increase.

. . . It is not just that once you get a customer you want to keep him. It is more a matter of what the buyer wants. He wants a vendor who will keep his promises, who'll keep supplying and stand behind what he promised. The age of the blind date or the one-night stand is gone. Marriage is both more convenient and more necessary. . . . In these conditions success in marketing, like success in marriage, is transformed into the inescapability of a relationship.[8]

The purpose of relationship marketing, or customer partnering, is, of course, to build loyalty. Although incentives such as discounts, prizes, and awards may bring in customers, they do not always build loyalty. Often the "loyalty" is to the incentive itself rather than to the establishment offering the incentive to purchase. As Levitt has so well stated, building loyalty comes from building a relationship. If the relationship is right, the customer may even be willing to pay more because of it. This means thinking in terms of the customers you have, not just the ones you want to acquire. This means customizing relationships.

The new database technology is one way to help customize a relationship. We have the ability to record and perform on each purchase occasion what a particular customer wants such as a feather pillow, a certain newspaper, a particular room configuration, or preferred seating in a restaurant. But databases are not enough. We have to get inside the head of the customer whether he or she is in our database or not. In other words, we have to think like a customer.

To do this is both complex and yet so simple. Consider how often customers are seated in a restaurant where it is convenient to the operation rather than where the customer would prefer to sit. Many restaurants on slower nights, for example, will close a section of the dining room. Fair enough. But which section is closed? Often, it is the one farthest from the kitchen to make it easier for the waitstaff to service their guests. Thus, the customer gets to sit closer to the noise and mayhem of the kitchen instead of the more relaxing and typically more inviting section of the restaurant. As customers ourselves, we have encountered this scenario many times, too many times.

Many hotels now ask "Smoking or nonsmoking?" when customers are making reservations. Yet, still, many do not. How simple. But, then, even when reservationists do follow this policy, they often say that it cannot be guaranteed. If this request, which is very important to many customers, cannot be guaranteed, should the hotel even take the reservation with a "We will do our best" approach to the request? Not fulfilling the smoking/nonsmoking request can be a sure way to lose the customer forever.

Again, management and employees have to put themselves inside the customer's head to build a relationship and loyalty. Why? Because to not do so is probably the greatest failure in building customer relations. The very frequent traveler gets his name and preferences entered into the database. His needs and wants are presumably taken care of; he becomes a loyal customer. But that's only a small percentage of our customer base. We have to reach out to new customers, too, until they all become loyal customers. And then we have to constantly remind ourselves that today they may be loyal, but what about tomorrow?

Relationship marketing is a way of thinking. It reinforces thinking about the long-term relationship with our customers including today, tomorrow, and the day after that. And what about next month? Next year? And the year after that?

> [R]elationship marketing goes to the heart of the marketing philosophy. Traditional definitions of maketing focus on the primacy of customer needs . . . relationship marketing as a philosophy refocuses marketing strategy away from products and their life cycles towards customer relationship life cycles.[9]

Yes. The customer does have a life cycle. And we need to think how we can best appeal to that customer throughout the course of the life cycle continuum.

In Chapter 2, we introduced the sales process as consisting of five basic steps. Step 1 is opening the relationship, step 2 is qualifying the account, step 3 is presenting the message, and step 4 is closing the sale—asking for the business. Step 5 is service delivery, delivering as promised. Relationship marketing, in a sense, is going one step further. It requires asking the customer, "Will you come back? What more can we do for you to want to come back?"

Relationship marketing is a mindset. It is a way of perceiving what hospitality management is all about. Who are our customers? What are they really buying? What do they need today? What will they need tomorrow? The only way to find out is to ask. Probing is a continuous process. It never ends.

The customer is king, and always will be. Customers dictate what our product is today and what it will be tomorrow. So we can't just think today. We have to think tomorrow, too, from a *customer* perspective. Relationship marketing is truly what hospitality is all about. Getting and keeping a customer. If we don't get and keep that customer, someone else will.

SUMMARY

Partnerships are when two or more firms join forces to enhance sales. Hospitality partnerships include reservation networks, consortia, and affiliations; frequent-traveler programs; hotel and restaurant partnerships; like-kind and related business partnerships. Partnerships with customers have come to be known as relationship marketing.

Reservation networks are organizations that provide central reservation systems for independent and chain hospitality organizations. Although large chain operations have their own CRSs, joining a reservation network can give them more exposure, especially in the international marketplace.

Consortia are niche-based marketing organizations. Membership in these organizations comprises largely upscale independent hotel operators. Most consortia have central reservation systems and each member hotel actively promotes other members of the consortia to which it belongs.

Affiliations are joint partnerships that are more loosely organized than consortia and reservation networks. Independent hotels often affiliate with a branded hotel company. Although not owned or managed by the chain operation, affiliated hotels are included in the central reservation system. In return, the chain operation can offer customers hotel accommodations in locations where they are not present.

Frequent-traveler program partnerships are common today. Many hotel, airline, and car rental companies have teamed up with one or more of the others to offer joint frequent-traveler programs. When a customer stays at a Marriott, for example, he or she has an option to get hotel or airline mileage points. In other words, the customer is given a choice as to where he or she most prefers to build the frequent-traveler awards. The two noncompeting hospitality organizations share the customer database that is created as a result of the partnership.

Hotel and restaurant partnerships are growing in hospitality. Full-service hotels are increasingly leasing their food and beverage outlets to outside operators. Thus, the hotelier focuses on the lodging side of the business and the restaurateur focuses on their expertise in foodservice management. Limited-service and budget hotels are also hooking up with foodservice operators. Joint arrangements are being made to build side by side or nearby. Lodging management needs to offer foodservice, and restaurant companies are looking for growth opportunities. Together, they are joining forces and benefiting the customer, too.

Like-kind partnerships are those where two or more organizations in the same business form an alliance. The purpose is to share resources and enhance sales and marketing to similar target markets. Hotel companies such as Radisson based in the United States and SAS formerly based in Scandinavia partnered to increase awareness and marketing clout in their respective geographic locations. This partnership is expanding the presence of both companies in Europe, the Middle East, and North Africa. Like-kind partnerships also share advertising and related marketing expenses.

Related-business partnerships refer to organizations from different sectors of the hospitality industry partnering together. Theme parks partner with foodservice companies. Cruise lines partner with hotels. The idea is that customers often seek several hospitality venues when traveling. So why not join forces and offer joint package options to vacation and business travelers alike. It is similar in concept to wholesale tour operators developing tour packages. Yet, in related-business partnerships, there is no wholesale tour operator involved in the process.

Relationship marketing is building a lifelong partnership with customers of a hospitality establishment. It is creating, developing, and maintaining customer relationships. Marketing is creating and keeping a customer. Relationship marketing focuses on the "keeping" of that customer. What are their needs today? What will their needs be tomorrow? How can we keep customers coming back again and again? Customers have a life cycle and their needs will evolve and change. Hospitality sales and marketing is understanding what they need today, tomorrow, and the day after that. In hospitality, it is too easy to fall into the trap of being overly focused on product. It is the customer who purchases our product, not us. The customer is our reason for being in business in the first place, and always will be.

DISCUSSION QUESTIONS

1. Briefly describe the essence of hospitality partnerships.
2. Compare and contrast reservation networks, consortia, and affiliations. Give an example of each in a hospitality context.
3. In hospitality, there is growth in the development of hotel and restaurant partnerships. Discuss.
4. What are like-kind partnerships? Suggest a hospitality example to support your response.
5. Compare and contrast like-kind partnerships with related-business partnerships. How are they similar? How are they different?
6. As stated by Theodore Levitt, "success in marketing, like success in

marriage, is transformed into the inescapability of a relationship."
Discuss.

7. What *is* relationship marketing?

NOTES

1. "Inter-Continental Sells Muscle," *Hotels*, August 1995, p. 18.
2. Adapted, in part, from Robert W. Strate and Clinton L. Rappole, "Strategic Alliances Between Hotels and Restaurants," *Cornell Quarterly*, June 1997, p. 51.
3. "Winter Perks Abound in Caribbean," *Orlando Sentinel*, 1997, p. L-2.
4. Thomas A. Stewart, "A Satisfied Customer Isn't Enough," *Fortune*, July 21, 1997, p. 112.
5. Cited by Stewart from Thomas Jones and W. Earl Sasser, "Why Satisfied Customers Defect," *Harvard Business Review*, November–December, 1995, pp. 88–99.
6. Stewart, "A Satisfied Customer Isn't Enough," p. 112.
7. Adapted from L. L. Berry, "Relationship Marketing," in *Emerging Perspectives of Services Marketing*, L. L. Berry, G. D. Shostack, and G. D. Upah, Eds., American Marketing Association, Chicago, 1983, p. 25.
8. Theodore Levitt, "Marketing Intangible Products and Product Intangibles," *Harvard Business Review*, May–June 1991, pp. 94–102. © 1981 by the President and Fellows of Harvard College. All rights reserved.
9. Adrian J. Palmer and Richard Mayer, "Relationship Marketing: A New Paradigm for the Travel and Tourism Sector?" *Journal of Vacation Marketing*, Vol. 2, No. 4, 1996, p. 330.

Glossary

Account: Refers to a customer or a grouping of customers from an organization, such as a business enterprise or a professional trade association, that has ongoing needs for hospitality services.

Actual Market Share (AMS): Comparing actual occupancies of competing hotels to the overall combined occupancy for these facilities over a given period of time.

Advertising: Indirect, nonpersonal communication to prospective customers through various media including radio, television, newspapers, billboards, and the like.

Affiliations: Partnerships among hospitality organizations providing mutual benefits primarily in the area of sales and marketing. They are less stringent (or less binding) then consortia and reservation networks.

Association executive: A person who assumes the responsibility of planning meetings for an association. (*Note*: In some associations, this title may reflect other positions within the organization.)

Association market: A market segment composed of state, regional, national, and international associations. These organizations are formed to serve the common interests and goals of its individual members.

Average daily rate (ADR): Average room revenue per occupied room, calculated by dividing total room revenue by the number of rooms sold. Establishments may or may not include complimentary rooms, out-of-order rooms, and day-use rooms in the calculation.

Banquet manager: Individual within a catering department who is assigned and responsible for delivery of specific banquet events. This person works closely with the catering services manager.

Bartering: The exchange of goods and services between two business organizations with no cash transactions.

Binding contract: A legal document indicating that each party has accepted the obligation to fulfill his or her part of an agreement; signed by the parties in question.

Brochure: Indirect, nonpersonal printed material describing a hospitality product offering.

Bundle pricing: When two or more aspects of a product or service are priced as one.

Casinos: Gaming operations including traditional casinos, hotel and resort casinos, theme casinos, and riverboat casinos. Casinos usually provide food and beverage services; some provide lodging accommodations.

Catering sales manager: Individual who solicits local banquet business such as weddings, rotary club luncheons, and local business functions.

Catering services manager: Individual who attends to the specific details of a catering event once the function has been booked.

Central reservation system (CRS): A computerized reservation system that contains a data bank of available guest room inventory for sale for multiunit hospitality organizations.

Client: A regular customer of a hospitality establishment.

Cold calling: Essentially "knocking on doors," it is a process used to garner information on the hospitality needs of a potential customer, find out who the decision maker is, and, in turn, determine if a true prospect has been identified.

Communication mix: Communication tools used to reach identified target markets including personal selling, advertising, direct mail, public relations, brochures, merchandising, and special promotions.

Conference services manager (CSM): Individual responsible for coordinating the various aspects of an event being held at a hospitality establishment. The job includes client contact, preconvention meetings, convention resumes, and function room setups.

Confirmation: Gives details of what was agreed upon between two or more parties.

Consortia: Loosely knit groups of similar yet independently owned and operated hotels that share joint marketing efforts such as advertising and a central reservation system.

Contract foodservice: Firms that provide food and beverage management on a contractual basis for institutional organizations. Some corporate organizations also use contract foodservice for their office complexes.

Convention and visitors bureau (CVB): Municipal, state, or provincial non-profit organization involved with the promotion of tourism for a specific area.

Convention centers: Exhibit halls providing large amounts of unobstructed space for exhibits and trade shows. Most convention centers are owned and operated by state or local governments.

Convention resume: An internal document that details all aspects of an event scheduled to take place at a hospitality establishment. It is normally prepared by the convention services manager.

Convention services manager: *See* **Conference services manager.**

Corporate market: A market segment composed of employees who travel for individual or group meeting needs.

Cruise lines: Hospitality organizations that offer cruises at sea. Cruise lines provide passengers with lodging accommodations, food and beverage services, entertainment, and ports of call.

Database marketing: A technology-driven tool to reach out to identified customers in the marketplace. It is precision marketing, a one-on-one sales approach to individual customers and clients.

Database mining: A process by which a well-defined group of customers or prospects can be extracted from a database.

Direct mail: A form of advertising that is nonpersonal, non-face-to-face yet direct communication to a clearly defined target audience. It is written communication promoting a product—a letter, a special promotion, an electronic message—sent to current and/or potential customers.

Director of marketing: Individual responsible for the marketing efforts of a hospitality establishment.

Distribution mix: Addresses the issue of accessibility and availability of the hospitality product to its target markets.

Double booking: When two salespeople mistakenly book the same dates and space for two different clients.

Environmental scanning: A checklist or means to ensure that external factors including economic, political, technological, sociocultural, regulatory, and ecological environments impacting the marketplace are included in the supply-and-demand analysis.

Escorted group tours: Tours where a representative of the wholesale tour operator meets the group at the departing airport and travels with the group throughout the tour. The group is met and assisted by local guides once they arrive at the destination.

Executive summary: A brief yet concise summary of a marketing plan recapping main points covered in the plan.

Exhibits and trade shows: Events where exhibitors display their wares and meet face to face with current and prospective customers. A venue to communicate directly with customers about product and service offerings.

Extended-stay market: A market segment composed of business travelers who stay at a lodging establishment five nights or longer.

Fair market share (FMS):   Compares a hotel's inventory capacity to the total capacity of direct competitors in the marketplace.

Floor supervisors: Individuals within a convention services department who supervise the employees who set up rooms for meetings and/or meal functions.

Free independent travelers (FIT):   *See* **Individual customers.**

Frequent-traveler program: Loyalty programs whereby travelers can build points through frequent patronage of a hospitality business. Points accumulated can be converted to free purchases, upgrades, etc., depending on the number of points earned.

Function book coordinator: Individual within a convention services department who oversees which group is assigned to which function room.

Global distribution system (GDS):   A network of worldwide computer reservation systems for booking hotel, airline, car rental, and other related travel reservations.

Government market: A market segment composed of government employees who travel on official business.

Heterogeneity: Refers to the variability of the hospitality product offering, especially aspects of people interaction.

Hoteling: When a sales manager travels to company or corporate headquarters and is assigned a cubicle or office space to work on a temporary basis.

Incentive house: *See* **Incentive travel house.**

Incentive travel: A reward given to employees, especially sales personnel, for reaching and/or exceeding company set goals.

Incentive travel house: Organization that is in business to develop, package, and sell incentive travel programs to companies that offer such rewards to their employees.

Independent meeting planners: Entrepreneurs who manage their own firms and specialize in meeting planning. They are hired by organizations (on a contractual basis) to plan meetings or other events for them.

Independent meeting planning firm: An outside firm that is contracted by an organization to orchestrate the logistics for a meeting or other events. This includes making travel arrangements, arranging for lodging, food and beverage, function rooms, and ground transportation.

Individual customers: Customers who travel independently for business or leisure purposes. They make their own travel arrangements or do so through a travel agent. Also referred to as free independent travelers (FITs) and transient customers.

Institutional market: A market segment composed mostly of institutional organizations such as colleges and universities, hospitals and health care facilities, primary and secondary school systems, and corporate facilities.

Intangibility: Refers to the intangible nature of the hospitality product. This aspect of the hospitality product cannot be pretested prior to purchase.

Intermediaries: Third-party organizations that assist in the development, promotion, and/or sale of hospitality product offerings.

Inventory management: Managing the sale of inventory in a hospitality establishment.

Leads: Potential customers with whom no contact has yet been made.

Leisure market: A market segment composed of people traveling for non-business-related purposes including singles, couples, families, and the mature market.

Letter of agreement: A formal document outlining key requirements for an upcoming event with space given at the end for each party to sign the agreement. When signed by both parties, a letter of agreement becomes a legally binding contract.

Like-kind partnership: When two or more organizations in similar businesses form a partnership to benefit all parties.

Marketing: Communicating with and giving customers what they want, when they want it, where they want it, at a price they are willing and able to pay.

Marketing management: Entails an analysis of supply and and demand, an external environment analysis, followed by segmentation, target marketing, and positioning decisions, and marketing mix decisions.

Marketing mix: Addresses hospitality marketing management decisions including product/service, presentation, price, distribution, and communication to targeted audiences.

Marketing plan: A formal document detailing the marketing management decisions of a hospitality establishment.

Market segment: A grouping of buyers having similar characteristics and similar needs and wants.

Market segmentation: *See* **Segmentation.**

Mature market: A market segment comprised of leisure travelers aged 50 and over.

Meeting planner: Individual who makes or assists in making decisions related to meeting design, objectives, content, and logistics including facility and travel arrangements.

Meetings and conventions market: A market segment composed of groups of individuals meeting together for a common purpose. The association, corporate, and government segments make up the bulk of this market.

Merchandising: Personal and/or nonpersonal communication directed to an in-house captive audience.

Off-premise: Refers to scheduled events that take place at a location other than that of the organization.

Partnership: Two or more firms joining forces to mutually benefit from better selling and marketing and enhanced customer satisfaction.

Performance appraisal: Evaluation of a sales manager's activities, development, and goal attainment. Performance appraisals are normally done on a semiannual or annual basis.

Perishability: Refers to the short shelf life of a hospitality product.

Personal selling: Direct person-to-person, often face-to-face, interaction with a prospective customer.

Person-trip: One person traveling 100 miles or more away from home.

Point-of-sale system (POS): A computer-based system designed specifically for foodservice operations. Commonly referred to as POS system.

Port of call: When a cruise ship pulls into harbor and passengers can spend time on shore at their leisure. These shore excursions can be a half day to several days, depending on the cruise line's itinerary.

Positioning: Creating an image of a hospitality product or service in the mind of the consumer.

Presentation mix: Refers to how hospitality products and services are presented such as the dress and attire of employees, the location and decor of the hospitality establishment, and atmospherics.

Pricing mix: Refers to what price, what level of pricing, and, most important, what the customer is willing to pay.

Probing: Asking questions to learn as much as possible about the wants and needs of potential customers.

Product-line development: When a company that is in a core business, such as lodging, offers several product concepts that reach out to separate and distinct markets.

Product segmentation: A grouping of similar products, such as budget hotels or fine-dining establishments, that target similar market segments.

Product/service mix: Refers to actual hospitality products and services developed and offered to guests of a hospitality establishment.

Property management system (PMS): A computer-based system that facilitates and electronically expedites interdepartmental communications in a lodging establishment. It is a highly integrated system connecting sales, reservations, front office, accounting, housekeeping, purchasing, POS, security, and other facets of hotel operations.

Prospecting: Searching for, making contact, and establishing relationships with new potential customers.

Publicity: Indirect/nonpersonal forms of communication in public relations. It is often a "story" (good or bad) printed in the media about a hospitality organization, a person within the hospitality organization, or an activity at the hospitality establishment.

Public relations: Direct/personal or indirect/nonpersonal forms of communication to the general public.

Referral: Learning of prospective customers from current customers, national sales offices, and other sources.

Related-business partnership: When two or more organizations in different, yet related businesses form a partnership to benefit all parties.

Relationship marketing: The building and maintenance of customer relationships based on a solid understanding of their needs and meeting these needs on an ongoing basis.

Reservation networks: Organizations that offer central reservation systems and services to independent and chain-affiliated hospitality organizations including hotels, car rental companies, and cruise lines.

Revenue per available room (RevPAR): Total rooms revenue divided by total guest room capacity of a lodging establishment.

Sales: The direct communication link with current and potential customers of a hospitality establishment.

Sales account management: Assigning sales managers to identified target markets, geographic territories, and/or specific customer accounts within an identified industry, corporation, and/or profession. Examples include Ford Motors, Federal Express, American Society of Engineers, or the insurance industry.

Sales office automation: The automation of various aspects of the hospitality sales process and sales management. This is largely done through computer software.

Sales management: The training, development, motivation, and directing of the sales force of a hospitality establishment.

Sales manager: Individual responsible for soliciting and booking business for a hospitality establishment. Also referred to as sales account executive, sales associate, or sales representative.

Sales organization: Refers to the internal organization of sales efforts in a hospitality establishment. This includes departmental organization, team effort coordination, and individual planning of sales activities.

Sales process: A five-step process of personal selling that includes opening the relationship, qualifying the account, presenting the message, closing the sale, and delivering as promised.

Sales support tools: Tools that support the personal selling effort including printed brochures, videos, CD-ROMs, and Web sites.

Segmentation: The act of dividing a market into meaningful groups or segments of buyers having similar needs and wants.

Simultaneity: Refers to simultaneous production and consumption of a hospitality product or service. The customer, in many respects, is part of the assembly line or the production process in hospitality.

Single-product pricing: When a basic price is set for the basic product.

Site inspection: When a prospective client comes to the premises and is given a tour of the hospitality facility.

Special promotions: Short-term product offerings designed to stimulate sales on a short-term basis.

SWOT analysis: Analyzing the strengths, weaknesses, opportunities, and threats of a hospitality establishment's marketplace environment.

Target marketing: Choosing which segments of demand the marketer is going to go after or target.

Telemarketing: A form of cold calling by telephoning potential customers from lists such as the Yellow Pages, an association membership directory, etc.

Theme parks: Large amusement parks providing entertainment for people of all ages such as roller coasters, water rides, animal shows, cultural attractions, cartoon and storybook characters, sports complexes, etc.

Tourism destinations: Geographic areas or regions having multiple product offerings for the leisure traveler. These include lodging, foodservice, transportation, and entertainment accommodations. A tourism destination is a product in itself. Cities, counties, states, provinces, regions, and countries often promote themselves as tourism destinations.

Trace system: Setting a date when an account needs to be reviewed and acted upon.

Transient customers: *See* **Individual customers.**

Travel agents: Individuals qualified to sell tours, cruises, transportation, lodging accommodations, sightseeing, and other elements of travel to the public.

Travel coordinator: A person within an organization who makes travel arrangements for employees traveling on business. The travel coordinator may or may not handle meeting planning activities.

Travel manager: *See* **Travel coordinator.**

Vacation ownership: When vacationers own a block of time in an apartment unit (or similar accommodation), usually in a resort- type location. It is similar in concept to owning a condominium, yet one owns only a specific period of time. The time period is usually in one-week increments.

Wholesale tour operators: Organizations that contract with transportation, lodging, foodservice, and other hospitality companies to develop and manage tour packages. Tour packages are typically sold through the retail division of wholesale tour operators and/or travel agents.

Yield management: A revenue management concept that maximizes yield by raising or lowering prices depending on anticipated levels of demand. Yield management is a tool used to maximize revenues for a hospitality establishment.

Index